The Future of Political Science

The Future
of Political
Science

Harold D.
Lasswell

GREENWOOD PRESS, PUBLISHERS
WESTPORT, CONNECTICUT

Library of Congress Cataloging in Publication Data

Lasswell, Harold Dwight, 1902-
  The future of political science.

  Reprint of the ed. published by Atherton Press, New
York, in series: The American Political Science Asso-
ciation series.
  Bibliography: p.
  1. Political science. I. Title.
[JA71.L3 1974]   320   74-3623
ISBN 0-8371-7444-9

Originally published in 1963 by Atherton Press, a division
of Prentice-Hall, Inc.

Reprinted with the permission of Aldine Publishing Company

Reprinted in 1974 by Greenwood Press, Inc.,
51 Riverside Avenue, Westport, Conn. 06880

Library of Congress catalog card number 74-3623
ISBN 0-8371-7444-9

Printed in the United States of America

10 9 8 7 6 5 4 3 2

The American Political Science Association Series

Preface

The present discussion of the future of political science has grown out of the phenomenally rapid expansion of the study of government in the United States and elsewhere. Leading figures in the American Political Science Association backed the initiative taken by Charles S. Hyneman during his presidency to encourage exhaustive consideration of the policy problems now facing the association, university and college departments of political science, and individual scholars and students presently or prospectively connected with the discipline. The idea was to encourage active members of the association to publish sustained reflections on the issues at stake. It was assumed that each contributor would emphasize the conceptions of political science with which he had the deepest experience, but that he would relate what he said to a comprehensive set of questions concerning the study of government.

Political scientists have not been studied with the care that has gradually built up a body of knowledge about physicians, lawyers, and, to an increasing extent, physical scientists and engineers. For the data that appear in the first two chapters, I am chiefly indebted to Evron M. Kirkpatrick and his staff at the national office of the American Political Science Association, particularly to Miss Cora Prifold. I have also had the benefit of comment by several members of the Yale Department of Political Science and by colleagues and students in many official and unofficial agencies with which I have been connected.

The book deals mainly with the American scene, since this country has encouraged the relatively unfettered study of government on an unprecedented scale. In some bodies politic, the formidable potentialities of freedom to research, teach, and publish are so well understood by the political elite that every effort has been made to commandeer political science as a tool of the Establishment. In countries where the dominant aims of the community are industrialization and modernization, the lack of a competent political science profession has contributed to the turmoil of transition. As it happens, our programs of what was styled economic growth suffered in the early stages from one-sided guidance by specialists unaccustomed to thinking comprehensively about the value goals and institutions affected by intervention in the lives of others.

For opportunities to explore many problems in political science at home and abroad, I thank several sources of support, without incriminating them in the positions taken in this volume. I have especially in mind the Ford Foundation and Yale University. Within Yale, I am under lasting obligation to the Law School, which manages to keep alive over the years the creative intellectual tension that became endemic in the deanships of Mr. Hutchins and Judge Clark and continued to flourish under Deans Gulliver, Sturges, and, presently, Eugene V. Rostow.

I especially desire to acknowledge the importance of my closest collaborators at Yale, among whom Myres S. McDougal plays the most redoubtable part. On technical matters, M. R. Campbell, of Washington, D.C., is as skilled and judicious as ever. In New Haven, Miss Theresa V. Brennan met every challenge with characteristic distinction.

I trust that Charles S. Hyneman will not feel too acutely discomfited by this partial result of his high-minded initiative.

Harold D. Lasswell

June 1963

Contents

The Future
of Political
Science

1
Political
Science
Today

The present period of world transformation could with equal justice be called the age of science or that of astropolitics. No one imagines that political science alone among the arts and sciences will remain unaffected by the changes through which the world is moving. The distinctive concern of political science is with the political process itself, and it is impossible to believe that government and law will lie outside the accelerating tempo of history. In this inquiry, directed mainly to those who are seriously concerned with the study of government, we shall consider the future of political science from the viewpoints of scope, method, and impact.

Any problem-solving approach to human affairs poses five intellectual tasks, which we designate by five terms familiar to political scientists—goal, trend, condition, projection, and alternative. The first question, relating to goal, raises the traditional problem of clarifying the legitimate aims of a body politic. After goals are provisionally clarified, the historical question arises. In the broadest context, the principal issue is whether the trend of events in America or through-out the world community has been toward or away from the real-ization of preferred events. The next question goes beyond simple inventories of change and asks which factors condition one another and determine history. When trend and factor knowledge is at hand, it is possible to project the course of future developments on the pre-liminary assumption that we do not ourselves influence the future. Finally, what policy alternatives promise to bring all preferred goals to optimal fulfillment?

PAST CONTRIBUTIONS

The problem-solving frame of reference is no novelty to political scientists. It is and has been, for example, common for members of the profession to concentrate on one or another of the intellectual tasks involved. A few reminders will establish the point.

Among the enduring contributions to the study of politics we number treatises that have undertaken to clarify the goals appropriate to political activity. The principal writing of this kind falls roughly into two categories, the first directed toward the specification of goal, the second toward justification.

The most successful method of specifying a positive vision is an imaginative essay in the manner of Plato's *Republic* or More's *Utopia*. There are also the counterutopias, full of hell-fire and damnation, to which Orwell's *1984* belongs.

The treatises that seek to justify more than to specify desirable goals rely on many modes of argument. Perhaps the principal tool is rhetoric properly keyed to the receptivities of a waiting audience. This was true of Rousseau's *Social Contract*. It is also possible for a writer to dispense with eloquence almost entirely and to depend on the cumulative impact of evidence and analysis. Such was the method of Marx in *Capital,* which sets forth a theory of power in the language and framework of economic history. Many famous works of justifica-tion dispense with rhetoric, empirical detail, or historical analysis and trust the razor of logic and the weight of authoritative citation. This mode of expression is particularly congenial to theologians and jurists.

The great bulk of writing on politics is more devoted to history than to any other dimension of the subject. It would, however, be a mistake to assume that history is written for its own sake. Even the most dreary account of changes in the structure of government is typically inspired by the hope of making available a body of data that will eventually help discharge the obligation shared by all political scientists to explain the rise and fall of political institutions. The immediate technique, however, is historical, bound to the collection and criticism of sources and to the establishing of sequences of events in time and place.

In the United States, political scientists have been captivated by the task of tracing the roots of government, law, and politics in this country to the soil of England or elsewhere and distinguishing between the original design and subsequent adaptations to American experience. Woodrow Wilson's treatise on *Congressional Government* is a classic work of the kind.

Systematizers deal directly with the problem of explanation by putting forward propositions that are confirmed, or open to confirmation, by empirical data. One irony of history is that writers have sometimes been identified with a single factor, a set of factors, or a single generalization that does scant justice to the scope and subtlety of their approach. Michels, for example, is known almost exclusively for his formulation of the oligarchical tendencies of mass political parties. Even Aristotle is more commonly referred to in connection with the role of the middle classes in politics than for his discussion of other subjects.

It is not inappropriate that Hobbes is immortalized as the exponent of psychological motives for political action or even that the fecund Bentham is identified with a calculus of felicity. But it does little justice to Montesquieu to narrow his originality to comments on climate, geography, and politics or to condense Spencer to axioms on centralization and external threat.

Grand theories of the probable course of future development only occasionally rise to enduring influence. In this select company, Marx and Engels take the prime position. On a far more modest scale, political scientists are continually engaged in estimating the probable strength of trends in the immediate and remote future. For example, students of American government have been substantially of one voice in predicting such developments as the further centralization of the federal system, the rise of metropolitan regions and the decline of states, the concentration of executive power, the liquidation of ethnic discrimination, the continuation of the two-party system, the increase of litigation over civil and political rights, the continuation of con-

troversy over civil-military relations, and the extension of social insurance coverage.

Contributions of this kind are often made jointly with proposals
in the realm of public policy. No historian of the American Constitution is unaware of the attention paid by the most active drafters and
defenders of the document to classical and contemporary treatises on
government and law. Several of the founding fathers attained a command of the theory of government that is impressive to this day. It
is necessary to go no further than to name James Madison, Thomas
Jefferson, and Alexander Hamilton. Among political scientists of the
present century, we think of the role of Woodrow Wilson, A. Lawrence
Lowell, and others in founding or promoting the League of Nations.
Whatever the problem, political scientists frequently appear as innovators or critics of policy. This is in fact the intellectual task that
many professional students of government find most congenial.

FUTURE PROBLEMS

Political scientists, we have said, possess a tradition of distinguished achievement in many areas of problem-solving importance.
As we face the future, it is safe to say that the challenges are of far-
reaching and unprecedented variety and importance. It is perhaps
useful to glance here, however briefly, at the scope of these developments.

Will questions of value goal, of overriding objective, become more
or less acute as science and technology continue their explosive
course? In all probability, these issues will not recede from sight. On
the contrary, the chances are that the immediate future contains a
unique challenge to man's conception of himself and to the values to
which he is presently committed.

I do not intend to emphasize the potentialities of modern knowledge for the destruction of man and his works, formidable as these
implications are; I refer to another dimension of the problem. Among
all faiths, "man" is traditionally assumed to be an identifiable and
usually a cherished form of "life." In Europe-centered civilizations—
and America unquestionably belongs in this company—prevailing
images of man were shaped by classical philosophy and the Judaeo-
Christian religion. Asia-centered civilizations have a more varied religious inheritance, mainly Buddhist, Taoist, Hindu, and Muslim. In
whatever doctrinal terms the affirmation is grounded, the articulate
leaders of the world community presently employ the language of
deference to human dignity. Although many differences of specifica-

tion exist, it is generally understood that human dignity implies an opportunity for mobility on the basis of merit; human indignity, on the contrary, assumes the blind immobility of caste.

The most obvious forms of "man" and "life" are easy to locate on the cosmic map of science. There are also marginal forms, and sooner or later the question of identity will be posed by these marginal phenomena. Computing machines perform many intellectual tasks more quickly than men do. Even today it is no longer out of the question to design machines that repair themselves or reproduce their kind. More to the point, machines can be made with built-in criteria of "enjoyment" and with the capability of learning through experience. The original criteria, if not specified in fine detail, permit novel responses.

As it becomes more widely recognized that the differences between man or life and machines have reached a vanishing point, the question becomes: Shall we treat machines with the same deference that we give ourselves as advanced forms of life?

The same question will be posed somewhat less starkly in connection with products from laboratories of experimental embryology and related sciences. It is not easy to overcome the original image of "thingness" where a machine is involved. Induced mutants have at least the advantage of belonging to the traditional realm of "life." We must be prepared, of course, to meet living systems whose central integrative plan is organized quite differently from the brain and nervous system of man.

The central issue will hinge on how the overriding goal of human dignity is to be interpreted. Shall the idea of "human" be redefined to bring within its field of reference many phenomena that we now tend to exclude? Shall we retain the current identification of the "human" with the biological envelope called Homo sapiens and merge the "higher" characteristics of man with a larger category—"advanced forms of life"—in which the human species may some day play a subordinate role? More specifically: When shall we extend the protection of the Universal Declaration of Human Rights to machines and mutants?[1]

In whatever terms we eventually define the commonwealth of life or delimit the forms to be called advanced, it is plausible to believe that we will feel some residual loyalty to the symbols of what we today identify as human. Looking back from a future vantage point, the story of man will continue to seem, in some intimate sense, "our" history.

When we consider the trends that have carried the species toward or away from a conception of human dignity, it is apparent that the decisive steps toward a positive self-image were taken during the tens of thousands of years that elapsed before written records were invented. Living in migratory and occasionally settled bands, early man was in contact with protohuman forms, forms that were not always easy to distinguish from Homo sapiens. As protohuman types dropped out, the biological environment grew more stable. As "reality" was more sharply defined, man was able to achieve a clear, affirmative self-image.

The conception of the dignity of man includes an ordering principle *among* men as well as *between* men and other forms of life. It is not farfetched to conjecture that, in early generations, human survival depended on the cultivation of discipline within bands. Entirely egocentric conduct could bring disaster to everyone. When we take into account the propensity of individual members of the species to act egocentrically, it is possible to perceive the evolutionary significance of what may be called the syndrome of parochialism. Included in the syndrome are demands by the self on the ego (and on all group members) to sacrifice for the power of common defense and for other shareable outcomes. Among the added outcomes were physical safety, comfort, convenience; those related to intimacy and respect; and those of cultivation or transmission of know-how and of physical facilities. There are indications of the presence of common themes of fantasy and ritual and of common conceptions of cosmic order. We can summarize by saying that it was the experience of interdependency that enabled man to survive and to develop his peculiar cultures.

All this lies in the shadow before records were written. The appearance of written records is a manifestation of the greatest invention of man—urban civilization. Cities are the launching pads of mankind's meteoric rise. Urban civilization dates from about 3000 B.C., when the first cities emerged in the valleys of the Nile, the Tigris-Euphrates, and the Indus.[2]

During the preceding tens of thousands of years, man had been divided into small, independent folk societies, bound by ties of family identification, mutual sacrifice, and self-preoccupation. It was in urban communities that traditional bonds of kinship were attenuated for the benefit of territorial units; hence, the simultaneous rise of law, legislation, and the techniques of impersonal administration. Cities brought literacy, and with literacy came records and the expansion of knowledge in all departments. The accelerated productivity resulting from the new division of labor encouraged capital formation and the building of fortifications, monuments, temples, palaces, and whole cities. The new skills of production were also turned to destructive use, and empires spread from an urban hub. In the new cities and states, the social gap between ruler and ruled was not always filled by middle-class formations. Hence, revolutions as well as wars were fought on an unprecedented scale.

It was in city-centered civilizations that the conception of human dignity became articulate.[3] Generalizing beyond the obvious differences that divide mankind—of physiognomy and ways of life—an occasional thinker, poet, or religious innovator envisioned a single family of man and an inclusive commonwealth where everyone obtained a basic minimum of consideration, supplemented by value indulgences according to need and to the meritorious exercise of capability. Any dream of a common humanity unified in a commonweal of merit challenged the ideological residues of a thousand wars and indicted every vestige of caste.

The record shows how ideologies of human dignity rise and fall, spread and retract, in the ebb and flow of world affairs. On the whole, however, the conception has been moving toward universality, and today the dominant elites of the globe give at least lip service to human rights.

It is directly within the scope of political science to identify the factors that impede the realization of policy goals and to assess their relative significance. Even a cursory examination fixes attention on the discrepancy between our articulate deference to life and the continued practice of death. How can we account for the continuing facts of war and preparation for war? We shall briefly consider some of the factors involved as a means of underlining this component of the total problem-solving approach.

The perennial tragedy of the uncounted millions who despise violence is that, in concrete circumstances, they feel constrained to engage in organized killing as an alternative to something worse. They are victims of a factor that is often overlooked or taken for granted and hence underemphasized. I refer to the expectation of violence, the expectation that, despite many formal renunciations of war, it is probable that collective violence will continue to be used in general and limited war.[4]

It would carry us too far into the study of a single problem to analyze in detail the disastrous role that continues to be played by expected violence. Perhaps it is enough to think of the position of the effective head of a modern state. He may cherish the dream of leading his people, and ultimately all mankind, from the shadow of annihilation. He is, nevertheless, aware of many factors that hold him in check. For instance, he cannot order serious reductions in armed force without spreading consternation among trusted colleagues and strengthening the hand of opposing leaders and factions within his party. His opposite numbers abroad are simultaneously trapped in the same bog. Given the prevailing fact of a divided and militant world, there are plausible grounds for perpetuating the structure of precaution that we call national security. The situation is further complicated by the growth of vested and sentimental interests in continuing the situation indefinitely. The threat to the general peace that results from a divided world fluctuates through time as a function of a combination of factors whose net impact determines the level of crisis. Among major factors is the demand for intensity—of subjective life, of communicative expression, and of overt action. The demand for intensity is variously distributed among the cultures of the globe. American civilization, for example, is organized to encourage a strenuous life of vigorous self-assertion. Intensity also varies from one social class to another and among interest groups. And we know enough about the structure of personality to see that intensity is a significant personality variable.

Intensities are particularly dangerous when they are joined with severity, the factor that is present in a "pure-power" approach to human relations. Latent severity demands may at any time spring to life and add to the destructive potential of diplomacy and of other modes of international intercourse. The central feature of severity is the obtaining of deep gratification in the act of imposing significant value deprivations on others. (It should be expressly noted that demands can be intense without exhibiting this admixture of sadism.)

It is not within the scope of the immediate task to go further with this analysis of some of the critical factors that condition the future of destructiveness and the attainment of a world in closer harmony with the ideal of human dignity.[5]

We turn for an equally brief discussion to the fourth dimension of our political task and project the course of certain developments that bear on the realization of preferred events. Undoubtedly, the attainment of human dignity will be intimately bound up with the future of science and technology, which have already brought us to the threshold of an age in which man's habitat is changing.

It is worth underlining the point that, despite their spectacular successes, science and technology have been singularly without effect on the fundamental structure of world politics. When we look closely at technological innovation, we are not surprised to see that improvements begin at highly localized centers. During recent decades, innovations diffused from originating centers that were almost exclusively in Western Europe and North America. New instruments of production cut the cost of production when the scale of output was sufficiently enlarged. Hence, the manufacturing interests of a locality sought to obtain translocal markets.

At some stage in the spread of these economic activities, power institutions entered the picture. Seeing the local market diminish, local producers turned to politics in order to exclude foreign competitors and to protect their local position, or strong competing manufacturers, equally interested in translocal trade and raw materials, turned to politics in the hope of obtaining exclusive markets.

The piecemeal introduction of science and technology led to the subordination of the productive and destructive potentialities of the new pattern of civilization to the basic structure of the world political arena. Scientists and engineers have not abolished politics; they have not liquidated the division of the world arena; they have not changed the domination of public affairs by rival syndromes of parochialism. Hence, prime loyalties are less than universal; values are sacrificed for goals less inclusive than the commonwealth of man; the expectation of violence continues to sustain the institutions of militant division.

Is it likely that a turning point in the relation of science to power has finally come? The question is whether the joint exploitation of the potentialities of man's newly accessible astral environment will provide a set of goals for the whole of mankind and for all advanced forms of life that will appear to be of such overwhelming importance that traditional differences will rapidly become obsolete.[6]

Political scientists are increasingly aware of the task of projecting to the age of space. They are also aware that their participation in problem-solving does not stop with the passive projection of future development. The "creative flash" of policy innovation is no monopoly of the man of action; it may, in fact, elude a mind dusty with everyday affairs. Of course, it is not necessary for political inventors to assume that their proposals will change the course of history. One may, for instance, hold grave reservations about the probability that the age of space will be a new era of science, order, and freedom. At the same time, no wise man is dogmatic about present visions of future reality, including forecasts of what *cannot* be done.

PROFESSIONAL ROLES

The attention that we gave above to eminent names and treatises has drawn a somewhat unbalanced picture of the profession as a whole. It is no use pretending that every professional student of government is primarily engaged in the writing of masterpieces. It is not to be assumed that he writes at all. Many advanced students become civil servants. A considerable fraction stays out of the civil service, writes little, and instructs much. The active teachers shape the curriculum and control the organized aspects of the profession in countries where it is possible for relatively free professions to exist. It is also true that teachers are heavily involved in advisory activities of a part-time character.

The sustained study of government, politics, and law was undoubtedly a feature of the first urban civilizations that arose in the Nile, Tigris-Euphrates, and Indus valleys. Some of the early legal codes suggest the presence of thoughtful minds interested in the theory of what they were doing. Nevertheless, voluminous treatises of a theoretical character did not appear until about twenty-five hundred years ago. This is true whether we look to China and Confucius, India and Kautilya, or Greece and Plato and Aristotle.[7]

The principal difficulty in the way of identifying members of the political science profession in many civilizations is uncertainty about the theoretical context of the training received by public officials. The transmission of know-how is not enough to constitute a profession. The scholar class in traditional China was unquestionably a profession, since scholars were supposed to entertain comprehensive conceptions of the place of politics in society and nature. Specific skills were acquired "on the job" or in clerkships occupied to obtain the funds needed to continue studying for examinations.[8]

Careers develop by playing several roles at the same time or in sequence. For convenience, we speak of the following professional roles that may be taken by persons who have received advanced training: teaching; research and equivalent activities; advice (participation in public affairs short of leadership or administration); management (civil service, staff of unofficial organizations); and leadership (community commitment on controversial issues). Many of those who receive advanced training migrate into other activities.

Teaching about government is formally organized and carried on at many levels. The United States Office of Education reports that there are over two thousand universities and colleges in the United States (2,040 in 1961). About one-third of these establishments offer sufficiently sustained instruction in the field to award a degree (B.A., M.A., Ph.D.) in political science or international relations. Approximately 700 schools offer courses in political science.

At the precollege level, the study of government is frequently merged with history and the social studies generally. No dependable information is at hand to estimate the number of qualified professors and teachers who are engaged in offering instruction about government. Ambiguity rises in part from the fact that no separate department of political science is organized even at some universities and colleges, where it may be joined with history, economics, or another related discipline. An unknown percentage of the courses in government are taught by persons whose primary training is not in political science and whose exposure to the subject is slight.[9]

In recent years, the demand to upgrade instruction throughout the American educational system has favored the engagement of qualified personnel. In this connection, the staffing policies of junior colleges are indicative. The National Education Association has reported on the new full-time teachers in 343 public and 187 nonpublic junior colleges. The figures show that over 55 per cent of the new teachers of political science had completed the M.A. and at least one additional year of study or the Ph.D. No other group had a higher record of academic qualification.

It is clear that about two-thirds of recently graduating doctors of philosophy enter college and university teaching.

Although teaching is the principal responsibility of advanced students of government, the obligation to contribute to the advancement of knowledge is taken seriously. Higher degrees are awarded to candidates who demonstrate, among other capabilities, their competence to complete an acceptable piece of research. In the case of doctoral dissertations, it is usual to require publication or evidence of suitability for publication.

The number of doctoral dissertations in political science fluctuates rather sharply from year to year. The Office of Education records 191 Ph.D.'s in 1959 and twenty in 1960 (plus twenty-seven Ph.D.'s in international relations). The responding universities and colleges reported 649 and 722 M.A. degrees during these years.[10]

It is common knowledge that the doctoral dissertation is the only substantial piece of research or writing that many political scientists complete during their entire career, and this is not unusual. The term "research" is often stretched to include the preparation of textbooks whose novelty is mainly typographic. There are, it is reassuring to add, textbooks that are more suitably described as treatises, since they introduce intellectual order where little could be discerned before. Without a separate research project, it is impossible to say what percentage of postdoctoral publications can be regarded as new knowledge or as critical interpretations of the field deserving of equal recognition.[11]

A quick way to obtain some estimate of the body of "live writing" in scholarly political science is to find how many titles have been put out as paperbacks during the current revolution in publishing. The 1962 figure is 900, which covers 691 authors and ninety-nine publishing houses.[12]

The scholarly journals publish research and critical writing in political science and adjacent fields. *The American Political Science Review* has for many years reflected the varied intellectual interests of the profession. The *Review* has, of course, been unable to provide a channel for the many specialties within the study of government. New—now old—journals have come into existence in public administration, public opinion, international relations, social and political philosophy, public law, and jurisprudence; and new periodicals are in prospect.

The special issue of established journals and the yearbook or symposium volume are devices that have provided an immediately effective and stimulating outlet for systematic, critical, or empirical expression.

It has been implied, and correctly, that the most significant research has been done by political scientists who retain their connections with colleges and universities. There are, nonetheless, important reservations to this statement. The scientific and technological innovations of recent days have coincided with and exacerbated a continuing crisis in world affairs. Political scientists who are associated for long or short periods with new and largely government-financed agencies of research and policy critique have played an increasing part in the recent development of political science. The practice of subcontracting Defense Department and other official projects to universities has done much to break down the personal and intellectual isolation that formerly prevailed.[13]

I have briefly characterized the teaching and research roles of political scientists. It is also important to describe the advisory function. In the present context, the advisory role is understood to be a part-time activity carried on by political scientists who are otherwise absorbed in research and teaching. It is widely assumed by his fellow-citizens that a professor is, or purports to be, an authority on current events; that he is willing and able to make public statements and to lecture on practically everything from the assassination of X to the politics of Zanzibar; or that he is on tap as a consultant on charter reform, the reorganization of state government, or the politics of foreign aid.

A rough indication of the advisory activity of political scientists can be gleaned by examining how many are engaged as official consultants at the international, national, state, or local levels of government and how many spend some time writing for private media of communication or working with unofficial organizations concerned with public questions. At present, no exhaustive inventory of these diverse connections exists. I have, however, examined the *Who's Who* entries of professors of government in a few institutions with which I am acquainted. There are, perhaps, political scientists whose advisory roles are negligible, but they would be as rare as unicorns.

Despite the high proportion of advanced students of government who make their careers in teaching, research, and consultation, it is not to be supposed that career alternatives end there. A sizable fraction steers toward government and enters the federal civil service; the armed forces; the diplomatic corps; or state or local levels of employment. I use the term "management" to cover the holding of an official or party job and regular responsible participation in the decisions of an organization that tries to influence public affairs.

The gradation between advice and management is not distinct, since advisors sometimes become so deeply involved in a particular activity that it absorbs their available time over many years. But it is not difficult to identify the tenure of a definite, full-time job.

For present purposes, I distinguish advice and management from each other, and I give separate consideration to the role of leadership. This term is intended to designate the public leader, the one who plays an influential, conspicuous part in public affairs. Leadership goes beyond advice to commitment; it goes beyond management to goal-setting and high-level integration. The full-time public figure or active politician comes in this category.

Many young people have studied government in the hope of pursuing active political careers, and they have done so. Given the variety of ladders by which an ambitious young man or woman may become a political leader, it is common for students of political science to approach the goal somewhat indirectly. They may, for example, begin by teaching and move into active participation in civic and party affairs. An increasing number find that the most direct route is to serve an apprenticeship with an active leader, starting as a research or administrative assistant and moving up. Some young people have organized, or taken an active part in, civic or issue organizations. For others, the media of mass communication are the obvious choice, since journalists or commentators have high public visibility. By tradition, many students of government have added legal training to their equipment and obtained a foothold by practicing law and participating vigorously in public affairs.[14]

The five roles described above refer to the major specializations in the official and informal government of our society. As indicated above, many students of government move away from careers of this kind, often going into business and dealing with public affairs in the intermittent fashion that characterizes most citizens. It is not to be assumed that the study of government is lost on the hundreds of thousands of students who receive some exposure to the study of politics at the collegiate, secondary, or presecondary level. On the contrary, there is little doubt that some permanent impressions are left. We are at present in no position to assert that these effects importantly determine conduct or to establish whether—to face unwelcome contingencies with candor—the exposure to political science, as usually taught, leaves negative conceptions of the field and, indeed, of the aims and potentialities of citizenship.

POLITICAL SCIENTISTS IN THE DECISION PROCESS

We have cursorily inspected the role of political scientists as seen by themselves. Our inquiry goes deeper, however; the most pressing question about the study of government relates to the adequacy of political science when assessed in the wider context of past and prospective community decisions. Hence we shift the standpoint of observation and sketch the relationship between political scientists and the decision process in each functional phase.

At this stage we shall not insist on precise definitions of these phases. It is important, nevertheless, to call attention to two sets of meanings. We distinguish between *functional* definitions which are set up to serve the analytic needs of political science and the *conventional* usages current in a given community. In conventional usage, the official decision process of the United States is carried on by various authorized participants, among which we mention the electorate; Congress (state and local legislatures); the presidency (governorship and local chief executives); the federal departments, agencies, and authorities (and any corresponding structures at state and local levels); and the Supreme Court and the federal judiciary (state and local judiciaries). In conventional terms, the world decision process is said to be carried on multilaterally among authorized representatives of state authority or in intergovernmental agencies set up for the purpose (United Nations and other transnational structures).

No agency is authorized to tell the scholarly community what terms must be used or how they must be defined and applied. This is left to the judgment of each scholar, who is free to accept or reject the terms proposed by other scholars on the basis of criteria that seem good to him. His chief professional responsibility in the interest of clear communication is to be explicit about the "referent" of his labels. The rapid growth of political research in our day has brought with it an accelerated tempo of experimentation with new concepts and terms. Conventional usages are data of reference for functional categories. One result of terminological change is the discovery of concealed or tacit meanings in the conventional language of the United States or, indeed, of any body politic that receives close study.

As analyzed here, the decision process includes both formal authority and effective control.[15] Thus, "lawful" power is authoritative and controlling; "naked power" is controlling and not authoritative; "pretended power" is not controlling. When the decision process of any body politic is described, it is necessary to examine the pattern of perspectives that constitute recognitions of authority and the patterns that exemplify effective control.

Think of any act of decision. We conceive it as beginning in an influx of information from sources at the focus of attention of participants in the decision process, some of whom perceive that their goal values have been or may be affected in ways that can be influenced by community decision. We refer to this as the *intelligence* phase.

The next phase is *recommending,* or promoting, which refers to activities designed to influence the outcome. The *prescribing* phase is the articulation of norms; it includes, for instance, the enacting of enforceable statutes. The *invoking* phase occurs when a prescription is provisionally used to characterize a set of concrete circumstances. When a prescription is employed with finality, we speak of *application.* The *appraisal* phase characterizes the relationship between policy goals and the strategies and results obtained. The *terminating* phase involves the handling of expectations ("rights") established when a prescription was in force.

Every interaction in the political process at a transnational, national, or subnational level can be examined with all seven phases of the decision process in view. Consider, for paradigm purposes, the publication of a volume such as Charles A. Beard's *Economic Interpretation of the Constitution*. This was, of course, a private venture by the author and publisher of the book. It therefore belongs to the unofficial stream of activity. In terms of phase analysis, it obviously belongs to the general stream of intelligence relating to the history of a major institution of American government. Given the constellation of factors in the political process of the time (1913), the book was immediately interpreted as offering or implying an appraisal of the Constitution as part of a conspiracy of various economic interest groups to use political power through a new institution of government to their own advantage. It is true that a literal reading of Beard's book does not lend support to the conspiracy theory, since no evidence is presented of a secret strategy among the principal groups named as beneficiaries of the new form of government. For that matter, the assertion is not flatly made that *all* who stood to benefit in the enumerated ways were aware in advance of ratification of their advantageous position and exerted themselves for adoption. There are no actual estimates of the alleged impact of the calculation of economic advantage on the behavior of the persons most actively engaged in promoting the Constitution. Nevertheless, many phrases in the book are sufficiently ambiguous to lend themselves to the "liberal" view prevalent in many American circles at the time that both the Constitution and the Court originated as part of an antidemocratic movement.[16]

Small wonder, then, that Beard's book was turned to active propaganda use by crusaders who claimed to be completing the democratic revolution in America. Monopoly finance and industry were the principal enemies, and Beard's volume was said to confirm the allegation that financial influences had been active and successful from the beginning of the constitutional system.

It can also be suggested that the prescribing and applying phases of decision were affected by Beard's contribution, since it fostered a "sociological" and "realistic" approach to the work of the courts. American sociological and realistic schools of jurisprudence were actively forming at the time. They emphasized the importance of thinking about the social consequences of decision and especially of giving weight to economic repercussions, rather than remaining at a formalistic level of doctrinal analysis. In effect, Beard had written a brief on behalf of a problem-solving method that emphasized the importance of bringing economic causes and consequences to the focus of judges' attention. And judges—as is today widely understood—make law whenever they affirm or deny the relevance of a prescription to a controversy. When the intellectual method of judges is modified, the repercussions go far, since the bar now advises clients to adopt a new approach to the judiciary. It is conceivable, though difficult to demonstrate conclusively, that the economic interpretation influenced the readiness of community decision-makers to deal generously with private claims for compensation. If past privileges came into existence as a result of the undue influence of monopoly interests, why deal gently with them in controversies growing out of the exercise of eminent domain or franchise termination?

That Beard's publication interacted with every phase of the decision process is not, in principle, an exception. It is true that few recent books have had such an immediate *succès de scandale* or a more solid impact on the tools of thought. When a new trend of thought begins, many publications are necessary to build the predispositions required to accept a "famous" culminating volume. Subsequent contributions, though individually minor, largely confirm the trend.

The interplay between political science and the total process of decision goes far beyond the effects obtained from book publication. This will be more evident as we give separate, though necessarily brief, consideration to each of the seven decision phases that we have identified.

The Intelligence Phase

Every government develops a network of structures specialized in obtaining information about the intentions and capabilities of actual and potential allies and opponents in the world arena and detecting subversive tendencies at home. Relatively covert channels of information are supplemented by overt data-gathering operations conducted by census agencies and by diplomatic, military, economic, and cultural attachés abroad. The information is organized in terms of trend, analyzed as to cause, projected into the future, and related to clarified goals and to potential alternatives of policy.

Political scientists are among the specialists who are heavily relied upon to supply personnel for information and planning agencies of government at all levels. The literature of political science has a long tradition of concern with the strategy and tactics of intelligence. In ancient monarchies and tyrannies, the theorists of government were well aware of the difficulties of obtaining reliable information. Thus we find in Kautilya's *Arthasastra* explicit consideration given the choice of agents for covert operations; guidance is also provided for open intelligence.[17]

In open societies, the channels operated by government are supplemented, and often eclipsed, by the flow of information provided by the press and by other private agencies. We observe in connection with the press that, as it seeks to achieve professional status, its relationship with political science grows closer. In the United States, this is indicated by the role that has been played by individuals who combine journalism with political science in changing the curriculum of schools of journalism.

To the intelligence agencies of any body politic must be added the universities and private organizations of research and planning. In many countries, the rise of centers of advanced instruction has been furthered by political objectives; and these objectives have included obtaining a large supply of knowledgeable specialists in public law, international politics, government, and administration. That knowledge is perceived as a base of power is emphasized in the history of institutions of higher learning. The German university system took shape in the shadow of Napoleon, and L'École Libre des Sciences Politiques was born after the humiliation of 1870. More recently, the institutions of higher learning among the defeated powers underwent varying degrees of reconstruction, especially in political studies. Modernizing and industrializing countries are everywhere alert to the fact that the complex fabric of world society cannot be grasped unless an adequate supply of trained specialists are produced at home as well as abroad. In such programs, the study of political science occupies a place, occasionally of great emphasis.

American universities have been welcomed abroad by many reviving civilizations or modernizing societies, and political scientists have been actively involved in the development of programs designed to increase the supply of competent administrators of the public services and to widen the vision and the skills at the disposal of the rising generation of American students. In 1957–1958, there were 382 exchange programs at 184 American universities, covering a vast range of subjects. In 1960–1961, 53,107 foreign students from 143 countries and political areas were enrolled at 1,666 institutions of higher learning in this country. More than 15,300 American students were attending foreign universities. More than 3,600 members of foreign faculties were affiliated with 304 American colleges and universities, and more than 2,200 members of American faculties were teaching abroad. Edward W. Weidner calls attention to the fact that the Center for International Studies at the Massachusetts Institute of Technology and the Michigan-Okayama project in area studies are among the programs that have been effectively used for research as well as other purposes.[18]

The Promoting Phase

Where popular government exists, the official agencies of persuasion are often less potent than political parties, pressure groups, and other private associations. Nevertheless, as "big government" grows, the line between purveying intelligence and promoting policy is dimmed. In closed systems, no pretense is made that a proper function of government is the providing of pure information. In the arena of foreign politics, it is everywhere taken for granted that news and comment are slanted in order to influence policy commitments.

In the United States, modern information and propaganda services began by relying on newspaper reporters and editors, since it was obvious that a large part of the job was to win the confidence of other media men. In many cases, however, there were advantages in reaching government officials at the national or subnational level, and expert knowledge became an asset. Hence, political scientists were often involved. Since promotional activity to some extent entails negotiation between government officials and party leaders or other group leaders, lawyers are often chosen to do the job. This is partly because many party leaders have legal training and because many managers of private associations are lawyers or ex-lawyers. Political scientists, especially those with training and experience in international relations, have an advantage in various transnational operations.[19]

The study of government often leads to the invention of proposed lines of policy innovation. Political scientists typically feel under an obligation to provide civic leadership where leaders are few or weak. Hence it is possible to call attention to many policy innovations at the national, transnational, or subnational level that owe a great deal to the promotional zeal of individual political scientists. I shall undertake no definitive summary of these activities, although it may be serviceable to cite a few cases. In world affairs, the United Nations, the movement toward international arbitration and adjudication, and the

pursuit of collective security were causes with which prominent political scientists actively identified themselves. Perhaps the names of
J. W. Garner and of Quincy Wright, the dean of academic students
of international politics, are sufficient reminders of the scholars involved.

The reform movements that aimed at improving the mechanisms
of government in the United States included many campaigns with
which students of government became prominently identified. Think
only of the council-manager movement or the demands for women's
suffrage; for the direct election of senators; for primary elections; for
a simplified ballot; for the initiative, referendum, and recall; for permanent registration and voting machines; for separation of national
and local elections; for redistricting (antigerrymandering); for poll
watchers and safeguards to ensure honest tabulation of ballots; for
organized civil service; for administrative consolidation (county and
local); for independent, dominant-purpose "authorities"—and I have
barely made an inroad on the list.

The Prescribing Phase

A legislature is the most distinctive official structure specialized in
the prescribing function. It is common knowledge that legal training
is a major asset in running for elective office, and no one is surprised
to learn that research confirms the established image. However, there
are indications that, as professions become differentiated, the dominance of the lawyer is somewhat weakened. Leaving aside the fact that
legal training is often preceded or combined with advanced training
in political science, we note that full-fledged members of the political
science profession sometimes appear in Washington in the Senate or
the House.[20]

Political scientists have been active in varying degrees in state
legislatures and in the municipal councils of many communities, large
and small. In some countries, legislators are heavily recruited from
the civil service and hence have received advanced education in government.[21]

In the last few decades, the legislatures have become increasingly
aware of the magnitude of the responsibilities that they bear in
complex modern societies. The chief executive has the advantage of
drawing on the entire administrative establishment for intelligence and
recommendations. Legislatures, on the contrary, are handicapped by
lack of control over sources on which they can rely. As a result, new
agencies have been brought into being, or greatly expanded, in the

hope of overcoming current limitations. The Library of Congress, for example, has steadily extended its Legislative Reference Service. Furthermore, the committees of Congress have augmented their staffs with professionally qualified personnel. The committee investigation device has been given a new lease on life in recent years as a means of coping with the almost overwhelming burden on Congress. Political scientists have played an active role in strengthening the intelligence agencies specializing in the immediate requirements of legislatures at every level.[22]

A comprehensive functional analysis of the prescribing phase of decision in the United States must await research bringing the principal private organizations into the picture with government. A prescription is not identical to the words of a statute, although the statute is of importance in stabilizing the perspectives that constitute a prescription. The text of a statute can be used to make a tentative inference regarding the labor-management code, for example. However, the inference must be verified by ascertaining whether the alleged prescription is in fact applied to most of the situations to which it is presumably applicable. By examining concrete circumstances and by discovering the views of "insiders," it may be possible to confirm the original hypothesis regarding the content of a prescription. On the other hand, the pattern may be so confused that no prescription can be said to exist.

The relative independence of law from the phraseology of constitutional charters or legislative statutes is well brought out in the case of customary regulation of a market.[23] It often happens that the statutes-at-large lack definite statements about fair-trade practice. Yet, if one interviews representative traders, it will be apparent that practically everyone expects participants in market transactions to live up to rather clear norms. A consensus also exists about the sanctions that will undoubtedly be used against an occasional offender. In the context of the market, or even of the body politic as a whole, some of these unofficial sanctions are classifiable as severe, rather than mild (for example, exclusion from all markets). If our functional definition employs the term "law" to refer to norms enforceable by means of severe sanctions, we classify community-tolerated severe unofficial practices as law. Conversely, we do not accept the face of the statutory text as establishing the existence of a law. In fact, research may show that nobody expects a given statutory norm to be enforced and assumes that whatever sanctions are applied will be mild, not severe.

It is appropriate to refer to the wider context of community life because it calls attention to the fact that effective legislation is in course of enactment in interactions that take place outside legislatures. We speak of the "minds and hearts of men," or, less rhetorically, the prescribing phase of the decision process is carried out as expectations change or remain the same.

One implication of this is that political scientists affect the prescriptive code of a body politic by engaging in the scholarly act of reaffirming or altering research conclusions about severely sanctioned norms. These affirmations influence the assumptions of public officials, party and pressure group members, and effective figures in other private associations.

Community expectations are also modified in the classroom or the tutorial session. The instruction of future decision-makers is a matter of consequence in any body politic. We are aware of acute sensitivity in all matters that affect the rearing of the heir apparent of the monarch, the heirs apparent of an oligarchy, or the leaders of a popular government. The deference accorded by the emperor of China to his tutor—the tutor was exempted from the usual forms of etiquette—is well known. In the Indian classics, the rearing of the princes especially emphasizes the role of companions. The preoccupation of classical Greece with the political socialization of the entire citizenship is justifiably celebrated. In the vast democracies of contemporary times, the educational task is channeled through huge installations in which professional students of government play a prominent part in crystallizing basic expectations—or in failing to do so.

The teachers and researchers, then, perform a legislative, a prescriptive, function which is insufficiently recognized in many formal treatises on government. Unless they transmit fundamental expectations regarding the allocation and the objects of power, they fail to transmit the constitutional framework of the body politic. In this way, they perpetuate or amend the constitution.

The Invoking Phase

It is comparatively easy to identify the official organs of government whose responsibilities are highly specialized in the invoking phase of the decision process. The policeman who makes an arrest alleges that a specific act violates prescription; so, too, do the prosecuting attorney who seeks an indictment and the grand jury which indicts. The health inspector who tickets a violation or the building inspector who finds a deviation from the building code is confronting a concrete case with a provisional application of what purports to be authoritative community prescription.

In our society, the bulk of the invoking function occurs unofficially. Think of all the controversies among private individuals and groups in which the argument is about the "law" and an alleged violation. If legal counsel is brought in, negotiations may continue until a settlement is reached without introducing into the controversy the official decision-makers of the whole community.

Although the role of the lawyer in acts of invocation is prominent, the trained political scientist is actually involved at many points. Political scientists are often engaged in administrative activities where questions of conformity to regulation are conspicuous. Indeed, the entire stream of administrative action is supposed to stay within the channels laid down by the basic prescriptive code, and the legality of alternative courses of action may be impugned at any moment. A large part of the routine task of administration is to act directly on private individuals and organizations which are required to show that they have lived up to officially prescribed standards. In this connection, we think of the regulatory agencies concerned with commerce, finance, industrial and agricultural production, relations of employer and employee, transportation and communication, resource conservation, and private education.

To an increasing extent, regulatory agencies draw their commissioners and staff from among political scientists. The literature includes many attempts to arrive at working principles of administrative regulation. When are objectives best served by formal invocation? When is it enough to refrain from initiative?[24]

The Application Phase

When an administrative tribunal or court has the last word in a dispute or an executive decides to proceed with a project, a "final" commitment is made in the decision process. Most of the personnel engaged in public administration are presumably absorbed in activities of this kind.

The continuing operations of government—which we call enterprisory activities—make use of most of the facilities available to public authorities. Although we are in no position to give precise estimates of the number of political scientists who are engaged in the application phase of government, there are grounds for saying that perhaps a third of all who do advanced work find their way into government service rather than into private research or teaching.

The literature of political science reflects the breadth of professional interest in the widely ramified tasks of application. Practically every field of administrative specialization has been enriched by this literature. Recall the treatises that focus directly on problems of organization, personnel selection, management, and fiscal administration. Every value-institution process that is touched by government has generated an inter-disciplinary collection of books and journals. This is abundantly true of education, public health, and welfare administration. The last-named tends to fan out to include all government contact with the family. In recent times, American political scientists have concentrated on the use of the established instruments of national policy for the achievement of the overriding goals of the system of public order. The quality and quantity of contributions to the strategy and tactics of military, diplomatic, and communications policy have risen sharply.

The Appraisal Phase

Official agencies set up specialized structures to report on the degree to which objectives have been fulfilled, to account for performance or nonperformance, and especially to assess the impact on the result. In many cases, reports from operating branches are reviewed to discover degrees of fulfillment or nonfulfillment of task. Auditing, inspecting, and censoring units participate in the appraisal function. In large modern governments, it is not unusual for management, often supplemented by outside consulting services, to study the efficiency with which operations are carried on and to weigh the effect of "the organization chart" on results.

Legislative bodies spend a large part of their time employing the mechanisms of committee inquiry in attempts to perform the appraisal task. The "watchdog" role is congenial to many legislators and legislative assistants. In many instances, we cannot discover without new investigation precisely "who does what" in connection with appraisal. It is, nevertheless, clear that political scientists often gravitate toward this phase of the governmental process.

It is obvious that many individuals and agencies whose main job is appraisal perform other distinguishable functions. Inspectors may go beyond factual reporting and performance analysis to recommend changes of personnel, of operating policy, or of organizational structure. Censors may be authorized to suspend or to indict (invoking or applying functions). Control commissions may proceed to reorganize units of government—unmistakably an applying or even a prescribing activity.[25]

When we turn from official to unofficial appraisal, the part that political scientists play looms in the foreground. A significant proportion of all political science publications has to do with the assessment of policy or of specific factors that influence the outcome of official acts. Given the ideological structure of the United States, it is predictable that systematic students of government will contribute to the appraisal of such external policy commitments as participation in (rather than isolation from) international organizations and programs of military, economic, diplomatic, and cultural aid (or refusal of aid). On questions of internal policy, an audience is always ready to give attention to studies showing that an expanded federal government program has positive (or negative) effects on individual freedom, pluralistic enterprise, or state and local government. Our ideological heritage prepares us to listen to appraisals of the balance between civilian and military elements in the body politic or to evaluations of more (or fewer) limitations on freedom to speak, listen, or investigate. The American ideological system provides an explicit or implied agenda for the perpetual review of the place of government in society, with particular concern for individual development.[26]

The Terminating Phase

When public policy changes in ways that disturb established expectations, the community often seeks to ease the difficulties of termination and establishes agencies to settle the claims put forward. If land is expropriated for public purposes, "just compensation" clauses provide norms of adjustment. In public emergencies, various groups may suffer disproportionately, and, at the termination of the prescriptions authorized during the crisis, private groups may be given restitution or compensation. When private relations are ended—as in divorce, bankruptcy, or dissolution of a college—the community intervenes to safeguard public order.

Matters connected with severance of personnel and payment of pension benefits, as well as with the administration of sanction law, enter the terminating phase of public action. The authority to parole or pardon is included here. Political scientists figure in many specialized organs connected with the terminating function and are assisting in the evolution of a body of literature that undertakes to clarify this often-neglected dimension of community action. For many years, most of the questions at issue were left to the attorneys, on the tacit assumption that the aggregate impact of policy change was not worth looking into or that it could not be tackled with any prospect of success.

To summarize, political scientists are actively involved at every phase of the decision process of the commonwealth at all levels—national, international, and subnational. Although every phase of decision is directly or indirectly affected by what they say or do, the chief professional role of students of government is most immediately linked with the functions of intelligence and appraisal. As teachers and research workers, political scientists are responsible for presenting an inclusive, reality-tested image of the changing role of government in the social process of every community. Their responsibility includes the linking of descriptive and explanatory knowledge and estimates of the future with clarified interpretations of community goals and evaluations of major policy alternatives.

Although leadership is not the primary function of political scientists, many students of government possess the additional qualities that make for active and conspicuous influence. The framers of the American constitutional system were often learned men who, if they did not devote themselves to the full-time study or practice of government, nevertheless sought enlightenment from every promising source, ancient or contemporary, on the pressing questions of public policy with which they were confronted. For a few outstanding Americans, notably Woodrow Wilson, professional inquiry into government provided a career that culminated in high office and a source of guidance that led to a complex achievement of dazzling success and crushing defeat.

NOTES

[1] I have referred to such problems in my presidential address to the American Political Science Association, "Political Science of Science: An Inquiry into the Possible Reconciliation of Mastery and Freedom," *American Political Science Review*, 50 (1956), 961–979.

[2] V. Gordon Childe, *What Happened in History* (Baltimore: Pelican Books, 1954).

[3] J. A. Wilson, *The Culture of Ancient Egypt* (Chicago: University of Chicago Press, 1951), particularly Chap. 5; but see S. N. Kramer, *From the Tablets of Sumer* (Indian Hills, Colo.: Falcon's Wing Press, 1956), Chap. 13. Further sidelights in H. and H. A. Frankfort, J. A. Wilson, and T. Jacobsen, *Before Philosophy*, "The In-

tellectual Adventure of Ancient Man" (Baltimore: Penguin Books, 1949).

[4] Some current models of world politics are M. Kaplan, *System and Process in International Relations* (New York: Wiley, 1957); G. Liska, *International Equilibrium* (Cambridge: Harvard University Press, 1957); T. C. Schelling, *The Strategy of Conflict* (Cambridge: Harvard University Press, 1960); A. Rappoport, *Fights, Games, and Debates* (Ann Arbor: University of Michigan Press, 1960); K. Boulding, *Defense and Conflict,* "A General Theory" (New York: Harper and Row, 1962); W. H. Riker, *The Theory of Political Coalitions* (New Haven: Yale University Press, 1962).

[5] Cf. M. S. McDougal *et al., Studies in World Public Order* (1960); M. S. McDougal and F. P. Feliciano, *Law and Minimum Public Order* (1961); M. S. McDougal and W. T. Burke, *The Public Order of Oceans* (1962)—all New Haven: Yale University Press—and M. Kaplan and N. de B. Katzenbach, *The Political Foundations of International Law* (New York: Wiley, 1961).

[6] Concerning the use of past-future constructs as a component of problem-solving method, see H. Eulau, "H. D. Lasswell's Developmental Analysis," *Western Political Quarterly,* 11 (1958), 229–242.

[7] See D. S. Nivison and A. F. Wright, eds., *Confucianism in Action* (Stanford: Stanford University Press, 1959); E. Barker, *Greek Political Theory,* "Plato and his Predecessors" (4th ed.; London: Methuen, 1951); Kautilya, *Arthasastra,* trans. R. Shamasastry with introductory note by J. F. Fleet (4th ed.; Mysore: Sri Raghuveer Printing Press, 1951).

[8] Cf. T. S. Ch'ü, *Local Government in China under the Ch'ing* (Cambridge: Harvard University Press, 1962).

[9] The figures concerning the United States come from National Education Association, *Teacher Supply and Demand in Universities, Colleges, and Junior Colleges* (Washington, D.C.: National Education Association, 1962), and the national office of the American Political Science Association, Washington, D.C. John D. Millett's Committee on Standards of Instruction (American Political Science Association) found that 786 colleges and universities offer political science courses. Of these, 466 have separately organized departments. In 162 instances, political science is joined with history; in 129 cases, political science is part of a department of social studies. Cf. *American Political Science Review,* 56 (1962), 417–421.

[10] Some information about political science outside the United States is available through the International Political Science Association and UNESCO. Cf., e.g., "Teaching of the Social Sciences in the U.S.S.R.," *International Social Science Journal,* 11 (1959), No.

2; J. Barents, *Political Science in Western Europe*, "A Trend Report" (London: Stevens and Sons, 1961).

11 *The International Social Science Journal* publishes current news and research in the United States and other countries. Representative numbers: "The Study and Practice of Planning," 11 (1959), No. 3; "Citizen Participation in Political Life," 12 (1960), No. 1; "Technical Change and Political Decision," 12 (1960), No. 3; and "The Parliamentary Profession," 13 (1961), No. 4.

12 H. Holland, *Paper Backs and Reprints in Political Science* (Washington, D.C.: American Political Science Association, 1962).

13 New types of institutions or modifications of established institutions are the RAND Corporation, Santa Monica, Calif., and the Operations Research Office, Johns Hopkins University.

14 Cf. R. E. Lane, *Political Life*, "How People Get Involved in Politics" (Glencoe, Ill.: The Free Press, 1959), and the literature of elite analysis.

15 I adhere to the usages in H. D. Lasswell and A. Kaplan, *Power and Society*, "A Framework of Political Inquiry" (New Haven: Yale University Press, 1950), and H. D. Lasswell, *The Decision Process*, "Seven Categories of Functional Analysis" (College Park, Md.: University of Maryland Press, 1956). Among the analyses of decision, attention should be given to the suggestions of R. A. Dahl, C. E. Lindblom, R. C. Snyder and associates, H. A. Simon, and G. A. Almond—among others.

16 For example, the concluding sentence of the book says that the Constitution "was the work of a consolidated group whose interests knew no state boundaries and were truly national in scope." Cf. the sharp critique of Beard on factual ground in R. E. Brown, *Charles Beard and the Constitution* (Princeton: Princeton University Press, 1956); also, B. C. Borning, *The Political and Social Thought of Charles A. Beard* (Seattle: University of Washington Press, 1962).

17 On intelligence problems, especially in reference to questions of external policy, R. Hilsman's work is especially useful: *Strategic Intelligence and National Decisions* (Glencoe, Ill.: The Free Press, 1956). The older literature on public opinion—by Walter Lippmann and John Dewey, for example—is concerned with what the intelligently participating citizen needs to know and what stands in his way. We can expect more empirical studies oriented to gauging the effect on aggregate decisions of various total patterns of statement available to decision-makers.

18 Among political scientists who have joined with others, particularly educators, to guide or evaluate programs may be mentioned E. W. Weidner—whose *The World Role of Universities* (New York: Mc-

Graw-Hill, 1962), is the standard summary—R. N. Adams, B. L. Smith, F. A. Pinner, H. F. Cleveland, W. H. C. Laves, C. D. Fuller, J. Gange, G. A. Mangone, C. H. Wells, W. Y. Elliott, and many others.

[19] Political scientists have been especially active in increasing the level of awareness that modern politics is, at least, highly manipulative. I refer to the stream of publications on the promotional activities of governments, political parties, pressure groups, other private associations, and individuals.

[20] At the moment, Sen. Hubert Humphrey (D., Minn.) is the most conspicuous example.

[21] Scattered data are in the Hoover Institute Studies on Comparative Elites (D. Lerner, I. Pool, R. North *et al.* (Stanford: Stanford University Press, 1952—); D. Marvick, *Political Decision-Makers* (New York: The Free Press of Glencoe, 1962); R. D. Matthews, *The Social Background of Political Decision-Makers* (Garden City, N.Y.: Doubleday, 1954); S. M. Lipset, *Political Man* (Garden City, N.Y.: Doubleday, 1960).

[22] A key figure in the growth of the reference services is E. S. Griffith. G. Galloway is the outstanding analyst of Congressional mechanisms. Cf. K. Hofmehl, *Professional Staffs of Congress* (Lafayette, Ind.: Purdue University Press, 1962).

[23] Many of the issues involved are examined in M. S. Massel, *Competition and Monopoly,* "Legal and Economic Issues" (Washington, D.C.: Brookings Institution, 1962).

[24] Information on regulatory bodies is to be found in the work of E. P. Herring, M. E. Dimock, E. Latham, M. Bernstein, M. Grodzins, and others.

[25] Suggestions are to be found in the writings of E. L. Redford and other specialists on administrative strategy.

[26] On civil-military relations, for example, see, among others: W. T. R. Fox, S. P. Huntington, L. I. Radway, J. Masland, A. Vagts, W. R. Schilling, P. Y. Hammond, K. N. Waltz, S. Melman, M. J. Janowitz, D. C. Rapoport, B. M. Sapir, and R. C. Snyder.

2

Growth
and
Ambiguity

The present inquiry into the future of political science is an outgrowth
of factors more specific than those described in the preceding chapter.
As we shall presently demonstrate, the profession has been rapidly
expanding in numbers and diversity of activity; and the result has
been considerable ambiguity in the conception of the roles proper to
political scientists.

EXPANSION

A convenient point of departure is the formation of the American
Political Science Association in 1903, an organizational step that had
been taken by the economists in 1885 and the historians in 1884. The

initiative for a distinct organization is to be seen as a manifestation of the process whereby the mother discipline of philosophy was losing intellectual and organizational control of the study of social and political life. As the nineteenth century wore on, the reorganization of higher learning and research had accelerated.[1]

In the United States, the formation of centers for advanced study and research proceeded with some rapidity after Reconstruction. The Johns Hopkins University came into existence at one stroke in 1876, and both The University of Chicago and Stanford were launched in the 1890's. The older institutions were responding to the same expansionist forces. (The Ph.D., for instance, was inaugurated at Yale in 1861.) Of particular importance for political science was the Faculty of Political Science that was approved at Columbia University in 1880.

The rise of political science benefited from the superimposition of features borrowed from the German university system on those of the English college. The study of government and other social sciences as independent professional disciplines was inadvertently furthered by the disappearance of the European-style faculty of law in the migration of university traditions to America. The tradition that training for the bar is strictly technical was established early in this country. The basic task was conceived as preparing students to pass state examinations for admission to the practice of law. With this background, the law schools attached to American universities did not become faculties of law in the European sense after the university movement reached America in the 1870's. In the universities of Berlin or Paris, for example, the faculty of law was part of the faculty of philosophy and included lectures on subjects that we classify as political science, economics, or some other social science. In the United States, it was definitely established that the dominant law-school figures had no interest in European-style faculties of law. At Columbia University, for example, Prof. John W. Burgess undertook to broaden the scope of the Law School by lecturing on comparative constitutional law in the manner with which he had become acquainted as a graduate student in Germany. His lectures, which began in 1876, were not popular and were presently discontinued.

The resistance of American law schools to becoming faculties of law proved a blessing in disguise to the social sciences. In the European faculty of law, specialists other than lawyers were privately or openly regarded as second-class citizens who had little claim on university resources to develop new directions of inquiry. At Columbia's Faculty of Political Science and Public Law, the social sciences were no longer subject to the faculties of philosophy or of law. A distinct Faculty of Science was responsible for "natural philosophy." It was administratively unwieldy and intellectually incongenial to group all the social sciences with philosophy or with arts and letters. The result was a tripartite university structure in which the natural and biological sciences, the social sciences, and what were presently called the humanities occupied separate administrative realms. The tripartite system was varied at different places—by the separation of physical and biological sciences, for instance, or by an outer breastwork of such professional schools as law, medicine, and engineering. But the American plan was trinitarian, a tripartite separation of responsibility in place of the unitary conception of philosophy as pure, and the professions as applied, knowledge.

Concomitant with the rise of the social sciences within the university was another organizational development that reflected and further crystallized the intellectual currents of the time. I refer to the growth of organized departments for the administration of advanced instruction and the cultivation of research. As the departments began to compete for graduate students, they became more aware of the market. As the demand for graduate schools and departments spread throughout the country, the new schools and departments constituted their own best market and fostered the intellectual consolidation of each field of specialization. When departments were completed at the main universities, new outlets were found at lower echelons of the educational system itself. Hence, departmental plans of organization were extended or confirmed at college and secondary levels. At the same time, new career opportunities were sought or opened spontaneously outside the educational network. For departments of political science, this meant chiefly the civil service at all levels of government.

The expansion of the American Political Science Association depended on the emergence at several universities of strong faculties for teaching and research. The association began with 214 members and by 1960 had grown to 9,000 (including institutions). These figures convey an accurate picture of the expansion. The impression is confirmed when we glance at other associations in which political scientists predominate or take an active part (in public administration, international law, law teachers). Further, we take note of regional organizations that cover the country.[2]

DIVERSIFICATION

More significant than the simple fact of expansion is the growth of diversified activity. A recent indication is the establishment of national headquarters for the A.P.S.A. in Washington, D.C., and the launching of programs of service to the profession and to the local, national, and international community. The congressional internship program is an excellent example of a service to the profession and to the body politic as a whole. The program brings academically trained students and instructors into intimate contact with one another and also with the organs, procedures, and personnel of statecraft. The headquarters staff coordinates preparation for periodic conventions and looks after publication, placement, and consultative activities.

In the educational system of the nation, the growth of political science instruction and research has been rapid. When the A.P.S.A. was founded in 1903, there were 977 colleges and universities in the United States. Not many departments of political science were in existence either separately or jointly with history or some other discipline. Present figures do not reflect the relatively modest numbers of graduate programs that were then available or the number of advanced degrees awarded at the turn of the century.

The diversification of political science is reflected in many ways. Long before the twentieth century, instruction in political philosophy, law, and government policy was included in the curriculum of colleges of liberal arts. At some of the better-known colleges, it was the custom for the president to participate directly in the induction of the senior class into these mysteries.

In contemporary decades, the field has been prodigiously subdivided and extended. The history of political philosophy has continued to emphasize Greek and Roman thought. It has, however, been modified in many ways. More attention has been given to the political inheritance of non-European civilizations, notably Chinese, Japanese, and Indian. The accumulating weight of precedent in the American legal system has had a parochializing effect on instruction and investigation in the study of constitutional, municipal, and administrative law, an effect only partly compensated by the attention given to international law and occasionally to jurisprudence.

The most massive change has been in what is often called descriptive political science. Even the most cursory review of curricular offerings in representative departments confirms the fact of course expansion in the study of political parties; pressure (or interest) groups and leadership; public opinion; public administration, with emphasis on organization, personnel, and finance; and with state, metropolitan, and local government. Descriptive courses have gone well beyond the traditional account of the British parliamentary system, the governments of Western Europe, or even the totalitarian or near-totalitarian leviathans of recent times. Under the impact of America's expanding role in the arena of world politics, instruction is offered in international organization and in the regional problems of the Americas; Africa; and the Near, Middle, and Far East.

THE PUBLIC IMAGE

That the relationship between political scientists and the environment has been changing need occasion no surprise. The transformation indicated in the preceding paragraphs could not have occurred without community support.

A link between the professional study of government and public affairs is occasionally brought to general notice when an academic specialist plays a prominent part in national politics. Woodrow Wilson is the only president of the United States who spent the early years of his adult career as a professor of government. There are, however, senators, representatives, governors, mayors, and political bosses who have received degrees in political science or taught the subject. The mention of Woodrow Wilson may bring to many minds the image of a public figure whose effectiveness was flawed by an aloof and self-righteous personal style of the kind that is often supposed to betray the academic man. A tendency to overgeneralize in this direction may be partially corrected by recalling the late Bois Penrose, of Pennsylvania, who was taken by many of his contemporaries as a symbol of unscrupulous practicality. Penrose appeared in print in the publications of the graduate school at Johns Hopkins University.[3]

A significant trend is discernible in the public image of political science and political scientists. It is not too much to say that, until recent years, there was no such image in general circulation. A political scientist was not appreciably different from any other academic "long hair" (or "crew cut"). One searches the *Congressional Record* in vain for other than an occasional matter-of-fact or derisive reference to the political scientist. The *Congressional Record* now contains many appreciative references to the work of the American Political Science Association. Dozens of congressmen have come in touch with capable and earnest young political scientists through the internship program. Many public officials, committees, and agencies have learned to recognize a special field of competence, thanks to their experience with staff members of the Legislative Reference Service of the Library of Congress. The headquarters of the association have become a clearinghouse for routing requests for information to qualified persons. Daily contact is creating an image of political science as a contributor to the intricate tasks of official and unofficial participation in public affairs.

The image, it must be repeated, is recent and dim and contains both ambiguity and contradiction. And this public image is not unrelated to the corresponding self-conception of many, if not most, members of the profession. Ambiguity and confusion betray the inner tensions that have accompanied the rapid development of the field.

Ambiguities in the Self-Image

The clearest evidence of inner stress is the unsettled character of advanced training, especially at the graduate level, particularly in the first year and in the basic survey of the field. Traditionally, the fundamental course was "political theory"; in practice this was a chronological review of political philosophy in classical and post-classical Europe. In recent years, however, the expansion of descriptive political science has led to dissatisfaction with the traditional course as an introduction to the field. The trend has been toward surveying the "scope and method" of political science. The survey is expected to provide a systematic view of the field and some training in the chief data-gathering and processing procedures available. Difficulties arise from the fact that members of the political science department who have specialized in the history of political thought are not always acquainted with the methods of research into the contemporary political process. Nor are they necessarily adept at systematic presentations that take into account the findings and potentialities of contemporary research. In many cases, they are intellectually alienated from the "new" political science and are unwilling to undergo the discipline required to achieve more than lay acquaintance with the appropriate methods.

Lack of agreement about the goals and procedures of political science is reflected in the range of solutions, often temporary, that have appeared in various places. Some graduate schools are unable to agree on a "scope-and-method" course and provide no unified picture of the past, present, and prospective future of political science. In a fragmented department of this kind, the power process is more likely to be practiced than investigated. In such an academic arena, feudal fortresses are built to defend various provinces called "political theory," "political parties," "comparative government," "public law," "international relations," and the like. Treaties and agreements establish courses of instruction (major and minor fields) which permit theses to be accepted and degrees to be granted without mutual deadlock. Every prospective appointment to the faculty is weighed in terms of its probable impact on the balance of power and hence on the appropriations available for salaries, research assistants, physical facilities, and fellowships. Loving and not-so-loving colleagues lie in wait for opportunities to put one another in the wrong or to damage self-respect. Students learn that the choice of courses and topics of investigation are acts of allegiance or of treason and that the consequences may be felt for years in letters of recommendation (or lack of them) when occasions arise for faculty appointment, for research and fellowship grants, or for government appointment.

Faculty participants in the power struggle within the "Hobbesian" department characteristically seek to defend and improve their positions by contracting foreign alliances, especially with government agencies willing to subcontract research and with private foundations and individuals able to make research funds available. With these assets at their disposal, department support can be obtained by a research consortium that absorbs graduate students from enough "fields" to command bloc support. If the departmental arena is unpropitious, arrangements can be made for the autonomy of a "committee," "project," or "institute" or even to secede and form a school or department of international relations, of communication, of administration, or of thought. The arrangements call for the support of key deans, the president or the board of trustees, and of leading donors or alumni.

In this bellicose setting, intellectual differences of scope and method are transmuted into fighting ideologies and slogans. In this way "philosophy," "morality," and "religion" manage to oppose "science," "pseudo-science," and "administrative triviality"; in reply, the "pursuit of verifiable truth" stands over against the "arrogance" of purported "truth by definition" and "private revelation." Even "mathematics" and "statistics" are fighting words, and "behavioral," "metaphysical," and "legalistic" are expressions of opprobrium or encomium.

It has been fortunate for political science that some departments where intellectual differences are most pronounced have been led by men of integrity and sophistication who have been able to disagree without rancor and to avoid the "Hobbesian" trap. Under such conditions, a working agreement that accepts the fact of diversity has come into being and uses the collective power of the department to preserve a situation in which students are expected to have the "right of exposure" to able representatives of the leading currents of traditional and contemporary thought. The department achieves an order in which the pursuit of enlightened skill is a dominating concern. "Minority protection" is a majority policy.

It is evident that the inner tensions of the recent decades of accelerated growth are to be explained in part by the tradition that political science is a microcosm of the macrocosm of law, the humanities, and the social and psychological sciences. Small wonder that scholars of diverse traditions have found it difficult to live with one another. If we examine the history of older departments of political science, we find that the original inhabitants usually migrated from elsewhere in the academic universe, often from history, philosophy, or law. Modern developments have broadened the intellectual antecedents or brought closer contact with sociology, psychiatry, psychology, social anthropology, and related disciplines.

THE BEHAVIORAL UPSWING

It is possible to locate without difficulty the principal place and time in American political science at which the "newer aspects" of the subject gained momentum. The creative center was The University of Chicago, and the time was the 1920's and early 1930's. The leading figure was Charles E. Merriam, who encouraged the new emphasis at the university and through the American Political Science Association. He also took the lead in initiating the Social Science Research Council. Funds were made available for the most part through private foundations, especially Rockefeller and Carnegie. Merriam believed—and he was by no means alone—that political science was too much dominated by the "library research" tradition of historians, including historians of political theory. He sought to establish a better balance by making it feasible for students of politics to use specialized methods to describe political events that they observed directly. The transition from "library research" to the conduct of field work in surviving primitive societies had already transformed social anthropology. The "participant-observer" had become acutely conscious of the importance of systematic notes and of cultivating and disclosing his relationship to informants. Psychiatrists were accustomed to summarizing interview protocols and observations and to supplementing routine medical tests with psychological instruments of measurement. Sociologists and human geographers were interviewing in various communities and mapping in systematic fashion the distribution of physical habitats, artifacts, and usages. Psychologists and social psychologists were experimenting with instruments designed to test information, to discover evaluative judgments, or to measure the personality as a system.

The initiative taken by Merriam was to supplement, not supplant, lethargy of the chair by the activism of field and laboratory. However, he did desire to enrich the traditional methods of describing past political events. Merriam was impressed by the steady advance of economics after the advent of time-series techniques for the study of business fluctuations. It seemed probable that statistical procedures could be devised to describe the fluctuating political process with equal success, whether the phenomena in question were wars; popular votes; or votes by legislatures, commissions, chief executives, or judges.

Advanced students found their way from Chicago to many faculties of political science and were often given facilities to develop teaching and research and to work with colleagues who, though having no direct experience of Chicago, were interested in research on pressure groups and political parties, public opinion, leadership, and related dimensions of the political process, particularly in its international aspect.

The difficulties that accompanied the redirection of political science were met in many ways, some of which I shall consider at length elsewhere in this book. It is sufficient here to observe that theoretical-descriptive political science received meager and grudging admission to some faculties. The shoe was occasionally on the other foot, and traditional scholarship in the history of political theory suffered from deprivations of every kind; so, too, did teaching and inquiry in public law. Given the mixed provenance of political scientists, it was possible, in a fit of xenophobia, to tell the "philosophers": "If you are any good, you ought to be good enough to get an appointment in a regular department of philosophy." Similarly with the "public lawyers"; let them go jump in the law school.

A UNIFYING SELF-CONCEPTION

It seems to me that, as political science faces the future, it is in a remarkable position to take an important initiative in the creative integration of thought and organization at the higher as well as the lower levels of knowledge and policy. The prospect of realizing a working harmony among diverse approaches has provided political scientists with an opportunity, which they have only partially utilized, to achieve a coherent conception of a problem-solving discipline oriented to the larger issues of the life of man in society.

Political scientists with a theoretical-empirical bent have often looked enviously at departments of economics, where legalistic and evaluative issues seem never to interfere with the smooth course of theory-building and investigation. They have, however, overlooked the fact that these issues were not resolved, but provisionally delegated. The delegation was to schools of business, which were frankly oriented toward the policy problems faced by responsible managers of the institutions conventionally specialized in the shaping and sharing of wealth. Schools of business could not, however, maintain a university status without gradually coming to concern themselves with the social consequences of business systems. In short, professors of business became professional men and not shop assistants. They concerned themselves with the aggregate impact of economic institutions and enlarged the contexts of the business curriculum to include explicit awareness of the total interaction between business and community.

A closely connected change was willingness to recognize a responsibility for training managers other than specialists working for the profits of the stockholders. Trade-union managers have an important organized constituency in the economic process, and a comprehensive professional school can find a place for those whose role is to define the interests of the workers in the relevant context.

This gradually brings other participants into the picture, among them managers of such institutions as consumers' cooperatives. And there are government managers whose main role is the administration of enterprises, many of which are organized on private-profit or the consumer-profit plans.

Schools of business have become places where every type of specialist in personality and culture can involve himself in the study of the shaping and sharing of wealth by all institutional practices. Meanwhile, academic departments of economics are experiencing new strains as theoretical problems concerning wealth seem most interesting and rewarding when institutional diversity is put into the foreground, as it is for policy problems of industrialization and modernization. Voices are raised to demand a multivalued, multi-institutional approach to economic theory. Hence, academic and business school economists are becoming problem-oriented in the sense of increasing concern with the clarification of goal and questions of trend, condition, projection, and alternative.

Law schools, too, seemed enviable to members of political science departments perpetually confronted with "marginal" issues. But modern American law schools are also losing their innocence. Only a few years ago, the famous casebooks compiled to further the needs of the case method of instruction were remarkably homogeneous. They were composed for the most part of snippets of the appellate court opinions of American and English courts. Today, by contrast, a casebook is a fearfully and wonderfully heterogeneous object containing, besides appellate court opinions, material from many sources, and especially from the psychological and social sciences. The books that deal with family, criminal, labor, corporation, administrative, or constitutional law—or, in fact, with any branch of the subject whatsoever—bring the language of legal technicality into the context of social interaction.[4] It is more obvious than ever that jurisprudence is a problem-solving discipline whose task is to aid the scholar and the active participant alike to perform all five intellectual tasks related to goal, trend, condition, projection, and alternative.[5]

Quite recently, departments of sociology have also become capable of arousing envious glances from modern-minded political scientists who find themselves struggling against collegial resistance to obtain the facilities or the permission to enable a student of political science to augment his professional equipment by courses in mathematics, statistics, psychological testing, and related specialties. Although political scientists were among the first to foster the contemporary efflorescence of research in communication and had long been especially concerned with the study of public opinion, they were losing out in many research competitions to social psychologists and sociologists who had spent the time necessary to obtain technical training in the procedures essential to refined research. In another important problem—the investigation of elites—political scientists were sometimes at a disadvantage in relation to sociologists, who had more acquaintance with field work or methods of processing data.

Sociologists, however, do not escape the impact of contextually oriented problems, despite the delegation of various matters to schools of social work or to programs in industrial sociology, medical sociology, vocational and educational guidance, and the like. If an "applied" school begins with pedestrian intellectual standards and modestly tries to provide candidates for the payrolls of departments of social welfare or of private welfare agencies, the situation refuses to stay static. Able and ambitious minds insist on examining their part of the social process in the light of available knowledge of the whole and in the face of challenges to improve social institutions.

The story is the same wherever we look at graduate and professional training and research. Schools of medicine and public health, agriculture, education, religion, departments of anthropology and social geography—everywhere the unit sooner or later searches to comprehend its role by discovering a map of the whole.[6]

In political science itself, the problem has been made more acute by the intellectual insurgency of organizations that were once supposed to content themselves with a modest patrimony of intellectual equipment. Today, schools, departments, or programs in public administration are frequently the germinating beds of vigorous programs of research in which the tools of operations research are familiar aids.

The long history of secession from "philosophy" is to be understood in part as a consequence of the rigidity of the professors who were traditionally expected to provide an inclusive map for the guidance of every participant in the vast field of intellectual labor. As modern society expanded in numbers and variety of institutions, philosophers were often put in the position of repeating the traditional wisdom in abstract formulas that lacked specification to the newly disclosed configurations of nature or society. Although the "eternal" questions were always present, creative contributions depended on building a bridge between the prescriptive language of the past and the unfolding present. Since many philosophers were unwilling to undergo the discipline needed to acquaint themselves with the new knowledge of nature or the novel practices of society, they were unable to think creatively. At the same time, they were impatient with "fact-oriented" specialists and helped to establish an atmosphere of contempt for the discoverers of empirical truth.

As we look to the future, it seems unnecessary to make the error of mistaking a part of the intellectual problem of politics for the whole. The challenge is to find ways of focusing man's search for the clarification of his goals and for policies giving optimal expression to these objectives. Both intellectual tasks, when rationally and realistically conducted, must proceed within a framework of knowledge of past trends and conditioning factors and of contingencies of future development.

In succeeding chapters, we direct attention to various dimensions of the contextual task of political science. First, we outline the requirements of a continuing survey of world political phenomena adequate to the problem-solving needs of political science. Second, attention is directed to methods by which intellectual bridges can be laid between knowledge of trends and highly specialized laboratory knowledge, on the one hand, and the information required to guide large-scale policy intervention, on the other. Third, we consider procedures by the use of which the vast Niagara of pertinent information can be kept manageable. Finally comes the question of creativity at every level of participation.

NOTES

[1] On the long European background, cf. Frederick M. Powicke and A. B. Emden, eds., *The Universities of Europe in the Middle Ages by the Late Hastings Rashdall* (3 vols.; Oxford: Oxford University Press, 1936); Vol. 3 deals with English universities; S. d'Irsay, *Histoire des universités françaises et étrangères des origines à nos jours* (2 vols.; Paris: A. Picard, 1933–1935). The American Social Science Association was organized in the United States in 1865. It was chiefly concerned with humanitarian reform. The Archaeological Institute of America was founded in 1879, the American Anthropological Association in 1902, and the American Sociological Society in 1905.

[2] They include Southern, Oklahoma, Southern California, Western, Pacific Northwest, Northern California, Mid-Western, Southwestern, Iowa, New England, Missouri, New York, and Pennsylvania.

[3] B. Penrose and E. P. Allinson, "The City Government of Philadelphia," *Johns Hopkins University Studies in Historical and Political Science,* 5th Ser., 1–2 (Baltimore: Johns Hopkins University, 1887).

[4] Among contemporary casebooks, cf., e.g., the pioneer volumes on the social control of business by W. O. Douglas; by W. A. Sturges on arbitration; by M. S. McDougal on property; by F. Harper and F. James on tort; and the most recent type, exemplified by R. C. Donnelly, J. Goldstein, and R. D. Schwartz, *Criminal Law,* "Problems for Decision in the Promulgation, Invocation, and Administration of a Law of Crimes" (New York: The Free Press of Glencoe, 1962), and A. Westin, *The Anatomy of a Constitutional Law Case* (New York: Macmillan, 1958).

[5] My colleague M. S. McDougal and I have been outlining and testing such a jurisprudential conception for several years.

[6] Cf. B. Blanchard, C. J. Ducasse, C. W. Hendel, A. E. Murphy, and M. C. Otto, *Philosophy in American Education* (New York: Harpers, 1945).

3

The Basic
Data
Survey (I) Intelligence, Promoting, Prescribing

We now consider how the political science profession can organize
its own intelligence function (which it willingly shares with others) in
ways that enable the political scientist to be knowledgeable about the
nature and extent of political events. It is far beyond the competence
of any single investigator to make more than a small contribution to the
vast body of data required to describe the changes in the distribution
of power and in the structure and function of political institutions
throughout the arena of world politics. However, this is the task for
which political scientists have professional competence and responsibility, though it is shared with other specialists—among whom are
journalists and undercover agents—who may or may not have political science training and identity.

As matters stand, political scientists have only partially met the challenge of applying their tools of description and analysis to the flow and spread of events in the political process. I shall therefore outline a possible line of development in which the American Political Science Association and other professional organizations in the United States and elsewhere can play a major role.

Professional organizations are strategically located to encourage and in part to administer comprehensive surveys of world political change. We have in mind associations of scholars, including scholars in socialist and Communist countries to the extent that their scientific independence is in fact accepted and enforced. In a divided world, there will always be limitations on publishing the results of research into government. Under totalitarian powers, which subordinate enlightenment to power, any publication will be censored to fit the current interpretation of the power interest of the elite. In the United States and in many other bodies politic, power is subordinated to a more inclusive set of values. Policies of "free press" and "free speech" imply "academic freedom," since the academic task can be performed in a free society only when research can be conducted on almost any topic and the results made known in the interests of general enlightenment.[1]

A private professional organization such as the American Political Science Association already provides a well-established mechanism for intelligence. Annual conventions, conferences, and committee meetings provide forums for the review of problems, methods, and findings.

The A.P.S.A. is a mechanism through which basic data surveys might be fostered and coordinated. We note in this connection that the association could be used for survey activities calling on all the resources of political science as a teaching profession. This has never been done, and the resulting loss of opportunity has weakened every function of the profession.

Thousands of college students are exposed to courses in political science. It is commonly said by experienced teachers that the level of the advanced undergraduate is higher than that of beginning graduate students; and there is much justification for this view when we recall that undergraduates constitute a pool of talent that is later channeled through all the professions.[2]

In any case it is well within the scope of an undergraduate, when competently supervised, to gather research data having obvious importance for the describing of trend and the discovery of conditioning factors.[3] We propose that the mechanism of the professional association be fully employed for the purpose of correlating our pedagogical, research, and consultative objectives by bringing students at every practicable level into a comprehensive program.

One objective of a basic data survey would be to strengthen the teaching effectiveness of political science, particularly at the college level. In this connection, however, it is not necessary to think exclusively of college students. Many secondary school students are capable of excellent research when properly motivated, equipped, and directed.

At every level, teaching involves problems of motivation. A key to intense interest in political science, as in any subject, is the sense that one is participating in an enterprise of genuine importance. Many routine exercises required in the usual course of instruction are pedagogically ineffective because they fail to communicate the importance of doing them well.

It is not difficult to show that participation in a basic data survey would be worthwhile. Such a survey is part of the adult world of public responsibility. The information obtained enters immediately into the public intelligence on which judgment depends at all levels of government. Wherever the survey was competently introduced and conducted, it would be possible for students to see that they are engaging in a serious enterprise.

In recent years, many new procedures for research on man and society have been invented.[4] Some of these methods were introduced and developed by political scientists, although many originated with psychologists and other social scientists. We think immediately of tests of aptitude, motivation, and performance. Modern research on communication has led to the invention of techniques of content analysis to describe the messages found in various channels and techniques of both brief and prolonged interviewing intended mainly to describe audience response. The study of electoral and administrative statistics is well established. The investigation of war and other forms of conflict has also produced specialized techniques. Devices have been worked out for the analysis of political elites and for comparative analysis of statutes and judicial opinions. It is beyond reasonable doubt that in future years new instruments will be invented or remodeled to serve the manifold needs of political research. Methods will continue to vary in intensiveness, that is, in length of contact with the object of inquiry, in complexity of the data obtained, and in length of training required. But the basic aim is the same—to bring to the attention of a scientific observer the events to be described, to provide a faithful record of what is observed (employing indexes suitable to the purpose), and to process data in ways that link them to analytic concepts and hypotheses designed to explain the phenomena in question.

Partly because political science has expanded rapidly in recent years, a gap exists between research practice and teaching. Many new manuals are needed to make clear to students (and to teachers not primarily specialized in the use of a given set of procedures) how to apply the methods at hand. Once the flow of manuals has filled the present gap, it will be possible to keep them up to date.[5]

In proposing a basic data survey, we are not oblivious to the favorable effects that participation in the survey could have on members of the teaching profession itself. Activities relating to the survey would provide concrete evidence of the distinctive task of political science and aid in crystallizing conceptions of the political scientist's role. The manuals show the range of special procedures the competent application of which provides dependable answers to pertinent questions.

In the process, the questions themselves would gain specification. For example: How do the changes occurring among officeholders in this community compare to the changes in neighboring or distant communities? How do the sources of political intelligence differ here and in other communities? What are the characteristic contrasts in political participation as exhibited in party and pressure group promotional activity and voting? What are the significant contrasts in the course of prescription (legislation) here and elsewhere? What legislative prescriptions are invoked or allowed to lapse in practice? How do performance levels vary here and elsewhere in various administrative applications? Are there significant likenesses and differences in the self-appraisal activities here and elsewhere? What has happened in connection with the termination of existing patterns of interests, as in the exercise of eminent domain in redevelopment?

Once under way, the continuously reported survey would provide even the most isolated political scientist with a comprehensive and selective image of the principal political changes in the locality, province, nation, region, and world. It would no longer be possible for him to reflect morosely on the fact that he is little better prepared than any other member of the mass audience to illuminate events. The data would lend themselves to visual presentation in the form of maps, charts, and models that would help to show the contexts of specific incidents. It would become obvious that the political scientist does, in fact, differ from the layman in the discipline to which his words are subjected. It would be perfectly obvious that, when a scholar makes a descriptive assertion about the direction and intensity of political change, he speaks as an expert. This does not, of course, imply that a political analyst is or would be beyond challenge by other experts or by laymen. His role in a free society is to enter the political process with particular responsibilities of intelligence and appraisal.

The data provided by the survey would enable one to achieve a clearer image of himself in the historical process of the current epoch. The survey would produce a map whose successive editions would show the changing patterns of world politics. Hence, one would have at his disposal a means of clarifying his political goals and strategies.

In reference to the map as a whole, these recurring questions would be basic: What new political patterns have appeared? Where? Where have patterns spread or been restricted (even to the vanishing point)? These inquiries refer to patterns of every kind, whether petty and local or cases of emergence of world revolution.[6]

The scope of the proposed basic data survey can be suggested by directing attention first to the study of local units. We deal with these units first partly because the coverage of representative cases is a matter of great importance for the entire conception of an inclusive survey and partly because student aid is likely to be most readily available to describe local events. We would not, however, confine the survey to data that can be obtained only with the assistance of students. Many of the facts required call for the competence of the specialist. We shall not call attention to this distinction in all cases, since it will be obvious. The basic data survey includes projects of every degree of methodological complexity, and the use of students is one among many elements in the total undertaking.

In Chapter 1, we described participation by political scientists in the political process at any community level (international or local) in terms of seven phases. We follow the same outline here, thinking of each phase in the flow of decision as "outcome" events occurring within the decision process as a whole. At each phase, we subdivide the data in order to provide answers to the following questions: Who are the significant *participants* (official or unofficial)? What are the participants' *perspectives* of the outcome (values) they seek, their prospects of success, and the groups with whose fate they identify themselves? What *arenas* are specialized in the task? What assets (*base values*) are at the disposal of participants seeking to influence results? What *strategies* do they employ in managing base values to affect outcomes? With what immediate and long-run results (*outcomes and effects*)?

INTELLIGENCE PHASE

Participants

All individuals who affect the flow of intelligence are participants in the process. It is, however, economical of research time to concentrate on persons and organs who specialize in gathering or disseminating information and to inventory their audiences. Among officials, this points immediately to agencies of reporting and planning. From time to time, local officials leave the area to obtain information about events elsewhere. A check will also show the extent to which local officials depend on sources outside the locality for news of relevance to local decisions. Organizations of mayors and of other officeholding groups publish bulletins and reports of municipal activities and also state, national, and international news of possible interest to local decision-makers.

Unofficial local sources of politically significant intelligence in the United States include the mass media, which often maintain correspondents at the state or national capital, and the reports of party, civic, or other private associations. In turn, these channels rely in varying degree on outside press, party, civic, and other sources.

It is possible—assuming diligence and competence—to inventory the principal sources of current information on which participants rely for intelligence that affects local decisions. There are the questions of (1) amount of exposure to the source and (2) evaluation of the source. It is useful to focus on the specialists who are most easily identified (planning agencies, broadcasters, and the like) and to examine the network of personal contacts on which they rely for rumors of current happenings that bear on local decisions. There is likely to be a high degree of interchange among these specialists; each in turn may rely on an identifiable circle at clubs, homes, offices, street corners, and other gathering places. The sources of information can be mapped according to the structure of politics and of the community as a whole. The result will show, for example, the extent to which any specialist has familiar access to upper, middle, or lower strata of government, party wealth, enlightenment, well-being, skill, respect ("social class"), affection (popularity), and rectitude.

The point of these distinctions and the need for relevant data are obvious on reflection. Common sense and research agree on the selective effect of position in the social context on sources of information. A rich businessman (a member of the upper wealth class, in our terms) who talks mainly to other rich businessmen can be expected to have a version of news differing from that of a rich man who maintains contact with middle-income or poor people. Similarly, the editor who mixes only with persons having equally exhaustive "top-level" knowledge of public affairs is likely to get out of touch with the current scene as viewed by reporters who circulate among humbler people. If one moves only among healthy people, he is likely to overlook the world as seen by the ill. Similarly, in regard to any occupation or profession where skill is important, the current interpretations of events diverge to some extent according to the level of excellence. That social class is a selective factor in rumor and gossip has been heavily emphasized in contemporary social science. In addition, there are persons of exceptional popularity and unpopularity in any community, and this affects versions of events. Similarly, persons and organizations who are regarded as custodians of religion and morality are likely to report current affairs in distinctive terms.

We have been itemizing the broad value-institution categories that are worth applying in any examination of participants in the gathering, dissemination, and interpretation of intelligence. Further, in many communities major differences in ways of life show the impact of contrasting cultures rather than class distinctions within a culture. In the United States, the distinctions between white and Negro castes survive in many localities; the organization of intelligence sources is deeply affected by this alignment.

Political scientists are accustomed to searching for smaller groupings whose effect on the flow of intelligence is often decisive. It is a question of interest groups; by definition, these may include fewer than all members of a culture or class or cut across such lines. Much of the time spent on the job by political reporters is devoted to attempts to uncover interest alignments that may affect their sources of information and therefore influence the intelligence made available to others. Every sophisticated person concerned with municipal politics is aware of an enormous number of interests, such as particular offices, departments, or commissions; political leaders and factions; specific publishers, editors, commentators, or reporters; public-utility, banking, real-estate, department-store, supermarket, hotel, theater, sporting, gambling, prostitution, drug, employer, trade-union, or other economic interests; associations concerned with accident prevention and hospital care; interests relating to administration of tests or awarding of recognition for excellence; "society"; concern with personal popularity; and religious or denominational interest. Obviously, the list could be extended indefinitely. The research task is to see the political process as a whole and to concentrate on combinations of interests that seem most likely to affect intelligence content on significant matters.

Instruments for personality testing open a new field for the intensive study of those who participate in the flow of information. Preliminary research points strongly to the role of various personality types in distorting the flow of intelligence. One thinks of the standard image of gossipy and malicious old maids, of disgruntled characters sliding down the ladder of social respect, of "litigious paranoids" and "persecutory agitators." As crisis levels fluctuate in local communities, the role played by such personalities in private rumor and public print fluctuates accordingly. On-the-spot surveys are needed to enrich our scanty understanding of the importance of these relationships.

If the knowledge pertinent to participation in the intelligence process seems to become unmanageably complex under modern conditions, it is worth recalling that it is not necessary to do everything at once. Approximations can be made, and the whole enterprise becomes cumulatively more important as successive generations of students and others add to the data.

In addition to planning and news, all research activities, including political science research, whether official or unofficial, come within the intelligence category and are eligible for inclusion as objects of survey.

Perspectives

The participants in intelligence activities approach their tasks with differing values, expectations, and identifications. Students of government will presumably concern themselves mainly with discovering the truth about local politics and relating information about local affairs to a comprehensive view of the political process. The dominant value of such a person is enlightenment or skill in research. In contrast, many individuals look on their intelligence tasks as "just a job," a means of making a living. On the other hand, the appeal may be the respect potentials of the task, as with some by-line reporters and commentators. For some persons, camaraderie is the main job aim and satisfaction. Others are oriented toward power, their own or that of the political party with which they are identified. It may be that the intelligence worker is more involved in advancing the cause of his religion or in reforming society than in any other part of his task. There are also cases in which the job has a specific, deep appeal that can be understood only when we see it as a means of preserving precarious mental health. "Inside dopesters" occasionally come in this group.

Whatever the individual case may show, a main object of the survey would be a picture of the aggregate situation at a cross-section in time usable as a bench mark for future changes. It is conceivable that, in the future, fundamental shifts in the relationship among power and other values will be detected earlier in local situations than in larger aggregates. The intelligence flow in the United States has been colored at the local level by the influence of groups actively seeking many values. Will future tendencies give prominence to power, and especially to the power of parties and pressure coalitions seeking to move the people toward militant nationalism? Will this bring with it relative decline in the influence of wealth as traditionally exercised through advertising and social pressure? Or will the leisure and education fostered by an opulent economy bring greater intellectual curiosity and sophistication, with a resulting domination of the flow of local intelligence by journalists, commentators, officials, and research workers who take a political scientist's view of the task?

In surveying the perspectives of intelligence participants, we are cognizant of the strategic role that they play in advancing or limiting competing ideological systems. The relative strength of competing systems can be assessed at the grass roots by a survey of local units. There must, however, be preliminary studies of materials that reflect the most comprehensive and systematic structures of ideology. The Universal Declaration of Human Rights, for example, is a compendium of official interpretations of the dignity of man. The particular problem of the survey when conducted at the local level would be to discover to what extent members of the community are committed to these objectives in the immediate process of decision.

Many methods are already at hand for gathering the data required for a successful survey. Municipal charters and ordinances can be analyzed to find harmonies or discrepancies with the Universal Declaration and other pertinent ideological statements. It is reasonable to assume—subject to more intensive study—that members of the elite are giving utterance to accepted views when they make uncontradicted declarations in public. Content analyses may therefore be made of uncontradicted assertions found in speeches or other public expressions by leading planners, media controllers, and research workers during selected periods. When contrasted with similar declarations by top governmental and party leaders and by other elite spokesmen, the results would show what is stressed or left unstressed by the different groups.

Relatively brief private interviews or tests may be conducted in order to discover the goal commitments of the interviewee and his perception of the goals of other members of the body politic. Depth interviewing can be employed to give a clearer picture of the intensity with which the various views are held.

Alongside the data that have to do with doctrinal declarations of goal, two other types of information bear on fundamental perspectives. The first relates to the structure of the self; the second to political lore, or "miranda."[7] The pertinent question about the self considers the boundaries of the system. How identified am *I* with family, party, religious, and other groups? What images do *I* entertain of the self and of others?

We have called attention above to the challenge in future years to the continued exclusion of advanced forms of life and machines from the category "man." In the immediate future, however, we are more concerned with trends of reference to "race," since world political alignments may conceivably crystallize along racist lines. If we go back to the epoch of the Declaration of Independence in the United States and of the Declaration of the Rights of Man in France, it is evident that the symbols of identity which received emphasis were universalistic, legal, and moral. It was an epoch whose leaders sought to realize the "rights of man," without derogatory distinctions based on criteria other than merit and common humanity. However, the next great world-revolutionary wave spoke the language of "economic" or "material" relations and exalted one economic "class" over another in the hypothetical transition to classlessness.

Beginning with Nazi racialism, world prominence has been given to biological or pseudobiological distinctions. Ex-colonial peoples are usually nonwhite, whence an obvious temptation to propagate racism. In this context, an inhibiting factor of enormous weight is the Communist movement which has identified many ex-colonial peoples with Eastern Europe and played down the racial cleavages. The Communist area may split; if so, the Sino-Russian tension suggests that the reorientation may be along "racist" lines.

We do not ignore the possibility that, as the boundary between living forms grows dim, exclusionist ideologies with new lines of demarcation may appear. Superior forms of life—superior, that is, technologically and in capability—may be discovered as man probes outer space or mutants or machines emerge who possess sensational capabilities and who see no reason to take the claims of man seriously.

Surveys at the local level are especially well adapted to ascertain the facts of caste and class. It is in the sphere of family and friendship that caste distinctions retain most vitality. At the same time, this is the area of human association in which specific attachments exert their greatest effect on established strategies. The changing balance resulting from ambivalence can be described in detail in local units with particular regard to the whole decision process.

In the study of perspectives, we do not depend exclusively on what people say, especially in estimating degrees of intensity. Many of the data called for elsewhere in this prospectus would provide behavioral indications that would deepen our understanding of the perspectives that prevail among intelligence personnel and in the general community.[8]

Arena

The various participants in the intelligence function interact to form an aggregate; the aggregate constitutes an "arena," a situation relatively specialized in the power process. The fact of entering into or leaving off interaction is the important point in describing the expansion or contraction of intelligence operations during a given period. The official agencies are not necessarily identical with the effective arena of information-gathering and -dissemination or -withholding. On the contrary, the principal decisions affecting intelligence may be made by political party leaders or by the staffs of pressure organizations.

Political science is concerned with the original constitution of an arena and with subsequent admissions, exclusions, consolidations, and separations. The total context can be described according to the number and relative strength of participants as multipolar, pluripolar, bi-, tri-, or unipolar. In totalitarian societies, the formal monolithic structure seeks to receive information of local affairs without providing any counterflow of uncensored information or any comprehensive public image of the local situation. This unipolar pattern is never entirely successful, however, since rumor and informal routes of contact supplement the formal channels.

Base Values

As far as official agencies of intelligence are concerned, the formal language of constitution, statute, or ordinance provides authority for a voice in community decision and clears the way to obtaining those assets in addition to power which are required for effective operation. Surveys of base values can conveniently begin with an analysis of the assets and liabilities provided in the authoritative language.

It may be prescribed, for example, that all agencies of local government make information available to the intelligence or planning center. The intelligence organs themselves may be barred from giving information to anyone except the head of the government (the mayor or the council). The services may obtain funds by appropriation or borrowing, and they may be granted access to facilities and to personnel whose qualifications they may prescribe. These may affect the human resources, skill, loyalty, respect, and moral standing of the intelligence operation.

In addition to formal authority, an organ of intelligence can obtain base values of every kind informally for use in gathering information. Personal friendship with key politicians can augment the effective power at its disposal. The economic assets of the individuals connected with intelligence, their social standing, knowledge, dexterity, intelligence, and uprightness all count heavily.

Private operations in the field of intelligence may receive no more protection from the public order than is customary for voluntary organizations generally. But they may have important connections with politics and every other value-institution process in the locality and outside it.

Recall that the survey of "participants" would classify them according to class position in order to describe the sources open to them in the community.[9] In the present context, the values available or potentially available at any cross-section in time are evaluated as contributions to the total influence of the individuals and organizations involved.

Strategies

When we refer to the strategies of a participant in intelligence we have in mind the ways by which base values are utilized to effect the outcomes sought.

Two subobjectives of strategy—assembling and processing—are always present. Base values are not always in a form operationally adapted to the task at hand. Personnel may be available on assignment from other agencies, but training programs may be needed to equip the staff to gather or disseminate information. Similarly, broadcasting facilities must be built before the active processing of intelligence can begin. Surveys can show, for example, the man-hours of time devoted to assembling the units required for planning, news, or research and the man-hours given over to processing. Breakdowns of both sets of strategic activities can be made in minute detail as hypotheses are formulated to guide investigation.

An important question in reference to strategy is whether coercive instruments are used to obtain or block the dissemination of intelligence or to alter the prevailing structure of participation in intelligence. Many dramatic examples of the use of coercion to interfere with news reporting are known, notably in connection with gangs connected with illicit activities. More subtle are the interferences that come from economic pressure (for example, threats of foreclosure or boycott).

Agencies often employ the intelligence at their disposal as a means of augmenting their control of intelligence. For example, during periods of acute crisis in foreign affairs, local groups of retired intelligence officers may circulate "loyalty" information to discredit the leaders of intelligence groups active in civic affairs or in the government. The result may be an effective monopoly of many types of intelligence for the group. The association in question may be dominated by a single decisive figure who concentrates control in his own autocratic hands.

Outcome

An intelligence outcome is the culminating moment in the disclosure or nondisclosure of information. Thus, an official agency may decide to release or to withhold copies of a completed city plan, or a civic association may decide to suppress or to circulate a report on the gangster connections of a candidate. A publisher may defer or expedite the appearance of a book analyzing city government and politics.

Whatever the content of communication media at the outcome phase, it is always pertinent to political science to estimate the degree of influence exerted by whom on the product. This can be done for a given period by examining the source of proposed or of vetoed messages. Such an analysis reveals the coalition alignments for and against various alternatives and isolates the pivotal participants in determining the result.

For purposes of comparison, we emphasize the importance of classifying content according to the five intellectual tasks—goal, trend, condition, projection, and alternative. How comprehensive are community goals in reference to each sphere of value and institution? What parts of the whole process are ignored or given prominence? What is the relative prominence given to trend, condition, and projection, to various alternatives of policy?

At the outcome phase, it is possible to detect the appearance of new ideological patterns and to take note of the diffusion or restriction of the old. When we look at the grand scope of religious or political myths at the extreme of their historical spread, it is easy to lose sight of circumscribed beginnings. One purpose of surveying political change is to learn of new initiatives before they spread generally and to improve methods of evaluating their potential domain. As we describe the current scene, will we be alert enough to detect the incipient stages of a T'ai P'ing Rebellion or a Bolshevik Revolution?

Innovations which themselves have little future may be important indicators of a maelstrom of symbolic activity gradually veering toward new directions of belief, faith, and loyalty. In this connection, "nonpolitical" as well as "political" symbols must be kept in view. Symbolic structures whose manifest content is religious sometimes perform a cathartic function that drains off the pool of motivation open to political programs. Immediately after Japan's defeat in World War II, no fewer than two thousand new religious sects took shape in various parts of the country.[10] It seems clear in the light of subsequent knowledge that the immediate role of these sectarian movements was to provide small pluralistic groups with affection, respect, and enlightenment and thereby to forestall programs of political action. Among sharecroppers and isolated hill folk in the United States, religious revivalism appears to have a similar role of catharsis.

When we referred to outcome events in the intelligence flow, the reference was to such culminating occurrences as the dissemination or withholding of information and exposure to or isolation from information. Subsequent events are assignable to the category of effects. We are asking for data about the total impact of information to which various participant audiences are exposed in a given slice of time. Are their goals for the local commonwealth clarified? If so, in what direction? Are their images of trend, condition, and projection influenced in any way? Is their perceived range of policy alternatives modified?

We referred above to the need for outcome data in terms of new or old ideological systems. The question at this point is how to obtain evidence of results of exposure to communication channels.

Already there are apprehensions at combining signs with chemical factors in the transmission of intelligence, thereby fixing audience response more permanently than by means of signs alone. These methods would presumably be part of the educational channels dedicated to the transmission of established ideology and operational technique.[11]

PROMOTING

Participants

We now consider the requirements of a survey of activities of promotion at the local level. In some communities, the initiative for new policy lies with associations whose staffs are expected to go beyond the intelligence function to advocacy. This is often the case with crime commissions, tax reform associations, property improvement leagues, and the like. Promotional activities are included in various degree in the work of elected officials, party machines, and the press. One task of the survey would be to locate the full-time and part-time performers of the function and to place them in the contexts of culture, class, interest, and personality.[12]

Perspectives

What value effects are sought by those who engage in promotional activities? If we assume that the future holds greater freedom from work, is it reasonable to expect that human activities will become enormously more diversified than they are at present and that many new policies will be pressed on the community? Will one consequence be that professional promoters gradually disappear as citizens engage in voluntary civic efforts?

A related question is whether economic interests will become more or less important sources of pressure for change in countries where private enterprise continues. We are aware of the role that has been played in the United States by equipment manufacturers in improving municipal technology, whether we speak of water works, streets, lights, fire-fighting, police equipment, textbooks, teaching aids, school buildings, or parks and recreational equipment. As science and technology expand and obsolescence is cultivated by industrial laboratories, new materials and designs will abound. If we pursue this line of thought, it seems probable that business promoters will, in fact, multiply in a mixed economy.

What significance do these considerations have for corruption? Will participants in promotion become more grasping, ruthless, and subtle in the pursuit of advantage? It is sometimes predicted that an opulent society will be a virtuous one, since the desperation of poverty will be gone. On the other hand, it is notorious that, in an economy of graduated incomes, economic scope is offered for people to become greatly concerned with small absolute differences ("keeping up with the Joneses"). Since traditional morality has been closely bound up with the ethical imperative to work, an economy that dilutes this imperative is presumably open to moral confusion during transitional stages.[13]

As a means of classifying the demands put forward at the promotional phase of decision, I propose the following broad adaptation of value-institution analysis. Which demands relate to:

(1) The structure of decision at each phase (intelligence, recommending, prescribing, invoking, applying, appraising, terminating) and to participants, perspectives, base values, strategies, outcomes, or effects?

(2) The functioning of the structure of power in the pursuit or defense of predominantly power objectives in the external arena? In the internal arena?

(3) The functioning of power in primary reference to wealth and to institutions relatively specialized in the shaping and sharing of wealth?

(4) The functioning of power in primary reference to respect and to institutions chiefly specialized in the shaping and sharing of respect?

(5) The functioning of power in primary reference to well-being and to institutions which further it?

(6) Functioning in primary reference to rectitude and to institutions which further it?

(7) Functioning in primary reference to affection and to institutions which further it (family, etc.)?

(8) Functioning in primary reference to skill and enlightenment values and institutions?

Arena

The traditional biparty system in this country does not apply to many local arenas, where a unipolar pattern predominates. Pressure organizations are usually numerous, although in many local circumstances a single association or very small number is characteristic. The rise and fall of new parties and pressure associations would be one of the phenomena to be described by the basic data survey in any period.

Base Values

On the basis of survey data, it should be possible to follow trends in the dedication of value assets to promotional work. Lurking in the background of any study of promotion is the hypothesis that, if the commitment of resources reaches great magnitudes, the probability is increased that promotional activities may themselves be prohibited as a consequence of revolutionary change. The analysis runs in these terms: If conflicting policies are vigorously supported against one another, the level of frustration, uncertainty, and anxiety will rise, culminating in a social movement to restore order.

Another hypothesis connects a possible transition from peaceful persuasion to coercion with the magnitude of base values at the disposal of opposing promoters. If money and other assets are unsuccessfully expended on persuasion, the temptation to coerce is increased in the hope of obtaining a surprise advantage.

Surveys of base values need to measure values in various contexts, especially in terms of the perspective of each participant or total asset involvement, political advantage, and probability of net advantage. We are aware of the desperation with which rear-guard actions can be waged by cultural minorities who recognize that, owing to the exhaustion of resources at their disposal, they are near the end of their privileged position.

Strategies

The temptation to cut promotional costs and uncertainties by entering into monopolistic agreements with competitors or by drives to abolish competition are as common in politics as in other situations. Surveys of party strategy are often able to demonstrate collusion between a perpetual majority and minority party.[14] Why go to the bother of a vigorous electoral campaign if the minority can be "bought off" in advance with a guaranteed place? Or why should parties identified with the established order allow themselves to be harassed by a vocal minority? Majority parties often connive to erect insurmountable obstacles to organizing a new party and obtaining a place on the ballot.

When party or pressure campaigns expect to win through the support of an uncommitted and pivotal body of individuals or organizations, the strategy is to emphasize demands acceptable to the pivotal elements. This tends to universalize "issue" demands and to transfer tactical emphasis to "personalities." The appearance of issue unanimity may create an exaggerated picture of ideological unity; that is, the strength of the dissatisfied extremes may be understated. Hence one task of the survey would be to devise methods of describing campaigns which distinguish genuine "issue unity" from more doubtful cases.

The survey would follow the justifications employed by the advocates of the various demands during the preoutcome phase. A particular demand in regard to power, for instance, may be justified in terms of power, in the language either of legality or of expediency. The same demand may be promoted in the language of ethics or religion (rectitude) or as a boon to safety (well-being), family solidarity (affection), science and education (enlightenment and skill), economic growth (wealth), or prestige (respect).

Outcomes

Promotional activities culminate in alignments that win, lose, or draw—whether the situation is that of a candidate or an issue election. Who took the initiative to promote a given demand or to block a demand? Whose support was pivotal in the formation of a successful coalition in obtaining or blocking a result?[15]

Effects

In providing data for the assessment of effects, a major question is whether promotional activities as a whole strengthen or weaken an established ideology for the benefit of rival ideologies. Ideologies become phraseology when the key terms, though given great prominence, lose intensity of commitment among their adherents. The best evidence of intensity changes comes from depth interviewing. Important assumptions emerge, however, if discrepancies between the pattern of justification employed in elite-to-elite and in elite-to-mass promotions multiply.[16] One index of a secularizing policy, for instance, is the omission of religious justifications where elites are addressing one another and when they are attempting to influence a mass audience.

Thus, the comparative reporting of justifications would furnish the observer with grounds for affirming the rise or fall of various values as goals of community action. Economic considerations have had a noteworthy impact on the language of advocacy. In the United

States, for example, business decisions are supposed to be made for the benefit of the shareholders; hence, policies whose support is non-economic (such as rectitude, power, or respect) are phrased in monetary terms. In local affairs, economic policies have often been championed in the vernacular of "business efficiency." More recently, the threat of war has led to the use in municipal matters of "national security" (power) as a justification for programs.

PRESCRIBING

Participants

Formal participants in local units include legislators and chief executives; where the initiative and referendum are authorized, the electorate also participates directly. Local community studies presently provide scattered data about the relationship between prescribers and the social context. One of the most obvious tasks of the basic data survey would be to enlarge the coverage by region throughout the nation.

In coming years, a topic of particular interest in this connection will be the degree to which the rising elite of scientists and engineers enters the local picture. In the past, some localities have become strongholds of archaic social forms. Because local leaders engage in full-time political activity, these districts exerted an influence out of proportion to their numbers.[17]

Perspectives

Every specialized arena tends to establish norms that restrain the pursuit of power. Among legislators, in particular, procedural arrangements lend themselves to the cultivation of particular skills that may take priority over the individual's pursuit of power. Respect often goes to an adroit parliamentarian or debater or to the negotiator of coalition agreements. The rewards of "the game" can become so absorbing that the participant fails to adopt a realistic power strategy and neglects to look beyond the confines of the committee room or the chamber. He may lose contact with constituents, and the process may go so far that the entire structure of government loses support throughout the body politic.[18] This narrowing of the focus of attention to immediate opportunities for gain or loss carries with it some systematic distortion of reality. Participants who are spatially remote tend to drop out of sight, and developments at the periphery are greeted with surprise or shock.

By examining the focus of attention of the legislators at the local level, we may discover trends toward greater parochialism even within the local community, such as the neglect of neighborhoods or cultural minorities.

But data on "the game of politics" afford many clues to the value perspectives and ideological involvements of prescribers. Additional clues are obtainable from some of the data called for in connection with intelligence and promotion. Here the information is brought together for the whole community in order to disclose the commitments of the specialists in prescription.

Arenas

The aggregate of formal arenas at the level of federal government is tripolar. At the local level, the judiciary tends to drop out of sight, and sometimes the mayor; but the electorate may take a more prominent part. In many communities, the prescribing function is highly dispersed to include the board of education, board of public health, a number of other boards, commissions, and relatively independent commissioners.

As usual in the investigation of effective as against formal institutions, it would not be possible for the survey to present a valid picture of the function of any part until the entire context had been described. Meanwhile, of course, particular indexes would be gathered because they are of obvious pertinence, even though they cannot be definitive.[19]

Base Values

Local units of government in the United States are usually regarded as creatures of state or even of federal government, not of the narrower community. In practice, of course, the situation may be markedly different, since the economic and other bases of power of some metropolitan areas may transform the state unit into a subsidiary structure.

In the local decision process, the consideration of base values can be focused on the authority of the legislative body in relation to other organs of government that enter actively into community affairs. This brings into the picture a number of agencies (state, federal, or international) that may be engaged in local programs. Some of the suburbs of New York, for example, include citizens whose connections ramify to Washington, Albany, or Hartford, with potentialities that can modify the values at the disposal of local authorities. Pending data obtained by the direct study of outcome situations, the basic data survey might use panels of "insiders" selected from among knowledgeable politicians to estimate the influence potential of a given unit. The questions would deal with possible conflicts between local authorities and other units of government.[20]

Strategy

The distinctive tool at the disposal of a prescribing authority is language; hence, drafting tactics are especially relevant to the strategy of prescribers. Modern systems of logic lend themselves to the study of statutes and ordinances, and it may be that more attention to the content of municipal regulations would influence the future phrasing of such enactments. Carelessness often leads to ambiguities that affect the discretion of officials charged with administrative responsibility, and it is often alleged that unnecessary damage is thus done. In any case, the survey could report on the clarity with which prescriptions are formulated, perhaps noting the difference between original proposals and final statements.[21]

In the interest of putting citizens on notice of their obligations, it is often urged that laws ought to be simple and clear. Several criteria have been suggested for classifying the relative simplicity and clarity of prose, and sample studies can be made by students of municipal ordinances.

A further point made in the cause of simple clarity is that "constitutional" provisions should be separated from "statutory" matter. In the local context, this would mean that charter provisions or fundamental ordinances ought to be kept free of cluttering detail.

Outcome

The survey would regularly record the sheer volume of words put out by authoritative agencies of prescription and classify according to the aspect of the social process to which they refer. Ordinances dealing with participation in the decision process obviously relate to power. Some are focused primarily on the economic process (for example, taxation and commerce). Local legislation is normally concerned with education, health, information, and morals. Matters of respect and affection play a pervasive but typically unformulated role.

For comparative purposes, the flow of authoritative prescription can usually be classified according to several codes designed to emphasize the role of government itself.[22] The "constitutive" code is identical to the power category mentioned above; it includes the language that specifies "who, with what qualifications, selected how, and with what objectives and base values may decide what, under what circumstances, and by what procedure."

The "enterprisory" code includes all prescriptions about activities for which the government has continuing administrative responsibility, for example, public utility services. The "regulative" code deals with the norms according to which private activities are to be carried out. The "supervisory" code concerns matters that are voluntarily referred to the community for settlement, which include most of the civil controversies sufficiently petty to get into municipal rather than state courts. The "corrective" code covers the measures that may be used by the community to cope with non-responsible offenders. The other "sanctions" are considered parts of the appropriate code whose norms are to be maintained.

In this context, we should note that a complete prescription includes three sets of statements: (1) the norm to be lived up to; (2) the factual circumstances to which the norm refers; (3) the sanction to be employed in case of breach or conformity. It is relevant to emphasize the point regarding conformity because sanctions are positive as well as negative: they may involve citations, honors, tax exemptions, and the like.

The basic data survey could throw light on the trend to rely on coercion or persuasion by reporting the changing balance of prescriptions of positive and negative sanction and the values involved. These categories are especially relevant to state and other inclusive units of government which are commonly authorized to monopolize the most severe sanctions. But there are grounds for asserting that variations in local practice are especially sensitive indicators of the significant tendencies in any period.

If the scientific approach to human affairs becomes more pervasive, sanctions will not be applied against non-responsible deviants; further, sanctions will be subject to continuing adjustment according to the results obtained from past applications. Survey data on the total sanctioning process are of great importance to political science and public policy.[23]

Effects

We have already mentioned a major effect that may follow prescription. Most of the data on effects will appear as we move through the remaining parts of the outline.

NOTES

[1] R. Hofstader and W. P. Metzger, *The Development of Academic Freedom in the United States* (New York: Columbia University Press, 1955), show the slow growth of the doctrine and operation of freedom of teaching, inquiring, publishing, and of civic participation. Also, J. E. Kirkpatrick, *Academic Organization and Control* (Yellow Springs, Ohio: The Antioch Press, 1931).

[2] Information about the pool of talent is to be found in D. C. McClelland *et al.*, *Talent and Society,* "New Perspectives in the Identification of Talent" (Princeton, N.J.: D. Van Nostrand, 1958).

[3] Research by undergraduates is often acknowledged by professors in prefaces and footnotes. It is common knowledge that senior theses often reach the level of masters' theses in quality.

[4] Cf. G. Lindzey, ed., *Handbook of Social Psychology* (2 vols.; Cambridge: Addison-Wesley, 1954); S. Arieti, ed., *American Handbook of Psychiatry* (New York: Basic Books, 1959); P. F. Lazarsfeld and M. Rosenberg, eds., *The Language of Social Research* (Glencoe, Ill.: The Free Press, 1955); A. Ranney, ed., *Essays on the Behavioral Study of Politics* (Urbana: University of Illinois Press, 1962); V. Van Dyke, *Political Science,* "A Philosophical Analysis" (Stanford: Stanford University Press, 1960); C. Hyneman, *The Study of Politics* (Urbana: University of Illinois Press, 1959); R. Young, ed., *Approaches to the Study of Politics* (Evanston, Ill.: Northwestern University Press, 1958).

[5] Active efforts are being made to overcome the "method gap." The urgency of providing suitable manuals has been repeatedly stressed in the regional seminars conducted under the auspices of the A.P.S.A. in recent years.

[6] On the rise, diffusion, and restriction of political patterns, cf. H. D. Lasswell and D. Blumenstock, *World Revolutionary Propaganda,* "A Chicago Study" (New York: Knopf, 1939). The framework was originally outlined in the senior author's *World Politics and Personal Insecurity* (New York: McGraw-Hill, 1935).

[7] I follow in this book the terminology utilized in H. D. Lasswell and A. Kaplan, *Power and Society,* "A Framework for Political Inquiry" (New Haven: Yale University Press, 1950). Political myth is divided into three categories—doctrine, formula, and miranda, which are approximately equivalent to philosophy, law, and folklore. The term "formula" comes from G. Mosca, and "miranda" from C. E. Merriam. "Self" is defined to include identifications (or identities), expectations, and demands.

[8] "Perspectives" are defined as subjective events which can be described

according to symbols of reference and intensity or degree of stress toward completion of an act. Nonsubjective events which are, in addition to subjective events, parts of an act, are defined as operations. A relatively stable pattern of operations and perspectives is a "practice." Institutions are classified according to the value (preferred events) in the shaping and sharing of which they are relatively specialized. Perspectives can be inferred from self-observation and by observing the operations of others relatively specialized in communication or collaboration in the social process of interaction.

9 On the composition, recruitment, and role of intelligence personnel, cf. R. E. Carter, Jr., "Newspaper 'Gatekeepers' and the Sources of News," *Public Opinion Quarterly*, 22 (1958), 133–144; R. L. Jones and G. E. Swanson, "Small-City Daily Newspapermen: Their Abilities and Interests," *Journalism Quarterly*, 31 (1954), 38–55.

10 Prof. H. Kishamoto of the University of Tokyo has studied religious activities in Japan in detail. For background, cf. his *Japanese Religion in the Meiji Era* (Tokyo: Obunsha, 1956).

11 Cf. R. J. Lifton, *Thought Reform and the Psychology of Totalism* (New York: Norton, 1961); A. D. Biderman and H. Zimmer, eds., *The Manipulation of Human Behavior* (New York: Wiley, 1961); and the work of E. H. Schein, J. A. M. Meerloo, and others.

12 Cf. the early contributions of B. L. Smith and L. C. Rosten, especially Rosten, *The Washington Correspondents* (New York: Harcourt, Brace, 1937). Further, L. Lowenthal and N. Guterman, *Prophets of Deceit* (New York: Harpers, 1949); G. E. Swanson, "Agitation through the Press: A Study of the Personalities of Publicists," *Public Opinion Quarterly*, 20 (1956), 441–456. See the hints in S. Kelley, Jr., *Professional Public Relations and Political Power* (Baltimore: Johns Hopkins University Press, 1956).

13 A. Rogow and H. D. Lasswell, *Power, Corruption and Rectitude* (Englewood Cliffs, N.J.: Prentice-Hall, 1963). On socialization and norms, see D. Easton and R. D. Hess, "Youth and the Political System," in S. M. Lipset and L. Lowenthal, eds., *Culture and Social Character*, "The Work of David Riesman Reviewed" (New York: The Free Press of Glencoe, 1961), pp. 226–251; A. J. Brodbeck, "Values in The Lonely Crowd: Ascent or Descent of Man?" *ibid.*, pp. 42–71; S. de Grazia, *The Political Community* (Chicago: University of Chicago Press, 1948); H. H. Hyman, *Political Socialization* (New York: Columbia University, Bureau of Applied Social Research, 1957).

14 V. O. Key, Jr., *American State Politics* (New York: Knopf, 1956); J. H. Fenton, *Politics in the Border States* (New Orleans: The Hauser Press, 1957); A. Leiserson, *Parties and Politics*, "An Institutional and Behavioral Approach" (New York: Knopf, 1958).

[15] The analysis of electoral behavior is the principal source of estimates of impact on outcomes. See the standard works of H. F. Gosnell, A. N. Holcombe, V. O. Key, P. F. Lazarsfeld, A. Campbell, W. E. Miller, S. J. Eldersfeld, S. Lubell, D. E. Stokes, P. T. David, among many others.

[16] The technique of such comparison is exemplified by G. A. Almond, *The Appeals of Communism* (Princeton: Princeton University Press, 1954).

[17] Cf. A. J. Vidich and J. Bensman, *Small Town in Mass Society* (Princeton: Princeton University Press, 1958); M. Janowitz, ed., *Community Power Systems* (New York: The Free Press of Glencoe, 1961); R. C. Wood, *Suburbia,* "Its People and Their Politics" (Boston: Houghton, Mifflin, 1959). In preindustrial cultures, the impact of the old, though great, is not always against change, even at the village level. Cf. G. M. Carter and W. O. Brown, eds., *Transition in Africa,* "Studies in Political Adaptation" (Boston: Boston University Press, 1958); R. L. Park and I. Tinker, eds., *Leadership and Political Institutions in India* (Princeton: Princeton University Press, 1959).

[18] The technique of such analysis is exemplified by N. Leites, *On the Game of Politics in France* (Stanford: Stanford University Press, 1959).

[19] Studies of local government are beginning again. Cf. R. A. Dahl, *Who Governs?* "Democracy and Power in an American City" (New Haven: Yale University Press, 1961). A comprehensive survey is S. Humes and E. M. Martin, *The Structure of Local Government throughout the World* (The Hague: M. Nijhoff, 1961).

[20] The connections of metropolitan to larger areas are indicated throughout W. Sayre and H. Kaufman, *Governing New York City,* "Politics in the Metropolis" (New York: Russell Sage Foundation, 1960).

[21] On technique, cf. L. E. Allen, "Symbolic Logic: A Razor-Edged Tool for Drafting and Interpreting Legal Documents," *Yale Law Journal,* 56 (1957), 833–879.

[22] G. H. Dession and H. D. Lasswell, "Public Order Under Law: The Role of the Advisor-Draftsman in the Formation of Code or Constitution," *Yale Law Journal,* 65 (1955), 175–184. The five categories for the comparative study of systems are constitutive, regulatory, enterprisory, supervisory, and corrective; they are systematically applied by M. S. McDougal and associates to the law of nations in the Yale Law School series in course of publication by the Yale University Press.

[23] Cf. the technical devices used to assess legislative outcomes according to final or early alignment, pivotal position, or initiative: J. C. Wahlke, H. Eulau, W. Buchanan, and L. C. Ferguson, *The Legislative Sys-*

tem, "Explorations in Legislative Behavior" (New York: Wiley, 1962); D. B. Truman, *The Congressional Party,* "A Case Study" (New York: Wiley, 1959); D. McRae, Jr., *The Dimensions of Congressional Voting* (Berkeley and Los Angeles: University of California Press, 1958); J. Turner, *Party and Constituency,* "Pressures on Congress" (Baltimore: Johns Hopkins University Press, 1955).

4

The Basic
Data
Survey (II) Invoking, Applying, Appraising, Terminating

INVOCATION

Participants

Those who officially participate in invoking activities are prominent at the local level. Besides policemen and magistrates, however, we must not lose sight of the large number of private citizens who frequently initiate complaints of "criminal" breach or become involved in private controversies that are presented or referred to the courts.[1] The basic data survey would enable us for the first time to follow in detail the factors that affect the changing level of invocation.

Perspectives

In the lower levels of society, it would presumably be an indication of increasing self-confidence if more complaints were lodged against upper-class organizations and individuals who were formerly feared. Not all rate increases are likely to have this significance, however. They may reflect an "overproduction" of lawyers and a resulting multiplication of disputes.

Research at the local level for the survey could provide information needed to distinguish between the articulated and ostensible grounds of an invocation and the value goals actually pursued. Consider the enforcement policies of local officials. Why do they suddenly act against long-standing abuses? Why do they adopt more permissive policies toward gambling and other illicit activities? Why do trends toward vigilant or lax law enforcement continue for several years or change abruptly? A notorious feature of many law enforcement drives is the desire to raise money for party purposes or even as private graft.

Since many of the calculations that affect policies of invocation are private, it may be necessary to approximate the facts by relying first on panels of insiders, whose views would be reported anonymously.

A neglected area of research is the matching of cases of invocation with cases that seem quite similar yet led to no appeal to official tribunals. Investigation may show that various commercial organizations or religious and ethnic groups have worked out their own arbitration arrangements. One problem for the basic data survey would be to report the flow of informal invocation and to direct attention to situations in which acts of invocation are missing (despite evidence, for instance, of traffic "violations" or of considerable violence in husband-wife, parent-child, or neighbor-neighbor relationships).

Arenas

In any given period, the aggregate composition of the arenas specialized in invocation will emerge if the survey gives attention to the initiators and targets of action in the framework of prescription. It is especially relevant to watch for new groups and organizations seeking to stimulate the exercise of formal authority by public agencies in every field. Similarly, it is relevant to note the dissolution, absorption, or inactivity of previously active associations. Emergency committees to press officials to clean up unsanitary conditions or to remove traffic hazards are typical examples.

Base Values

The usual analysis of formal authority and of formally authorized access to values is relevant here. In the future, however, the survey would be justified in paying particular attention to "respect values." There are also many indications that a new field of professional specialization is emerging which has particular significance for the invoking function. I refer to "sanction law," or the study of the entire subprocess of sanctioning within the decision process as a whole.[2] Many adjoining or partial specialties are involved, including political science, especially police administration and criminal law and criminology. To the extent that war is superseded by police action, the army, navy, and air and space forces will fuse with the sanctioning process. My forecast is that, as sanction law improves in scientific strength and professional recognition, the status of local sanctioners will rise.

Strategy

We referred to the timing of law enforcement activities in discussing perspectives. In the present context, the survey would summarize, among other data, the justifications invoked on behalf of a particular policy demand. It is not a question here of demands to prescribe, but of claims in concrete circumstances to obtain a result allegedly authorized by prescription or to block a result alleged to be contrary to a prescription.

The survey would need to summarize according to the five codes mentioned above (constitutive, regulatory, enterprisory, supervisory, corrective) and according to the value norm invoked. For instance, a demand to remove X from office for alleged breach of discipline might be elaborated by asserting that other formal prescriptions have been violated or that informal prescriptions have been broken.

Outcome

The survey would report as outcomes such culminating acts as formal complaints or the filing of a controversial claim. Preoutcome activities include the formation of coalitions for or against action. In this connection, we may note that some invocations are entirely individual acts; others involve collective behavior.[3]

Effects

The most significant effect is application or nonapplication, as will be outlined in the next section.

APPLICATION

Participants

The survey would identify as participants all who are so identified by fellow members of the application process and groups which, though not explicitly recognized in a given context, are nevertheless visible to the scientific observer with comparable experience. Subject to certain exceptions mentioned elsewhere in this outline, all who are charged with the execution of the authorized prescriptions relating to a local community belong to the application phase of the decision process.

In general, then, official participants include all administrative personnel. They would be further divided according to rank or grade into upper, middle, and lower echelons; further subdivided by service (public works and so on); and further into central and field components.[4] In the most general sense, "centralization" refers to the inclusiveness of a pattern. Thus, authority may be centralized for a given service—as for the settlement of a given category of disputes—at one level and in one office. Or a service, like sanitation, may have a headquarters and several field stations. The scope of authority of the headquarters includes all the field stations. However, there may be only two echelons at the headquarters which outrank the man in charge of a field station, and formal authority over many outcomes is delegated to the station.

At any given echelon, we speak of the degree to which authority is "concentrated" in one office and official or the extent to which it is dispersed among several coordinate agencies or persons. Instead of one judicial officer, there may be several independent courts, some of which have more than one judge.

The survey would reveal basic trends in the structure of government by reporting the ratio of officials to population for various services and the ratio between headquarters and field staffs. Comparisons of field districts would be facilitated if ratios were related to population densities, since some parts of the local community may be sparsely populated. Reporting by rank and grade would bring into the open tendencies to inflate the upper levels, or the reverse. With the introduction of automated procedures, it is likely that the future balance of administrative organizations will be appreciably modified by reducing "clerical" personnel.

It would be useful to bring into the survey information about the state, federal, or international units within which the locality is included, since these have immediate effects in the local decision process, especially at the application phase. The report should summarize the ratio of the local population to the population of each district and the place of the district office in the structure of which it is a part. These figures would indicate something of the ease of access to the centers of policy for the entire area.

The survey would supplement the formal image by adding for each participant a list of the significant organizations and unorganized groups which exercise a relatively strong influence over what it does. Most of this information can be revealed only by intensive and time-consuming case studies. However, a valuable preliminary result can be obtained by interviewing panels of "insiders" and recording their estimates. The top health authority, for example, is continually subject to initiatives that originate with "client" groups which expect to be affected by what the authority does. Hospitals, physicians, drugstores, food processors and purveyors, manufacturers who use poisonous or noxious materials or processes—these constitute a brief reminder. In seeking to obtain appropriations and facilities, the health authority is able to enlist the support of some of these client interests. Support or pressure is not limited to the locality, since state and even larger official and unofficial groupings are potentially implicated in local health affairs.[5]

As usual, the survey would report the results of elite analysis of official and other groups.

Perspectives

A key question in connection with administrative activity is whether the responsible officials are determined to serve the common interest as that interest is currently interpreted by the leaders of thought in the profession concerned. The question is not whether the contemporary views entertained by public health authorities or traffic specialists are correct, but whether the officials of a given locality are attempting to give their community the benefit of the best available judgment, recognizing the restrictions within which they must operate. The surveyors would need to be kept abreast of contemporary perspectives in each field, a formidable task which should be performed for the local people by colleagues elsewhere. Panels could be set up, if necessary, to provide estimates of the perspectives that in fact prevail at top, middle, and low levels.

Such an inquiry would simultaneously weigh the importance of

other factors. For example, there may be agreement that special
economic, ecclesiastical, or other interests affect the outlook of officials
on discernible points.[6]

Arenas

As usual in portraying the arena as a whole, it would be easy
for survey purposes to take note of all the official agencies which say
a final word in concrete circumstances on the meaning of authorized
public policies. The difficult questions relate to organizations that en-
force conformity on themselves or others or, on the contrary, persist
in failing to apply the manifest norms laid down in formal documents.

The conformity-enforcing organizations may apply a regulation
directly that all business houses in a given area close by 7:00 P.M.
Perhaps such a standard is not found in the book of ordinances; inquiry may reveal that the merchants of the locality agreed on this
rule and to punish any nonconformist by refusing the use of delivery
trucks, by exclusion from the merchants' association, or perhaps by
harassment of customers and clerks. Effectively applied prescriptions
are sometimes enacted by other than the government as conventionally identified. In fact, there may be no formal enactment of any kind;
an alert surveyor will discover that something new has come into
existence "by custom" and that deviations have serious consequences
for the offender.[7]

Base Values

Here is the most convenient place for survey planners to consider
the economic and other assets available to various participants. To
some extent, this is a simple matter of reporting the per-capita
equipment and current income accounts (including all forms of extra-
local aid) of each activity (school system, urban redevelopment, and
so on). Interviewing can disclose the positive assets or liabilities of
public officials in terms of community respect and reputation for integrity. The principal asset of an organization for many purposes is
the legislative enactment that confers jurisdiction on it and provides
an authoritative claim on other organizations and individuals for economic and other bases of power.

Strategy

In the discussion of invocation, we emphasized the relation between concrete social situations and the uses of complaint and claim.

Although the examples were largely from the field of police administration, comparable phases are involved in every public service. Assume, for instance, that a public works administrator is authorized by community prescription to proceed with site clearance and preparation, and the construction of recreational centers. Despite informal suggestions that he begin, the official may decide not to invoke his authority until other projects are completed. A survey of authorized activities (permissive or mandatory) not begun by a given time would provide pertinent information. Activities begun (with or without completion) would belong to the survey's inventory of the application function.

In addition to the strategy of timing, it would be convenient to explore the instruments on which each participant depends in managing his external relations. Each value base could be considered in detail. It is, however, illuminating for purposes of comparison to think of strategies as employing diplomacy, mass communications, wealth, or weapons. Each unit of officialdom operates in an arena in which superordinate, coordinate, and subordinate units are involved; external relations can be understood as relating to superordinate and coordinate units as well as to any other identifiable entity in the official or unofficial environment with which coalitions may be made or against which coalitions can be formed. Diplomacy is elite-to-elite contact and is designed to make or break working agreements. (Thus, in cooperation with finance officers, it may be possible to deny funds to Y and free more assets for X.) Communication is elite-to-mass contact and includes word-of-mouth and other types of publicity intended to advance the aims of the unit under study. Economic assets can be used to induce or intimidate action, and in some cases actual weapons are available even at the local level. It would presumably be easiest for the survey to obtain information about the man-hours (or dollars) devoted to propaganda than to other instruments.

In the context of the community decision process, each decision sequence internal to a participant can be viewed as part of the strategy whereby the organization in question seeks to make itself effective. The internal arena can be examined in detail through the categories used in reference to the community as a whole (participants, perspectives, base values, strategies, outcomes, and effects). In this way, the finer structure of government is brought into view and the assumptions reflected in the opinions of the "insiders" can be subjected to independent check. Although most of the information called for in this connection would require case investigations, it would be possible in some instances to obtain usable results with little outlay of time and facilities.

For some agencies, it would be possible to summarize the man-hours per capita spent in patterns of various kinds—receiving or giving information, advocating or listening to advocacy, putting regulations into final form, invoking or listening to the invoking of prescriptions, applying prescriptions in concrete cases or being an object of such application, appraising success or failure, terminating prescriptions, and disposing of resulting claims.

Outcomes

The final application of the authority of an official to concrete cases is an outcome. A decision by a revenue agency may be appealed to the courts. In the context of the agency, it is, however, final. Similarly, the contractual agreements of an administrative unit, the grants of license or relief, or acceptances of gifts are final outcomes.

The survey would tabulate decisions made by agencies of application and provide some indication of the magnitude of the values at stake (for example, dollars of contracts, capital investment in licensed enterprises, persons given varying amounts of aid, or capital evaluation of the land and facilities received by gift for recreational or other purposes).

Many decisions are made with little effort to provide a formal opinion justifying the outcome. This is also true in low-level courts. But the lives of millions of people are affected by the functioning of courts that deal with minor offenses and quarrels, and the survey would perform a unique service if it provided a more inclusive and accurate view than we have today of how the tribunals that are most directly in contact with the population function.

Surveys can usefully compare the successes of the same participant in several arenas. Thus, a minority group may fare badly in influencing legislative votes, even though it usually wins court cases involving its members. The report may be refined to bring out the originating or pivotal role in the eventual solution.[8]

Effects

Many postoutcome events can be attributed without much doubt to the combination of factors that are crystallized in an outcome, and the survey would be on the lookout for instances of this kind. For example, some public health results can be imputed to the decision to vaccinate or immunize school children. Public enlightenment may be affected by a program that exchanges students with a foreign country. Employment figures rise after new industries are brought in by advertising, land development, and tax exemption. Divorce may decline after the inauguration of matrimonial clinics connected with courts. Levels of skills may rise sharply after the completion of technical schools. Discriminatory practices in many community institutions may be abolished after a decision to discover and eliminate differential treatment of minorities in access to civil service positions, hospitals, and the like. The political impact of the community in the state legislature may be increased if a lobbyist is appointed to push measures affecting the area. The juvenile delinquency rate may fall after the introduction of club programs in depressed areas.

APPRAISAL

Participants

Official appraisers include financial officers responsible for giving an over-all account of the success of fiscal operations when assessed in terms of solvency and liquidity. Departments often have specialists in the preparation of reports, including the statistics supposedly depicting the successes and failures of programs. In future years, the skills at the disposal of such personnel will presumably include the various versions of operations research, the employment of which would be tabulated by the survey.

Perspectives

Will the demand for competent and impartial appraisal continue to grow? Most pertinent to the assessment of this demand is the practice of consulting experts on any aspect of local government which comes into controversy. Many appraisal activities have been organized in modern society to provide data for private and public commitment. We are accustomed to quantifying the performance of many municipal services and to comparing results through time and among communities. This is true, for instance, of fire, police, traffic, schools, health, sanitation, and finance. And it is relevant for a survey to discover the degree to which current reports of this kind reach insurance agents, physicians, school board members, and other appropriate local audiences.

Arenas

Since appraisal units are less clearly identified in contemporary structures of government than some other functional units, it would often be necessary for survey purposes to encourage detailed inquiries into the actual operation of local systems. In this way, an aggregate picture could be drawn and the rise and fall of organized activities could be followed through time. Specialized private associations would, of course, be included.

Base Values

In view of the mechanization of reporting routines in modern administration, it is probable that large capital expenditures would be necessary for adequate appraisal.

Strategies

The acceptance of the idea of competent and impartial appraisal is often accomplished in different ways. The most persuasive argument is economic: what is the taxpayer getting for his dollar? But appraisal operations are often the children of scandal, being introduced in the wake of public consternation about bad policing, poor schools, or graft. Quiet research can gather the facts which the community is willing to consider when in the grip of alarm and revulsion. The survey would occasionally examine the activities of appraisal services in bringing their findings to the attention of community groups and of the public at large.

It is notorious that no single index is ever satisfactory to everyone as a summary of the effectiveness of a program. This comes in part from the spontaneous defensiveness of one who fears that his position is imperiled. In fact, however, reluctance to agree on a single master index rests on more solid ground. The values of a free society are plural, and the emphasis on them varies among members of the community. Furthermore, specific operational indexes differ and give rise to diverse judgments. Officials charged with appraisal tasks therefore resort to "defense by technicalization" in the sense that they typically refrain from flat, over-all assessments and confine themselves to comparisons between "partial indexes of performance" and "partial indexes of goal." Furthermore, they adhere as closely as possible to a plausible interpretation of authoritative prescriptions.

Unofficial agencies and individuals are freer to put forward definitions of community goals which may or may not coincide with the prescriptions currently in force. Part of the contribution that unofficial groups can make is to call attention to more exacting specifications of objective than have been fully accepted in legislation. In this they are invoking the political myth to appraise the political formula.

Basic surveys would perform a clarifying function if they called attention to agreements and differences that arise in interpreting objectives or in discussing the index used to define goals. In the past, for example, varying methods of estimating the net worth of public utilities have led to great differences in published figures. Contrasting methods of measuring unemployment lead to important divergencies, especially in reference to the partially employed (or people with two jobs). Expert opinion is not unified on the best way to describe how public services affect the standard of living—a point of no small significance in comparing socialist and mixed economies.

Outcome

The grand objective of scientifically minded appraisers is a comprehensive view of the community that can be relied on to show the degree to which policy objectives are realized. At a more sophisticated level, appraisers add a further complication—to what extent are governmental activities instrumental in producing the results described? Sometimes the answer to this question is obvious: the new hospital was struck by lightning, hence the government cannot be regarded as a factor in the failure to hit the target of improved hospitalization by building new facilities.

There may be evidence that appraisers have been sharply divided about what they should report. It may, indeed, be spread over the face of reports signed by majority and minority members. But the split may be disguised. It may be possible to describe preoutcome maneuvers in terms that show which contending coalition supported or opposed the appraisals finally published. The issue may be primarily technical and may serve mainly to show that trained economists differ from trained lawyers or political scientists.

Effects

Perhaps the most far-reaching effect of the basic data survey would be in the appraisal phase of the decision process. It would focus on goals and performances of the body politic and, by bringing fundamental questions recurrently to general attention, affect the frame of mind in which problems of government are considered.

As a convenient check list for thinking about the total context,

I use the value-institution categories employed in this book. Those responsible for the survey would need to keep this or an equivalent set of categories at the focus of their attention in order to achieve systematic coverage. To some extent, effect data are currently available regarding each local community (as remarked above in the discussion of strategy). But it will be obvious to political scientists that there are many important gaps limiting any appraisal operation. Many of these gaps will challenge the profession to improve its research programs and to stimulate other disciplines to participate.[9]

TERMINATION

Participants

If concern for human dignity and for the dignity of all advanced forms of life increases in coming years, it is probable that more attention will be given to obviating adverse effects of policy change. More government officials will be involved in listening to complaints and seeking to make adjustments in ways compatible with fundamental policy. Such a criterion implies sensitive consideration for human rights and freedoms. Termination problems are familiar; for example, they involve adjustments intended to reduce particularly burdensome effects when a community shifts from rent control to a free market or back again or when a city terminates the policy of unrestricted land use and substitutes urban redevelopment. In the past, these adjustments have often been "highly political"; one topic of the survey would be the composition of boards or groups of referees.

Perspectives

More direct evidence of the frame of mind in which termination officials approach their tasks could be obtained by an "insiders' panel." It is likely that officials charged with such responsibilities would develop a professional specialty in clarifying the appropriate criteria. Inquiry would show whether the local boards are cognizant of these activities and whether they participate in professional meetings and related affairs.

Arenas

Since termination is a category that is not used in the conventional classification of government operations in the United States, the survey would usually need to interview "insiders" in order to draw a preliminary picture of all units engaged in this function and to describe the appearance and disappearance of units.

Base Values

Perhaps the most interesting survey problem in this connection would be to follow fluctuations in the deference assets of terminators (respect, rectitude, and so forth).

Strategy

Estimates of damage to a value position depend in part on establishing expectations of their future value position that claimants could have rationally entertained prior to termination. Hence, it is necessary to consider evidence of past trend and projection; if this is to carry conviction, the sources used must be among the best available. The survey would report on the quality of information brought into the determination of claims (by expertness of source and the like).

Outcomes; Effects

The results would be examined as usual to bring out their significance for fortifying the established ideological system, undermining adherence to it, and for affecting the practices prevailing in the community. Do terminations provoke resentment in identifiable groups? Is one effect to cut down local financing of civic enterprises?[10]

ORGANIZATION OF THE SURVEY

The A.P.S.A. need not assume responsibility for the entire stream of data required to present a comprehensive and current map of political change. However, the association would be well-advised to initiate the entire enterprise and to keep an appraising eye on future attempts in this direction. Fortunately, a few data centers are in existence and would welcome a mechanism limiting their responsibility by facilitating a voluntary division of labor that might well be worked out by a committee of the association and revised as circumstances suggest.[11]

Although the specific examples given in this chapter refer with few exceptions to the level of local government in the United States, I want to repeat the caveat given at the start that this limitation was adopted only in the hope of providing a concrete sketch of the whole idea. The scope of the proposed basic data survey is restricted neither to local affairs nor to the United States. The framework outlined above is applicable with appropriate modifications to provincial, national, and international arenas.[12]

How should tasks be allocated among cooperating organizations and scholars? As usual in matters touching on politics, two principles must be combined if the results are to be workable. Some research and training programs are pitched at the international level and focus on transgovernmental, transparty, or transpressure activities. Others focus on selected areas of the globe and consider the decision process of each power within the region, its relation to other powers in the area, and the interplay between the region and the surrounding world community. Many institutions devote themselves to the affairs of their own nations or specialize in a provincial, state, or local area.

The topical principle cuts across all territorial processes and subordinates them to categories that stem from, or imply, an analytic model of the political process within the social process as a whole. The legal field—the realm of authoritative prescription—is a conspicuous instance. When philosophical concern is joined with the empirical study of philosophies in action, the principal interest is in ideology. The structures of government are so diverse and numerous that a broad distinction is made between studies of top policy and those of the administrative completion of policies. As a means of showing the connection between myth and organizational structure, some programs concentrate on unofficial groups or groups that, though official, are distinguishable from what is usually regarded as the government (political parties or pressure organizations).[13]

A recent tendency is to emphasize strictly political analysis and hence to operate with an analytic model of the decision process.[14] This will prepare the soil for research programs whose scope is narrowed to such selected features of decision as intelligence, promotion, prescription, invocation, application, appraisal, and termination or to the affiliations and perspectives of participants, arenas, base values, strategies, outcomes, and effects.

Although no important conditioning factor can be ignored in systematic political science, the emphasis can vary widely in terms of interaction patterns within the social process and between the social process, on the one hand, and the basic predispositions of man at birth and the resource environment, on the other. The interaction patterns within the social process are divisible by culture, class, interest, personality, and level of crisis. The study of crisis levels concentrates on such exceptional states as war, revolution, class reorganization, reinterpretation of interest, and personality conflict.

In sheer numbers, however, research projects are usually related to particular policy problems known by such currently popular symbols as "modernization" or "urban redevelopment" and "metropolitan planning." These inquiries can be classified according to each value-institution category.

The table summarizes the scope of research institutes and projects according to the primary emphasis of the topics studied.

Territorial	Analytic	Policy
Local	Legal systems (formula)	(According to value institution)
Provincial		
National	Ideologies (doctrine, lore)	Power
Regional	Decision process	Enlightenment
North Atlantic		Wealth
Inner Eurasia	Intelligence	Well-being
South Asia	Promotion	
North Pacific	Prescription	Skill
Mediterranean	Invocation	
South Atlantic	Application	Affection
South Pacific	Appraisal	Respect
World	Termination	Rectitude
	Participants	
	Perspectives	
	Arenas	
	Base Values	
	Strategies	
	Outcomes	
	Effects	

Conditioning Factors

Social Process
culture, class, interest, personality, crisis level

Human and environmental resources

In order to make full use of the training and research commitment of undergraduate students there would be advantages to providing special services through the American Political Science Association. Some steps have already been taken to foster the preparation of research manuals. Arrangements could be made to file duplicates of local-data cards at a national repository established by the association at Washington or at designated subcenters. From time to time, basic data sheets (maps or graphs) setting local findings in relation to one another could be issued. These could be released to the press and other interested parties.

Voting studies have recently been encouraged on a large scale. However, they suffer from the absence of such local data as the proposed survey could supply. National and regional polls of opinion have become established institutions; they, too, suffer from lack of local studies and from insufficient attention to the long-run needs of political analysis. The polling agencies have been slow to select re-curring topics for periodic re-examination.

As political scientists became more concerned with the basic data survey, the effects on historical scholarship would be many and deep. Some of these would reveal themselves in the collection of fundamental documents.[15]

Needless to demonstrate in detail, concern with the extension of trend lines backward in time would lead to more systematic ex-ploitation of past serials. It is only recently that equipment has been developed to a point that promises to make the content analysis of past records automatic. Machines will scan, code, and excerpt samples of newspapers, pamphlets, proceedings (for example, of conventions, legislative sessions, and administrative and court sessions), books, stat-utes, administrative regulations, records (for example, tax assessments and receipts, licenses, assistance, gifts, calendars of appointments, registers of correspondence and phone calls, registers of the flow of official documents within and among organizations, property titles and transfers, and court and administrative orders).[16]

The preceding outline of the decision process can be used to describe that of any community whatever, whether a participant in modern industrial civilization or a remote folk society. It is clear that, the greater the cultural contrast, the more the functional categories must be adapted by complex intermediate procedures to the realities of the local situation. In this connection, I shall make no concrete references here to my experiences in research on preindustrial societies, since a detailed report will presently be available. However, it may be helpful to give some clues to the procedures involved in compara-tive investigation.

It is essential once more to underline the distinction, fundamental to political science, between the functional categories for which the scientist takes full responsibility and the conventional usages embodied in any society. How does the scientific observer relate his functional terms to concrete occurrences?

The fundamental strategy for research is the use of successive approximations, which, for purposes of rapid exposition, I shall condense into a few steps. Step One is to collect and provisionally classify available information about the object of study. At this point in the development of travel and of anthropology it is rare to find any tribe or neighborhood wholly ignored in the literature. True, in extreme cases, one is limited to a traveler's tale or to allusions in missionaries' reports. It is usually possible to obtain enough information to assign a given "fact" to one of the eight value-institution categories for the comprehensive description of a social process. A report says that there is a "chief"; this is provisionally treated as among the "power—institutions of government." Or a report speaks of "silent trading"; this goes to the file on "wealthy—economic institutions." The reference may be to "bilateral kinship"; this goes to "affection—family and institutions of intimacy." And so on.

Sometimes Step Two can be taken early in the preparation for work in the field. If accumulated knowledge is fairly rich, each value-institution category can be provisionally subdivided into outcome, preoutcome, and postoutcome phases and each subsituation can be characterized according to the terms employed in this book—participants, perspectives, arenas (subarenas: organized, unorganized), base values, strategies, outcomes (specific; aggregated in time), and effects (specific, aggregate). It may aid in the conduct of research to isolate the power (decision) situations according to the sevenfold classification of outcomes used above: intelligence, promoting, prescribing, invoking, applying, appraising, and terminating and, further, to draw preliminary distinctions in degree of authority and control.

Perhaps enough data are at hand to make a provisional analysis of each situation according to the interactions involved. Who indulges or deprives whom (self, other) in terms of which value (power, wealth, respect, and so on)? The scientific observer may adopt more than one standpoint for the study of value changes by participants in any situation. He may, for instance, describe interactions from the perspective of each participant, or he may use third-party viewpoints.

When field work begins (or, in historical research, when standard authorities are abandoned for primary sources), Step Three can be taken. It is usually possible to focus successively on various kinds of situations chosen according to dominant value. For example, the observer may witness an assembly of all village males in a council meeting or sit with an elder who is listening to a complaint that X has taken his field and has no right to it. In field work, however, the sequence from situations largely specialized in one value to situations specialized in another can be followed only approximately, since an informant may introduce testimony about altogether different circumstances, and it then becomes wise to pursue the new topic further.

As data multiply, the reclassification of original data becomes a regular procedure (Step Four). The operation can be kept administratively practicable by reclassifying only when substantial increments of data have accumulated. It may begin to appear quite early that the original image of the decision process was badly out of harmony with the facts. The "governor" put forward by a village to meet strangers may turn out to be an insignificant participant in the internal process by which community decisions are made. Only at a late stage of investigation may it become apparent, for instance, that the key participants are the heads of the principal ceremonial associations into which all male members of the community are initiated at puberty.

The procedure of successive approximation allows the final picture to emerge—final, that is, from the investigator's perspective. At this stage, the conventional usages of the community have been comprehensively reanalyzed according to the functional categories of the scientific observer. Hence, the data are ready for inclusion in comparative political science, where they can be analyzed for the light they throw on alternative models of the political process.

I have indicated before that surveys have relevance to theoretical systems for the study of political dynamics. It would carry us too far from the necessarily limited scope of the present discussion to present a critique of existing models. However, I do give some attention to the problem in the Appendix.

NOTES

[1] Cf., e.g., R. B. Hunting and G. S. Neuwirth, *Who Sues in New York City?* "A Study of Automobile Accident Claims" (New York: Columbia University Press, 1962); J. Goldstein, "Police Discretion Not to Invoke the Criminal Law: Low-Visibility Decisions in the Administration of Justice," *Yale Law Journal,* 69 (1960), 543–594.

[2] Cf. R. A. Arens and H. D. Lasswell, *In Defense of Public Order,* "The Emerging Field of Sanction Law" (New York: Columbia University Press, 1961).

[3] Cf., e.g., C. Vose, *Caucasians Only*, "The Supreme Court, the NAACP, and the Restrictive Covenants Cases" (Berkeley and Los Angeles: University of California Press, 1959).

[4] Cf. W. N. Kinnard, Jr., *Appointed by the Mayor* (University, Ala.: University of Alabama Press, Inter-University Case Book Program, No. 36, 1956). For a system of distinctions, cf. P. M. Blau and R. W. Scott, *Formal Organization*, "A Comparative Approach" (San Francisco: Chandler, 1962). Note D. Marvick, *Career Perspectives in a Bureaucratic Setting* (Ann Arbor: University of Michigan Press, 1954). Also, the important trend studies of the prestige (respect position) of civil servants initiated by L. D. White and continued by M. Janowitz and others.

[5] Cf. R. C. Martin *et al., Decisions in Syracuse* (Bloomington, Ind.: Indiana University Press, 1961).

[6] The emphasis on interest groups in politics fosters the study of official as well as unofficial versions of advantage. Cf. D. B. Truman's influential study, *The Governmental Process* (New York: Knopf, 1951).

[7] The role of informal decision-making—which includes prescribing—is among the phases of the process described in R. Agger, D. Goldrick, and B. Swanson in their study of four communities in two regions (forthcoming).

[8] Cf. the techniques used in G. A. Schubert, *Quantitative Analysis of Judicial Behavior* (Glencoe, Ill.: The Free Press, 1959); C. H. Pritchett, *The Roosevelt Court*, "A Study in Judicial Politics and Values, 1937–1947" (New York: Macmillan, 1948).

[9] Strictly speaking, planning operations are classified in the present context as part of the intelligence function (when the activity does not proceed to the promotion, prescription, or other phases of the total decision process). When policy has already been formulated and put into effect, the problem of assessing results and analyzing the effects of various factors on results enters the picture. Hence, planning includes use of the findings produced by appraisals, which may or may not be carried out by the same structures. The International Institute of Administrative Sciences has had many sessions on the problems of intelligence and appraisal. An example of scholarly appraisal is C. Tunnard and B. Pushkarev, *Man-Made America: Chaos or Control?* "An Inquiry into Selected Problems of Design in the Urbanized Landscape" (New Haven: Yale University Press, 1963).

[10] Cf. P. H. Rossi and R. A. Dentler, *The Politics of Urban Renewal*, "The Chicago Findings" (New York: The Free Press of Glencoe, 1961).

[11] A Political Data Center was organized at Yale in 1962 and plans to work out cooperative arrangements. The Roper Center at Williams Col-

lege is an important repository of polling information. A newly
organized "Inter-University Consortium" unites, in the first year,
the Survey Research Center at the University of Michigan with
more than twenty institutions of higher learning in the United
States.

12 The university at Oslo, Norway, has been among the most dynamic centers
of modern social and political science and takes important initiatives in the direction of international research. Cf. S. Rokkan,
ed., "Citizen Participation in Political Life," *International Social
Science Journal,* 12 (1960). Also, G. A. Almond and J. S. Coleman,
eds., *The Politics of Developing Areas* (Princeton: Princeton University Press, 1960); and J. A. Robinson's continuing study of Congress, *Congress and Foreign Policy-Making,* "A Study in Legislative
Influence and Initiative" (Homewood, Ill.: Dorsey Press, 1962).

13 R. S. Lane has reconsidered the present and prospective state of knowledge of *Political Ideology,* "Why the American Common Man Be-
lieves as He Does" (New York: The Free Press of Glencoe, 1962).

14 E.g., R. M. Thrall, C. H. Coombs, and R. L. Davis, eds., *Decision Proc-
esses* (New York: Wiley, 1960); R. L. Chapman, "Data for Test-
ing a Model of Organizational Behavior" (Santa Monica, Calif.:
RAND Corporation, 1960; M. Haire, ed., *Modern Organizational
Theory* (New York: Wiley, 1959); J. G. March and H. A. Simon,
Organizations (New York: Wiley, 1958); A. Downs, *An Economic
Theory of Democracy* (New York: Harper, 1957); G. L. S.
Shackle, *Decision, Order, and Time in Human Affairs* (Cambridge:
University Press, 1961).

15 How fruitful such a task can be is convincingly demonstrated by W.
Jenkins at the University of North Carolina center of documenta-
tion.

16 Cf. W. N. Locke and A. D. Booth, eds., *Machine Translation of Languages* (New York: Wiley, 1953); J. W. Perry and A. Kent, *Tools for
Machine Literature Searching* (New York: Interscience Publications,
1958); B. Mittman and A. Ungar, eds., *Computer Applications—
1960* (New York: Macmillan, 1960); R. E. Machol and P. Gray,
eds., *Recent Developments in Information and Decision Processes*
(New York: Macmillan, 1962). Cf. especially Norbert Wiener's remarks. Current developments can be followed in *M.U.L.L.,* "Modern Uses of Logic in Law," quarterly newsletter of the American
Bar Association Special Committee on Electronic Data Retrieval in
collaboration with the Yale Law School, edited by L. E. Allen
and M. E. Caldwell.

Appendix
to
Chapter 4

DISCIPLINE BY THEORETICAL MODELS

Fortunately, political science is rich in theoretical propositions capable of guiding the choice of survey data. Hypotheses are also being welded into hypothetical models of how decision processes work, and the terms employed are intended to lend themselves to the choice of operational indexes. It is, of course, elementary that investigators must keep in mind the most comprehensive theoretical requirements of their discipline, especially at the moment when they make heroic simplifications as part of a program of research.

If, as political scientists, we were omniscient, we would have at our disposal descriptive and analytic tools enabling us to do the following: make a rapid survey of the predispositions found everywhere in the world; "predict" (retrospectively) the conditioning factors accounting for the direction and intensity of these predispositions; predict the way in which these predispositions would express themselves under the impact of any conceivable constellation of future conditioning factors; predict the probable occurrence of future constellations; outline the strategies by which the probability of future factor constellations can be modified (at stated cost in terms of all values); and connect past and prospective sequences of events with specifications of goal (in our case, the goal of realizing the dignity of man—and of other advanced forms of life—on the widest possible scale).

Any operation of this kind presupposes that we can describe the perspectives and capabilities (base values) of each participant. If we know the value preferences (demands) and the expectations of feasible strategies and outcomes, it is possible to predict the response, since behavior of advanced living forms is postulated as a function of expected net value advantage among perceived alternatives.

This point calls attention to the importance of devising procedures of value and expectation analysis (and also of identification, since identifications interact with all other perspectives). Moreover, each interaction requires that appropriate procedures be used to describe the effect of the environment on the focus of attention and on immediate perceptions. As implied above, expectations may be realistic or in error both in regard to outcome events and to capabilities. Presumably, the realism or unrealism of such perspectives depends in part on environmental impacts on the focus of attention and the immediate perceptions of the individual or the group. In principle, it must be within the competence of political scientists to describe *every* interaction according to its significance in the decision process of the social context under study.

The challenge is to invent or adapt instruments whereby we can describe any political interaction of value indulgence or deprivation as a function of expected net advantage and of actual capability in any arena.

Concurrently with value analysis, we are concerned with institutional analysis. The value categories, it will be recalled, are a *comprehensive* list of terms employed to describe any social process, particularly all culminating events (elections, loans, marriages, and so on). Having provisionally located such events, we describe the patterns relatively specialized in each, recognizing that all values are to some degree involved in every interaction. Various practices (perspectives and operations) comprise an institution, which can be described in terms of myth and technique—myth being patterns of perspective, technique being patterns of operation.

For many purposes, it is convenient to intensify the description of value or institutional events by treating them as patterns of *mechanism,* that is, as analyzable into fundamental common elements. The most useful categories of mechanism distinguish an act (or "interact") as a sequence in which actors affect the outcome. Further, an act is "externalized" or "internalized" according to the degree to which all actors are involved as the sequence runs to completion.

In terms of fundamental mechanism, we also characterize the degree to which symbolic or nonsymbolic events are implicated in the act sequence. Symbolic events are subjective; other events are not. The nonsymbolic events are signs or nonsigns. A sign is specialized in mediating among symbol events;

hence, it includes gestures and languages. A somatic event is a physical movement or structure of the body. Environing resources are physical events, and they are open to modification by actors to create culture materials.

Mechanism distinctions are valuable in the comparison of political and social styles, since they enable externalized or internalized patterns to be readily designated and provide ways of describing symbolic and nonsymbolic characteristics. For instance, symbols and signs may be greatly elaborated in some bodies politic where oratory and poetry are in flower, and images varying through time provide clues to the potential action, or tension, level.

As for the pursuit of power, the general hypothesis is that power is emphasized as an outcome when it is expected to yield greater net advantages than the pursuit of other values. In regard to strategies that rely on power or instruments of power, the general hypothesis is that they are expected to yield comparative net advantages.

Appropriately rephrased, the same formulation is applicable to the rise and fall of ideologies and technical operation and to the appearance of any pattern in competition with any alternative.

The data obtained by basic data surveys would be affected by developmental constructs of the future, since these constructs provide a sense of priority. In the preceding pages, we have mentioned the desirability of following certain events because our developmental constructs suggest their importance.

Contemplated strategies of future action also raise questions about past and current events that would influence the survey. However, the consideration of strategies almost invariably discloses the existence of not inconsiderable gaps between what we know and what we would like to know for the guidance of policy. Can we use methods that narrow this discrepancy and provide solid bases of inference for decision? In Chapter 5, we put forward suggestions in answer to this challenging question.

The basic data survey sketched in the preceding pages can be summarized in the form of a generalized outline appropriate to the study of the decision process in any social context or subcontext. The operational indexes appropriate to each category or subcategory depend on the intensiveness of the observational standpoint taken by the scientific observer and the discernible features of the field of events observed.

DECISION PROCESS

Prearena events   →   arena events   →   postarena events

Prearena Events

Includes all interactions that precede the involvement of authoritative or controlling decision-makers in the context. We may distinguish between *precipitating* events and *parallel* events, the former being interactions that lead up to entry into an arena; the latter, despite their resemblance to precipitating events, do not.

Arena Events

Includes all interactions in which decision-makers are involved. We distinguish *preoutcome* and *outcome* events, the latter being the events regarded as the culminating interactions in the sequence, since they are perceived as especially important for the value position of those involved.

Postarena Events

Includes all interactions that are influenced by the outcome.

The decision process occurs in the context of a larger social process which can also be characterized in preoutcome, outcome, and postoutcome terms. The political scientist must discriminate in the social process the frame of reference of special interest to him. This can be accomplished if the context is characterized by a list of terms that is kept fixed for potential use in designating any social context whatsoever. In this way, the observer uses the same "lenses" for locating comparable features of each situation that he approaches for comparative purposes. He is able to assign operational indexes to the terms in the fixed list. If other observers disagree with his assignments, the difference may be resolved by discussion, or equivalency of result may be guaranteed by discovering the magnitude of the difference in findings to be attributed to the index. One investigator may think that one or more terms in the fixed list (as generally defined) are not appropriately employed; another investigator, however, may use the whole list. This divergence, too, if not eliminated by discussion, can be dealt with by discovering the constants permitting intertranslatability.

The functional definition of "power" that I recommend designates interaction patterns in which the expectation prevails that severe sanctions are involved, either by immediate action, as in fighting, or potentially. Operational indexes must ultimately be chosen to designate "expectations," "severe" (rather than "mild") sanctions, and "prevailing" patterns.

At every phase of the decision process, the same components of the situation are open to study.

Participants

Conventional usage identifies many participants. Scientific observers may also note the existence of aggregates for which no symbol is found. (The general categories are culture, class, interest, and personality at various levels of crisis.)

Perspectives

Every value-institution process has a special myth. In specific situations, however, one myth (conventionally described) may blanket all others, making it necessary to investigate particular situations in detail if differentiations are to be found. Religious ideologies, for example, may include gods of health, good crops, victorious war, knowledge, expertness, love, honor, and salvation.

In the ideology of power, prescriptions may refer to each phase of decision, though inquiry may show that the nominal rule is not adhered to in actual circumstances. (Within each myth, we have further distinguished formula, doctrine, and lore.)

Arena

The observer must select some minimum frequency of conjunction of events to justify his identification of an arena. In world politics, for instance, an isolated and remote country may maintain such a low frequency of inter-action that it is not a "participant" (foreign relations, such as they are, may be administered by a foreign power; trade is negligible; news exchanges are inconsequential). Once an arena is established, the pattern of polarity can be described.

Base Values

The principal categories here are by value, actual and potential, under stipulated contingencies. Since the contingencies are as a rule incompletely considered, there is usually incipient ambiguity in the description of base values.

Strategies

The distinction in strategic objectives according to *assembling* and *processing* has been referred to before, likewise that in terms of *persuasion* and *coercion* and combinations of *indulgence* and *deprivation*. Differences by style (*mechanism*) are also appropriate, for instance in degree of symbol-sign-and-resource pattern. Communication and diplomacy depend on the former (symbol-sign pattern), military and economic strategies, on the latter. Strategies of *isolation* or *combination* depend especially on the polar structure of arenas.

Outcomes

The culminating events that affect value position are describable according to final *alignment* and weight, as indicated by initiative and by pivotal position in the preoutcome management of coalitions.

Effects

Particular effects can be followed for active participants in an arena, notably the subsequent fate of winners and losers as affected by this result. Aggregate effects are ultimately to be summed up in terms of value shaping and sharing and institutional stability or change.

It is possible to describe the whole decision process in terms of value indulgence and deprivation and of institutional stability or change. The basic data survey could supply indispensable information of trend toward or away from the goal of broad, rather than narrow, participation in value shaping and sharing. By correlational procedures, it would also provide some indication of the effect of various combinations of conditioning factors on trend variation and lay a foundation for inferences regarding desirable clarifications of goal and future projections and policy alternatives. However, the survey would have limitations requiring other methods to overcome.

5

Experimentation, Prototyping, Intervention

Trend data are in many ways insufficient to meet the criteria of science and policy. In the study of conditioning, the ideal is to formulate propositions that correctly state the relations among the factors involved. It is true that time series can be correlated with one another to verify explanatory hypotheses. However, a more satisfactory design would seem to be an experimental program conducted under circumstances that provide the widest variety of opportunities for the controlled investigation of factor combinations.

EXPERIMENTATION AND INTERVENTION

Contemporary social psychologists have made laboratory experiments providing valuable hypotheses for the analysis of politics. When, for example, a small experimental group agrees to try to make a decision within the constraints imposed on a flow of communication, results are affected by the pattern of flow. If each message must be routed through one member, rather than being sent directly between any pair, frustrations accumulate that are likely to take the intermediary link as the target of discharge. The outcome may be periodic disruptions of group work.[1]

It is tempting to extend the findings of such an experiment directly to field situations and to hypothesize that official prescriptions will produce frustration if they require that each message be centrally cleared. On reflection, however, the political scientist sees no grounds for assuming that this applies to all arenas. In actual situations, official regulations are circumvented in many ways. If obstacles arise to communication between A and C, A and C are likely in practice to establish informal channels. The hypothesis, however, is serviceable in directing attention to the importance of studying the actual flow of both authoritative and effective communication among officials. But this is no new idea, nor does the experiment provide a measuring device transferable to field situations. The data called for must, as usual, be obtained by the well-known methods of interview or participant observation.

Another laboratory experiment explores the effect of overloading a communication net. Let M be messages fed to an operator for translation from Code One (words) into Code Two (telegraphic code). Research may show that operators of equal skill (measured by test) will begin to increase their errors at a given level of M and that at some level of input the whole process breaks down. This is a suggestive finding for politics, since it calls attention to the fact that all communication systems can be overloaded and that overloadings at key subcenters can work havoc.

Moreover, the findings are immediately transferable to those parts of the decision process that employ word-to-telegraphic-code operations—transferable, that is, in the sense of providing hypotheses for the quantitative description of performance. When the input-output records of a group of (tested) operators in fire, police, military, or other services are analyzed, it may turn out that they make more errors under less pressure of input than were made by an experimental group. Further, the breaking point may differ, as shown by a few emergency situations of which there are records.

What variables account for the differences? Interviews may reveal that operators in field situations are not much interested in the job and make few conscious demands on themselves or colleagues to work hard. They make more errors; and, as pressure increases, they speed up very little, postponing personal breakdowns indefinitely, even though unsent messages accumulate. The operation is overloaded, but the human components do not "knock themselves out." Restudy of the laboratory group may show, by contrast, that the subjects who took part in the experiment were highly motivated to do well, since they wanted to win the respect of the scientists in charge, and they also felt competitive with one another.

In this case, the laboratory contributed more than calling attention to an interesting aspect of politics. Tests of performance could be transferred to the field—that is, to administrative situations—and the quantification of both laboratory and field results made it feasible to appraise government operators provisionally. A constellation of factors that condition administrative services was identified; their impact was precisely expressed.

Consider yet another variation in the relationship between laboratory and field. When experimental groups are given increasingly exacting tasks, behavior changes can be recorded by observers (who sit unobtrusively in the laboratory or look through one-way glass) or by instruments (for example, that trace the movements of chair springs or respiratory rhythms). Such random movements as directly observable frequencies of head or arm and instrumentally recorded respiratory frequencies or irregularities increase. These changes may be correlated with time (late versus early morning, early versus late afternoon).[2]

The results are pertinent to political science in several ways. Some procedures of data-gathering, especially the visual recording of random movements, can be directly transferred. These procedures can be adapted to studies of tension—a field that will probably attract much research effort in the future.[3]

Many laboratory procedures can be applied immediately to transnational and other group comparisons. For instance, important clues to the direction and intensity of world perspectives have been obtained from the Thematic Apperception Test (TAT).[4] There are grounds for predicting that tests of perceived body image (of the self and of others) will generate information about fundamental changes of political perspective. Preliminary results, with primitive methods, indicate that authoritative individuals are perceived as taller and heavier than one's self.[5] If this proves to be true of lower castes and classes, trends at all class levels can be disclosed by a program of periodic retesting. Democratization or the reverse is subtly registered by the phenomena of attention and perception.

Changes in communication style provide clues to trends that are not fully conscious. The demand to impose the self on others is likely to be revealed in gesture, intonation, and choice and arrangement of words. When commands are uttered, for instance, the sign components of the communication show "response-contrasting" in that they have a pattern which the audience is not expected to repeat. But in more equalitarian situations the style shows "response-modeling" (the hand outstretched in greeting is expected to be reciprocated).[6]

The foregoing discussion is intended to suggest both the advantages and limitations of laboratory experiments as tools of political science. From the point of view of basic data surveying, laboratories are now the chief innovators of data-gathering procedures and instruments. In the future, measuring instruments developed in the laboratory can be deployed in a comprehensive and perpetual survey of political "weather" (the direction and intensity of key predispositions).

It is rarely practicable or desirable to leap directly from the laboratory to legislative or regulatory innovations. It is not often practicable since the laboratory exercise may strike too many legislators, administrators, and publicists as "artificial," that is, as inappropriate to the values and institutional practices of the community affected by the proposed change. Furthermore, it is not desirable from the scientific point of view to extrapolate from the simplified and highly controlled conditions of the laboratory, since variables present in the field may modify or even reverse the results of the experiment. Typically, responsible politicians and administrators are concerned with value outcomes and effects in which the scientists' pursuit of enlightenment has a relatively low priority. If innovations are introduced by statute or after they have been incorporated into the platform of a political party, they have been justified on allegedly scientific grounds. But the scientists create a false sense of the scope of their knowledge if they claim to know all the significant factors of the institutional setting. Before political scientists can speak with scientific justification about an innovation in institutional practice, they need to know what they are talking about, namely, the pattern or variables whose interactions constitute the relevant political institution.

Several strategies are used to overcome the gap between laboratory experiments and full-scale innovation. The most important is the "pilot study," in which an official innovation is introduced in part of a jurisdiction with the expectation that, if results are satisfactory, the innovation will be extended throughout the nation or the region involved.

Pilot studies differ greatly from one another. At one extreme, they are conducted in the glare of publicity and controversy. The innovation may be under the direction of politicians who are determined to discredit the project or to score a seeming success at any price. At the other end of the scale, pilot studies may attract little immediate attention from the political parties, pressure associations, legislators, or administrators in the larger political arena in which it is conducted. Further, the direction of the study may be in the hands of scientists —including political scientists—who are deeply concerned with contributing to knowledge and professional skill.

Let us distinguish, as usual, between conventional and functional definitions. In the conventional sense, all official innovations, whether pilot studies or not, come into the same broad category of official prescriptions. It will be useful to isolate a functional category according to the importance of the effective pursuit of enlightenment. Prototyping is such a category, and I shall undertake a provisional formulation of the strategy of prototyping. My expectation is that prototyping will play an increasingly important part in the future of political science as a scientific and policy-oriented discipline.

As we shall see, prototypes are not necessarily official, since many institutional practices may be inaugurated for purposes of scientific research outside formal government. I think of prototyping as an innovation, typically small-scale, made in political practice primarily for scientific purposes. The institutional practice involved can be copied; hence, the practice may be incorporated into the institutional patterns of a body politic. An unofficial prototype may stimulate an official pilot project or an innovation that is authoritatively extended throughout a national or regional jurisdiction.

PROTOTYPING

We are principally concerned here with improving the scientific capability and achievements of political science. As the level of political science rises, so, too, will its significance for public policy. It is worth emphasizing the possibility of linking experimentation, prototyping, and intervention as a comprehensive strategy of policy innovation. At the same time, the sequence has great relevance to the strategy of knowledge.[7] In general, the scientist loses control over the relevant variables at successive stages. Clearly, his control is greatest in laboratory experiments and diminishes in a prototype situation. It is typically least in official intervention. In that case, the applicable methods of analysis are largely correlational. Prototyping is partly experimental and partly dependent on correlation.

A laboratory experiment is the procedure presumably least likely to be interfered with for partisan purposes. (However, the distinction is not likely to hold in totalitarian states or, for that matter, in relatively open societies if experiments conflict with genuinely effective norms of official and private life.) When a prototype is in process of formation, dangers from partisan interferences are usually greater than in the laboratory, since prototypes are likely to be identified by interests who seek to control results for their special benefit. However, the vulnerability to interference is greater still in the case of official innovations.

In some circumstances, the demand for knowledge outweighs all other considerations, even when officially prescribed patterns are under appraisal. For instance, leaders and led may be genuinely puzzled by failures of administrative efficiency; hence, political scientists are allowed a free hand to investigate and report. The typical advantage of prototypes is that they may be kept sufficiently small scale to stay out of sight until results have been rather fully studied. In this, they differ from a pilot project, although in the marginal case differences disappear.

In the present embryonic stage of political research, it is impossible to outline a body of verified principles of strategy for the construction of prototypes. Enough experience is at hand, however, to provide at least a degree of guidance. In the discussion of prototyping to follow, I make frequent reference to two projects, one at Vicos, Peru,[8] the other at the Yale Psychiatric Institute.[9] By agreement with the Peruvian government, the Vicos project was conducted under the auspices of Cornell University. The aim of the project was to prepare the Indians of Vicos for a decision-making process that would share the power in the village while making realistic demands and adopting realistic strategies for coping with the larger environment in which it was located (locally, nationally, internationally). The hope was to achieve a level of functioning that would encourage the government and other authorities concerned with the development of folk or peasant culture to repeat the prototype in pilot projects and eventually on an extensive scale, by intervention, throughout Peru.

The Yale project was also a prototype undertaking. The innovators sought to reach a level of operation that would present a new model of hospital practice and, if successful, encourage other psychiatric establishments to adopt its fundamental features. The aim was to enlarge participation in decision-making by patients on the hypothesis that this would have favorable therapeutic consequences.

One of the first problems in prototyping is when to regard an innovation as past the "preparatory" phase and effectively "introduced." After the introduction is made, the "results" of the innovation can be observed. Before valid comparisons can be drawn between the results of innovation X and established pattern Y, it is obvious that sufficient incorporation of X must take place to justify the assertion that the innovation has, in fact, been studied.

The principal question that arises in drawing the line between "pre-" and "post-" introduction is that human loyalties, beliefs, and faiths are involved. Unless a high degree of agreement has been reached, it can not be claimed that pattern X has been tried, since a precondition of institutional life is effective commitment to the operations concerned. From a scientific point of view, the task is to assess the consequences of pattern X after a specified degree of acceptance has occurred. From a policy point of view, the questions about pattern X are these: In view of the consequences of X in a situation in which it had a certain degree of support, should I support X in situations where it is not yet accepted, but where I can influence support?

It would make no sense to insist that every participant in a given prototype situation believe in the innovation before we regard the pattern as "introduced," since we live in a world where degrees of conscious and unconscious opposition are commonly present. Let us adopt as a working strategy, therefore, the requirement that a prototype is *"introduced" when an effective majority of the leadership is committed to try out the innovation and agrees that important results may reasonably be expected to follow from it.* At the Yale Psychiatric Institute, medical opinion was initially divided over the merits of the project, although the undertaking was an outgrowth of earlier work at the institute.

The anthropologist in charge at Vicos had formal authority to run the hacienda, and he determined to use it to bring into being a decision process that would continue after his withdrawal. The Vicos elders did not know what to make of the situation at first; but, by the end of a few months, they had got the idea that they did have a genuine voice in policy. At that point, we could say that the project was fully under way and that the prototype began to take shape.

When effective innovating support has been achieved, prototype managers should make it easy for the ideologically alienated and the

characterologically incapable among responsible leaders to withdraw.
We have said that, if the long-range implications of an innovation are
to be demonstrated, it is important that acceptance reach at least a
stated minimum. Otherwise, failure can be explained with the alibi
that the proposed policy "has never been tried," meaning that sincere
attempts were not made to discover the true potential of the idea. Of
course, the preparatory phase itself is of no little scientific interest,
since we need to improve strategies of obtaining acceptance of policies
under various original patterns of predisposition. But the fact that a
prototype must sufficiently overcome initial obstacles to achieve a
minimum level of support is not the distinctive problem or contribution of prototyping.

Once initial working acceptance is won, it is desirable to discover
the potential of the prototype by encouraging dissidents in the leadership to withdraw. A distinction was drawn above between "ideological
alienation" and "characterological incapability." Ideological alienation
is not difficult to detect if the situation encourages openness. It is a
question of leaders who are unwilling to agree that the project is
worthwhile or that it has a reasonable chance of success. In the Psychiatric Institute case, there were physicians who found the whole
approach distasteful, since it contradicted their conception of the
physician's role in the treatment of patients. For them, the proper task
of a psychiatrist is to work individually with patients and to authoritatively decide what changes should be made in the patient's hospital
environment. The prospect of being criticized in public by patients
and of becoming objects of public criticism by professional colleagues
was intolerable to them. In the Vicos project, it was important that
all outside innovators and the dominant element among the elders
adopt a positive approach. The innovators could enlist the cooperation
of others only if they indicated that they thought the project worth
trying. The approach recommended here is not blind faith that the
prototype will succeed; rather, the appropriate perspective is candid
willingness to give it the benefit of the doubt and to proceed with
determination.

The characterological point is more subtle. Many scientists are
unable to play the role that they consciously agree to play. Among
the psychiatrists, for example, were physicians who were consciously
in favor of patient-staff conferences and of a power-sharing approach
generally. But in the judgment of their colleagues they were unable
to live up to the requirements of a cooperative way of life. For example, one leading staff member seemed to sulk when adverse com-

ments on a hospital rule were made by a patient or when patients spoke on such particular issues as whether a patient was showing enough improvement to warrant a visit home. Similarly, an outside scientist who was active at Vicos for a time showed impatience with criticism and set a bad example for the members of the council.

A further principle of prototyping is that *clarifications of goal should be encouraged to continue intermittently even after minimum consensus has been achieved.* Not many creative projects begin with agreement in detail on the objectives to be sought or on the criteria appropriate to appraisal. Even when current perspectives are highly favorable and the point of "introduction" has been passed, explicit agreement on objectives may be inconclusive. In fact, a merit of prototyping is that it permits objectives to gain clarity through experience, enriching in this way the considerations to be taken into account in redesigning the basic proposal for later tests or for official intervention.

The idea of trying out patient-staff conferences was well received as a step in the direction of patient responsibility, although it deliberately stopped short of reinstalling the full responsibilities of ordinary life. It soon became clear that the medical personnel did not intend to give up their veto power over suggestions offered by patients. But it was equally apparent that conferences must go beyond "mere talk" and culminate in at least some outcomes that patients could attribute to their own initiative. Without attempting an exhaustive enumeration, it is possible to name several specific objectives that came to be regarded by the staff as among the legitimate goals: in general, to increase the therapeutic effectiveness of the institute; to discourage withdrawal by patients from active responsibility to larger social groups; to encourage a flow of information about hospital conditions that would assist in making better decisions; to encourage initiative on the part of patients (and all component elements of the institute) in proposing and advocating particular policy acts; to reduce the patients' sense of isolation from people by providing more knowledge of others; to stimulate realistic social judgment by supplying experience in evaluating the factual and preferential statements of staff and patients; to clarify the therapeutic goal of individuals and the institute by participating in attempts to evaluate situations and proposals; and to clarify the ideology of a social order of human dignity by giving concrete attention to the principles of democratic problem-solving.

Not many of these concrete objectives were in the mind of any one person at the beginning. Initial perspectives were decidedly fuzzy; but clarified objectives emerged once the staff-patient procedure was under way. We must bear in mind that the criteria applied by one scientist in assessing a prototype are not necessarily identical to those of another scientist or to all who participate in a given innovation. Even after the degree of unity that justifies one in saying that a prototype is launched has been achieved, important differences will probably occur within the framework of consent.

In the Vicos situation, for example, it is possible to isolate a few of the initial criteria that the originating anthropologist used in gauging the *short-run* effectiveness of the project. Would council members increase the frequency and extent of their participation in council meetings? It was also important to see from the attendance record and verbal statements whether the leaders thought things were going well in the council's deliberations. Other questions were whether more members of the community acquired the practice of listening to discussions and began to take a more positive part in talking about policy and in trying to affect the outcome of council deliberations. Another indication of effectiveness was the concern of council members for obtaining expert advice about the technical aspects of any problem that came before them.

The criteria of success or failure favored by the originators of the Vicos innovation went much further. However, many of these could not be tested before several years had passed and the Vicos community had taken the critical step of buying hacienda land and bringing local government entirely into its own hands. Would the community be able to act together without breaking up into struggling factions that might even come to blows? Could the community learn to obtain and identify expert advice given on behalf of common, rather than special, interests? That is, could council members distinguish a special pleader from a source both competent and disinterested?

As it turned out, the Vicos community did in fact operate with democracy and realism when the transition to self-government was made. Hence, the prototype model was regarded as successful by all who were willing to adopt these criteria. Judgment about long-range performance had to be reserved.

The Yale institute faced comparable problems of assessment. Before many months, the immediate participants agreed that the innovation was justifiable and even important. Key questions were: Did the recovery rate or rate of improvement change in either direction after the prototype was launched? Did rates for discernible categories of patients (for example, young schizophrenics, older schizophrenics) change? Did regressive behavior improve? Did physicians and patients come to agree more closely? Did patients try to pressure the staff into acting against the staff's judgment? Did physicians and patients carry more democratic perspectives and operational skills into other situations?

The preceding discussion distinguishes (1) the goal of an innovation, (2) the essential pattern of the new practice, and (3) the specific consequences in terms of which the degree of achievement can be described. Since all social values are to some extent affected, the goal (1) can be given a wide meaning, such as the sharing of all values in the social context. It is also useful to construe goals more narrowly, as at Vicos and the institute, where the chief goals were, respectively, realism and democracy in decision-making and improved therapy. If a political scientist had conceived the latter project, he might have formulated it as a means of exploring the degree to which power-sharing can be achieved in a therapeutic community without much or any sacrifice of well-being—the dominant value outcome sought in such a community.

The chief specific practice innovated at the institute was the patient-staff conference; at Vicos, the principal feature was the devolution of power to council and people. We have emphasized the point that a prototype is in being when an effective majority accepts the project as reasonable. This requirement implies agreement on (1) and (2), above. It is not enough to endorse a general value goal: a degree of precision concerning the specific practice to be launched and investigated is also required.

A significant distinction can be made between the early phases of the Vicos and the institute prototypes. The initiator at Vicos was clear about the broad objectives he sought in the project. By contrast, it is not easy to demonstrate the time at which the institute program became clarified as an identifiable project in the minds of the responsible members of the medical staff. The fact seems to be that the situation was moving toward greater deference to the patients, even though specific patterns of participation were not thought out in advance or assigned dates in a calendar of innovation. The patient-staff conference was a practice that grew out of the dynamic interplay of the variables of the situation. We can say that the prototype leaders, when they became fully aware of the situation, simply took advantage of tendencies already present. The strategy of prototyping is especially well adapted to the discovery and further development of newly emerging patterns of institutional life. Hence, it is appropriate to speak of "organic," or "structural," changes in the social process and to emphasize the opportunity that political scientists enjoy when they are sufficiently in step with change to use the technique of prototyping to expedite potential evolution. The method can also be employed to strengthen the forces working against the emergence of various patterns, such as ruthlessness in the pursuit of political objectives.

The preceding allusions to Vicos and the institute have called attention to problems that must be met in inaugurating any prototype. There are, in addition, conditions that may invalidate the prototypicalness of a given attempt. Exceptional circumstances may put far too many obstacles in the path of the project (or, less often, foster the project). The former conditions occur, for example, if war, flood, or similar disasters interrupt the test. The latter conditions might occur if the project suddenly becomes a focus of general policy interest and support, so that many remarkable inducements are added to those ordinarily available for inaugurating change. Money and talent may "bribe" the test community into becoming a "model." This fate almost befell Vicos because many public figures in Peru recognized the urgency of "doing something about the Indians" and thought that they could exploit Vicos in a big way. Fortunately, the barrage was avoided until after the actual transfer of power.

A prototype, then, cannot be "completed" unless the factors that condition its operation are representative of other than extreme circumstances. Views can differ on the question of representativeness. If there is difficulty in preparing a context suitable to a prototype, great faith is needed to continue the attempt. We know that some influential prototypical situations have eventually been completed because of the tenacity of a man of vision who foresaw the possibilities. In this connection, we note that modern research has been greatly influenced by Elton Mayo's innovations in industrial sociology. Although usually referred to as "experiments," they come more nearly into the category of prototypes, since the practices could be incorporated into modern industry. A "test room" was set apart so that output of the prototypical group could be easily measured. The nurse who kept physical measurements was also on hand to record and discuss personal problems. (The practice of holding management seminars on cases of labor-management difficulty could also be copied.)

We may find it profitable to review in more detail some factors that have conditioned the success or failure of prototypical innovations. An interesting point is the role of "faith" and "rational inference" in launching and carrying through such projects. When we hear people extol "the faith that moves mountains" (for example, the celebrated case in which a devoted teacher succeeded with Helen Keller, a severely handicapped child), they usually overlook attempts that were frustrated largely because of failure to identify and control factors that seem obvious on rational reflection. We have already paid some deference to these matters by referring to characterological limitations. Frequently, personality limitations are conspicuous among the agitators who originate or promote novel ideas. One combination is particularly noteworthy—the fanatic who is partly sound on scientific grounds and wildly unscientific in other respects. Schliemann is a typical case in the recovery of man's classical past and especially in the vogue of archaeology. (Cases might be chosen from reform in the treatment of children, mentally ill, women, castes, criminals, soldiers, and so on.)

The Vicos case draws attention to several factors that condition prototyping attempts. Devolution was undertaken in a community that had learned to regard any top man at the hacienda with grave suspicion. At least four hundred years of bitter experience had cured the Indians of whatever romanticism they may once have had about the good intentions of an outside boss. Hence, mere verbal assurances could not be expected to carry conviction. The project director began with a dramatic and tangible step. He announced that the crops from the boss's land would be turned over to the community. The impression was favorable but cautious, since the Indians wondered if this were part of a subtle plot to damage them in some way they did not yet grasp. Eventually they accepted the good faith of the project director, as shown by many expressions of respect and affection that went far beyond the demands of simple expediency.

The Vicos example is in harmony with the guiding principle for affecting conduct by persuasion—lead people to expect to be better off by acting in accord with a program rather than deviating from it.

In many cases, the assets available to a leader may be unreproducible until he has had time to mold a new generation which somewhat conforms to his image. If the leader is cut down early, his promising initiatives may collapse. The main Vicos figure approached everyone with a friendly style that offered human warmth and fellowship until an individual demonstrated himself to be undeserving. Furthermore, the leader was tireless in respecting the personal identity and opinions of the Indians and of all with whom he worked. He adopted a simple style of greeting and showed that the obsequious etiquette used to address bosses in the past was neither expected nor desired. He discovered the intimate worries of people and did what he could to be helpful; and he took in return nothing that could be regarded as a bribe or special favor. Here, too, he set up a new model for the community to follow, and it demonstrably spread to the relations between fathers and sons, elders and neighbors, and so on. We note also that he was no plaster saint; he did not fail to drink and be a good fellow, and at times he got obviously angry. He showed human weaknesses and admitted them; and, if he overstepped, he did what was necessary to put things right.

(Some of these descriptions rest on satisfactory data, such as field notes, that describe through time the dropping of old forms of prostration and the use of the handshake or salute. Other statements are less well grounded.)

If the members of a group become inspired with the significance of what they are doing, they create a mutually indulgent environment of congratulation for being in the project at all. A perpetual stream of reassuring remarks about the enterprise and hearty approval for cooperative conduct occur spontaneously.

At the same time, the invocation of these standards can be carried to censorious extremes, as when phlegmatic or explicitly uncooperative persons are made butts of indignation, boycott, or even violence. Since the Vicos and institute projects alike were oriented to persuasive action, the leaders set a model of patience with errors of ignorance or with persisting patterns that could not be expected to disappear in a day.

The prototypes were by no means developed in obscurity, though they were screened from general publicity until well along. Quite early in the project, the institute innovation aroused the enthusiasm of some patients who established contact with patient groups in other hospitals, suggesting that everyone seek to have a voice in policy. Administrators and staff members attached to other hospitals discussed the innovation and listened to brief reports of theory and progress at meetings and in less formal conversations. Vicos, of course, was always on the edge of potential eruption if anything happened to make a political football of the enterprise.

Obviously, the strategy of prototyping must aim at confidence without generating sanguine expectations that end in disillusionment or permitting the pessimism that invites paralysis. We referred above to the special environment of mutual support that "true believers" create among themselves. Since more than words and gestures (for example, affection, respect, and rectitude) are needed, it is always relevant to ask: What else do the participants get out of it? Whose value demands are indulged? Deprived?

Clearly, the demand of individuals for arbitrary power is exposed to value deprivation by any innovation of the type we are discussing. At the same time, individual demands for a share in common decisions are indulged. Some physicians did not go along with the idea of patient-staff conferences; and many staff members and patients at first resented the attention and time that the meetings took. There were patients who were accustomed to getting their own way by tantrum behavior or by using family wealth and respect to overcome difficulties; they felt endangered by the new power structure. Another element in the patient population consists of highly withdrawn and very timid people. They were passive resisters and practitioners of indirection, especially in making themselves a burden on others.

In Vicos it was tempting to project directors to build a vested interest in transition and to postpone relinquishing control to the Indians. There always seemed to be plausible grounds for waiting a little longer in the name of more education. The temptation, however, was successfully resisted.

It must not be supposed that economic values were of no consequence in these (or in any) prototype situations. One of the first programs that the Vicos council endorsed was a potato-growing experiment that during the first season actually did pay off handsomely to those who cooperated. The whole Vicos project depended on the willingness of private and governmental sources to make money and facilities available for staff and improvements. In common with many prototype situations, the investment in Vicos was not trivial, especially in relation to the amount of outside investment available to other villages in the Andes. This created a strong incentive to "make good" and to justify the money, no doubt partly in the hope of getting grant renewals to carry the program further. The Yale institute did not depend on a specific grant; nevertheless, economic considerations were not insignificant. If the innovation had initiated a wave of suicides or assaults, for example, the financial position of the institute would have been threatened, since the wealthy clientele on which it drew extensively might have withdrawn.

We mentioned respect as a factor; it is worth stressing the role that this played among the scientific leaders of both projects. The professional people concerned were connected with top-flight univer-

sities, and they were ambitious, not only to advance human enlightenment and skill, but to obtain a respected place among their colleagues
in the wider community.

Moral factors were involved throughout. Many American psychiatrists have been sensitive to the anomaly of exercising great power
over the lives of others in a society whose proclaimed goals are human
dignity and many of whose actual practices allow for considerable
power-sharing. However, the moral considerations were not all favorable to the project. Some physicians were shocked when traditional
conceptions of privacy were abandoned at the patient-staff meetings.
And the Vicos project invariably raised questions in the minds of some
participants and observers about the legitimacy of the degree of control exercised in shaping the future of Vicos. At least, the directors
would say in reply, the aims are frankly stated.

But is this strictly true? Did the project leaders go out of their
way to make clear to interested groups how their interests might be
affected? In the environment of Vicos—nearby and elsewhere in
Peru—there were groups which would have risen against the undertaking if they had been fully alerted to the threat that it implied to
their vested interests. It can be said frankly that the project director
did not go out of his way to stir up sleeping dogs. His self-justification
was clear: If this project succeeds it will supply actual knowledge
rather than mere polemic regarding the capacity of Indian communities in Peru for self-government.

The patient-staff conference, too, was begun without an effort
being made to spell out in detail the impact that it might have on the
component groups of the hospital community. Some physicians saw
that their type of therapy would be undermined; but it was impossible
to argue, in a scientific environment, that test projects should not be
undertaken. Perhaps the nurses were least prepared for what the future might bring, which was nothing less than posing a grave question of the usefulness of the profession as traditionally practiced.

The problem of balancing, or integrating, rectitude and disclosure
is one of the most delicate in the past and future of the sciences, and
especially of political science. New knowledge is likely to redefine the
value position of many members of the body politic. If the "sleeping
dogs" are alerted before knowledge is acquired, the resulting political
controversy proceeds with less pertinent knowledge for the guidance
of community decision than would be the case if the prototype had
not been established. Both the Vicos and the Yale innovations were
profoundly revolutionary in their potential findings, and they pro-

ceeded on the assumption that some sacrifice of disclosure in advance was a justifiable cost of the total enterprise.

The members of the Vicos community were soon aware of the fact that the project improved their health. This was not so obvious, however, to patients in the institute; it was also less certain from the physicians' standpoint. We note in this connection that discrepancies of interpretation are particularly likely to occur when ego-norms are in process of reconstruction. Psychiatrists are accustomed to welcoming as evidences of improvement acts that may be resented in more conventional circles. We know that, when patients have been exceedingly withdrawn personalities, others are accustomed to exploiting their timidity and dependence. As the patients improve and begin to externalize their attention over a wider range of objects in the environment and to assert themselves more often, conflicts usually develop with the former exploiter—the husband, wife, brother, sister, or friend. These people often think that the patient is getting worse, since he is becoming "unmanageable." However, this is not necessarily the psychiatrist's interpretation.

When ego-norms of inequality are called in question, the resulting tension and conflict are, in principle, signs of growth. As Vicosinos became more confident of their judgment in relation to the surrounding world, they were bound to seem less agreeable people to anyone who had previously thought of them as passively obedient toilers or maids of all work. The mixed, or "Spanish," population would certainly resent their new demands for political, economic, and respect values.

In the cases mentioned here, the prototype-builders were aware of these contingencies and sought by appropriate strategies to keep the tensions and conflicts of growth within limits (especially limits this side of violence). As a means of improving the strategy of prototyping, it is essential to view comprehensively the sequence of value deprivations and indulgences among all participants in any project and particularly to assess the role of the scientists as part of the indulging or depriving environment. From the perspective of each participant, the following questions need to be asked and answered: What indulgences or deprivations does the participant attribute to the innovation? In terms of what values? From the point of view of the scientific observers (who are active participants), what value changes are being experienced by each participant? In terms of what value? How are these questions to be answered from the point of view of scientific observers, nonparticipants in the prototype situation?

The experience of prototype-building usually includes partial failures that call attention to better strategic possibilities. As we have suggested, one justification for a prototype is that it stimulates the discovery of an improved program and lays the foundation for orderly replication of the revised prototype model. Timing, for example, can as a rule be greatly improved by experience. Possible modifications are suggested by these questions: Would a larger or smaller group learn more quickly? Should preliminary discussions of the project be long or short? Should the discussion style vary (for example, more or less hortatory)?

Which possible participants are likely to be favorably disposed toward the project? How can their predispositions be most efficiently dealt with without disturbing the basic structure of the innovation? What composition of project groups is likely to overcome adverse predispositions most economically (in terms of man-hours of talent)?

Questions of this kind emphasize the feedback relationship between prototype and experiment. As a prototype is built, ideas multiply for experiments that systematically modify various features of each prototypical situation. Ideas are also generated that can be meaningfully employed in laboratory experiments having little connection to the prototype itself. For example, every significant prototype situation to date has been handicapped by lack of efficient measuring instruments. How can simple procedures or tests be devised that will show *how much* incapacity an individual is likely to show in making his behavior conform to his proclaimed ideal? How can these tests be adapted to persons of diverse culture, class, interest, and personality exposure and predisposition? What simple tests will show how rapidly people of specified past exposure can learn to conform under conditions of mixed indulgence and deprivation (by value category)?

The prototype experience is not only a means of improving institutional practice and scientific knowledge in general; it creates a new body of assets and liabilities that can be utilized to spread or block the specific innovation. Successful prototype situations tend to create an elite of knowledgeable and skilled individuals who can gain further advantages by continuing their activity on behalf of the goal (the "cause"). Vicos prepared a few such people; so did the institute.

At the same time, a prototype often generates negative assets, or liabilities, perhaps because of clumsy technique in the early stages and because some opposition to the aims and methods of the project is crystallized by early exposure. Such professional jealousies as resentment at receiving insufficient acknowledgment or annoyance at the publicity received by a rival figure may be involved. Besides these egocentric motivations, there may be divergencies of outlook on plausible scientific grounds or from fear of eventual damage to political, ecclesiastical, or philosophic affiliations.

We have said that the prototype procedure adds to knowledge and that future political scientists will rely on it to bridge the gap between survey and experimentation, on the one hand, and official intervention, on the other. To phrase this more precisely: A prototype enables the observer to report that, when a given innovation was introduced by participants who were largely in favor of the attempt, the innovative practice was or was not stabilized in a given situation by the use of a reported strategy during a given period with reported results. The previous discussion provides an indication of what is involved in specifying each of the key phrases above—the characteristics of the innovation, of the innovators, and of other participants; the strategy; and the results.

Prototyping as a Strategy of Self-Observation

Prototyping can be effectively used as a contextual procedure that seeks to clarify to all who participate in a situation their role as interacting factors. The depth of self-observation varies greatly from one prototype to another. The environment of the Yale institute was full of ego-assessment, since the hospital attached therapeutic importance to understanding others and obtaining insight into the self. The Vicos project brought many insights to its directors. They learned to assess themselves continually as efficient or inefficient instrumentalities of the over-all objective. The elders of Vicos went along with this process to some extent, since they were obtaining tools of thought and talk with which to designate the decision process in which they were engaged and to refer to the cultural differences between Indian and non-Indian communities. They were set a model of candid acceptance of at least partial responsibility for the failures as well as the successes of the enterprise.

The political science of the future, especially in relatively free societies, will no doubt rely extensively on prototypical methods in order to influence the political process by means of the variables of insight and understanding. Our previous discussion has indicated the important role of subjective events and especially of expectations in the manifold of events. The role of the observer, with his total subjectivity, has been emphasized in connection with the fundamental operations of the physical sciences. Earlier versions of scientific method often presented it as a device for ignoring subjectivity, rather than for exposing subjective events to proper discipline. In the light of what has been said, it is clear that the older view was a misconception.[10]

However, the disposition to exempt the "I-me" from candid description and evaluation is strong; it is a subjective pattern of no inconsiderable importance in limiting the application of the scientific perspective to political events. But the culture of science in the modern world is gradually closing in and melting the ice floe on which the touchy ego has taken refuge. The total situation has been drastically redefined. The distraught ego is not faced with the humiliating alternatives of annihilation or admission that he is part of the ice; on the contrary, he is invited by the pursuing ego to join the common self of the age of science.

Political scientists have always been close enough to the perspectives of active politicians to appreciate the importance of the personal factor in politics. They have, however, joined with the adroit political leader in screening themselves from candid observation, using the screen to impose the prestige of "distance" on others. The scholar has fallen into this frame of mind willingly enough, since he often has much to conceal—such as why he shrinks from active political participation. He is not deliberately conspirative in obtaining deference and other values from the community, but distracting the focus of attention from incongenial features of the self is one of the automatic defense mechanisms of the ego. Neither the political scientist nor the practicing politician has to learn self-deception; rather, he has to unlearn it.

In the future it will become less easy for political scientists or politicians to escape from self-observation, chiefly because the observational imperative of science grants no more than temporary exemption from its searching eye. Prototyping is itself a cultural device of enormous potential for the reconstruction of politics, as of all of civilization, by providing a fundamental strategy for examining all the egos involved—including the initiating scientists'.

Prototyping provides an easy transition in many circumstances from an initial point of innovation to the eventual adoption of an institutional pattern by the official prescribing authorities of a body politic. In the past, many new ideas have been inaugurated under lay or scientific or combined auspices and have spread widely through the civic order, culminating as part of the public order.[11] In some of these cases, attention has been given to recording data that are useful in evaluating the consequences of the new practice. More often, scientific values have played a very subordinate role, and the full potentialities of prototyping have not been realized.

Where opportunities exist for prototypical situations to be multiplied at private initiative and guided by scientific considerations, it is possible to approximate a truly experimental approach. Theoretically, for example, the Vicos pattern could be deliberately extended to haciendas matched according to size of population, equality of land distribution among families or castes, levels of education, exposure to the outside culture, and similar variables. The program itself could be varied by emphasizing cottage industry rather than agriculture or by introducing a manufacturing plant (at first under outside management) able to absorb much of the local manpower. The program could be varied by enlarging the role of collectively managed resources.

On the other hand, the original project could be replicated in major outline, and the research directed to the study of factors affecting diffusion of the program. The aim would be to improve the strategy of encouraging community demand to obtain assistance in inaugurating such projects. For example, visits could be arranged to bring Vicos elders to new haciendas, where their testimony could be added to the presentation of the idea by the scientists.

Civic initiative, especially when strengthened by research evaluation, provides experience enabling the whole body politic to proceed with no little rationality to decide whether to extend a program. In popular government, this includes the possibility that a majority vote may be obtained in the face of substantial minority opposition; and it brings a new but familiar factor into the localities where the innovation enters actively into the balance of political power. A successful prototype is able to stay at the margin of the political arena and to avoid controversy among parties and pressure organizations.

When objectives and techniques are relatively noncontroversial, prototyping can be carried on within the framework of governmental authority. Political scientists are asked or permitted to initiate and control such projects, with heavy emphasis on obtaining data of scientific worth.

Prototyping and the Deeper Dynamics of Politics

Undoubtedly, the future use of prototyping in conjunction with other methods will greatly improve our knowledge of *intensity factors* in the political process and of the changing environmental and pre-dispositional elements that condition intensity. In turn, the strategy of clarification and consent will become more refined.

From one point of view, prototyping is a means of uncovering the predispositions of the political process at any particular time and place. It adds depth to the knowledge obtained by surveys able to describe one or only a few variables at a time.

Consider in this connection some of the findings at Vicos and at the institute. When contact was first established with Vicos, the pattern of excessive alcoholism was well established. It was usual for people to drink themselves insensible during fiestas or over the week end. Furthermore, the pattern was strengthened by the success of the potato-growing program, since ready cash was brought into the community. This cash was spent on fiestas to obtain respect by lavish hospitality.

We interpret the drinking as part of a boredom syndrome, not only at Vicos but perhaps in all folk societies at a stage of easy and partial accommodation to civilization. To the casual eye, the members of a folk society may not seem to suffer from devaluation of self. Nevertheless, many lines of inquiry often point in this direction. Evidently, the Vicosinos had gradually come to see themselves as cutting a somewhat ridiculous figure in their traditional costumes, since many villagers were discarding parts or all of the ancient garb and donning the clothes of "civilization." Furthermore, the respect given, grudgingly or not, to anyone who obtained a new gadget—a clasp knife, a wrist watch—was significant. This behavior was supported in intimate talk during which it became apparent that some parents were secretly determined that their children should have a better life and a chance to obtain some education and skills appropriate to the modern world, even if it meant spending time away from home.

Looking into the historical records kept by Spanish administrators and priests and assessing individual stories of the past, it was necessary to conclude that alchoholism had grown as Vicos culture was impoverished by the dropping of old rituals and the attenuation of the traditional ideology.

We predicted that alcoholism would diminish as life in Vicos got more interesting with the introduction of education and the multiplication of community activities. (This was, in fact, the case.)

Data from other folk cultures in many parts of the world tend to confirm that drugs may be used to excess as a self-damaging response to self-contempt and impotence in a changing world. The

Borneo head-hunters, for example, were restricted by outside authority from head-hunting, and the frustrations experienced by young men were intense. They no longer had an approved method for demonstrating their masculine status and obtaining respect, power, and other values. A substitute activity became the collective and excessive use of alcoholism; the drinking parties in the long house often went on for days.[12]

The boredom hypothesis goes much deeper than the assertion that, in transitional stages of exposure to modern civilization, the members of folk societies entertain self-contempt and internalize their aggressive impulses—which do not find gratifying expression against the external world—against themselves. They are internalized, for example, against their bodies and in the forms of factionalism, bitter gossip, ridicule, ambivalent overassertion, rejection of traditional patterns of culture, and boredom or distaste with the insipidity of life. Is it probable that boredom is a latent mood in all isolated small societies and that the temptations and limitations of contact with a universalizing civilization simply bring the boredom near to awareness? Boredom is itself a defense of the ego against such alternatives as explosive rage (running amuck, for instance). Alcoholism is a simple use of drugs to abolish the dullness and meaninglessness of life. It is characteristic of small communities to continually invade individual egos and to subordinate their latent demands to the parochially tolerated outlets of the culture. The perpetual interaction of the small community is a vigilant mutual censorship that smothers individuality.

That the human ego is endowed with a large repertory of strategies with which to protect itself from the steam roller of other people is becoming clearer to us in the perspective of modern findings on many topics. Not long ago, a team of psychiatrists at Yale tried hypnosis as a research method in studying a group of severely ill patients. They often seemed to be getting full cooperation. Eventually, however, the subjects would cast aside the façade of acquiescence and resume their original states, including the symptoms. In one sense, the experiment was negative, but it strongly confirmed the depth and subtlety of the protective devices at the disposal of the ego.[13]

The emergence of the modern urban metropolitan aggregate has brought the question of ego alienation into the foreground. Durkheim proposed the concept of *anomie* to describe the failure of the ego to achieve an identification with society. We analyze this as failure to achieve a self-system providing a satisfactory entity in terms of which value demands can be shaped and shared.[14] Marx's image of the alienated proletarian was in the same vein. The proletarian was presented as a man rejected by the culture of capitalism, since, deprived of ownership, he lacked security in any human relationship.

Recent research on metropolitan areas casts a great deal of doubt on the idea that human beings are in fact cut off from human association. Studies of Los Angeles and Detroit, for example, show that high percentages of the population are in weekly or even more frequent contact with relatives. Nearly everyone is in several networks of human association.[15]

Though accepting these results, we must emphasize that they do not destroy the point that crises of ego identity do in fact occur in civilized society and that many of the labile and even explosive characteristics of urban crowds are to be attributed to the inner tensions generated by exposure to such an environment. It is impossible to survey the figures for suicide, murder, rape, or major crimes against property and the indexes of petty quarrels and altercations without a renewed sense of the relevance of these factors. The picture is even more impressive if we add the incidence of psychosomatic disease and mental disorder.

When we reflect on the boredom of primitive man and the insecurities of civilized man, a major point emerges. The culture forms hitherto devised by Homo sapiens are in some profound sense maladapted to his needs. This is the large kernel of truth in the picture of "man versus society." It is, however, man (modified by early experience of other men) against man (similarly modified) in the sense that the forms of culture thus far invented both perpetuate and generate conflict.

Perhaps the most interesting hypothesis for future exploration is that the cultural forms thus far developed do not use or challenge man's fundamental capacities for creative expression. Man suffers from unused capability; his recurrent crisis is generated by excess capacity for value formation.[16]

It is at first glance paradoxical that man is only beginning to discover himself at the moment when he appears on the verge of bringing superior successors into existence or of annihilating himself altogether. Nevertheless, the pioneering achievements of science and technology contain the seeds of man's fulfillment, since the methods of science are able to disclose the capabilities of the human brain and to make a continuing appraisal of the cultural practices by which the potential can become actual.

Unused capability, therefore, may prove to be the key to the symptomatic generation of boredom and kindred forms of withdrawal and of intermittent explosions of rage and destructiveness. The relatively isolated items serialized in the basic data survey would gain depth, direction, and coherence when supplemented by the results obtained by strategically placed prototypes presenting the whole dynamic balance of local forces.

That prototyping provides a means of clarifying and disseminating the social practices of human dignity and of revealing the latent capability of man is evident. In particular, prototyping lends itself to discovering the limits of power sharing in various circumstances. The Yale institute research was undertaken on an island of autocracy in a prevailingly democratic order; it threw light on the strategy by which power might be fully shared without heavy adverse costs. Our society has many islands of limited participation in decision, of which the most obvious are perhaps schools, prisons, and units of such large, organized structures as the army and civil service.

The Vicos project was also a deliberate devolution of power, in this case by the boss of the hacienda and the government. In view of the structure of Peruvian politics and society, Vicos could hardly be called an island of autocracy. More accurately, it became, for the time being at least, an island of democracy on an archipelago of contrasting structures.

The prototypes discussed thus far have been limited to small community or small group units. However, prototypical units can be developed from top to bottom or from bottom to top of every existing hierarchical structure. All kinds of combinations are conceivable: the chief of a unit of a large organization plus deputies, assistants, and departmentalized subordinates; the members of a board plus major figures in the subordinate staff; coordinate chiefs of units plus deputies, assistants, and departmentalized subordinates; each of the above plus significant participants from outside the official line of authority (trade union officials, client agencies, supply agencies, and the like).

The future will probably see more attention given to the intermediate echelons of large-scale organizations and to other intermediate units. We have moderately satisfactory information at hand about the national cabinet and the smallest units of national government. But the intermediate level has been grossly understudied from the point of view of carrying the practice of shared participation as far as is compatible with other objectives.

Prototypes are nearly experiments when they can be replicated under appropriate conditions; they are also "case studies" in the sense that they take note of many variables which are not controlled. The conspicuous virtue of a case study—whether the observational field is a community, a small group, a personality, or some other subject—is that it familiarizes the scientist with what to expect in such circumstances. In this way, he is able to estimate the hypotheses that can be profitably tested in the context and what methods are best adapted to the task. However, only a handful of case studies oriented to a common objective seem rewarding.[17] As quickly as possible, correlational or experimental research should be designed, or cases can be put fully into the context of a prototype.

A problem that is certain to arise in prototyping is how to be as precise as possible in providing data on the basis of which pertinent appraisals can be made. An essential consideration is that data-gathering not be allowed to interfere with, in particular, the preparatory phase of the project since the precondition of having anything worth appraising is at least a minimum degree of harmony in the perspectives of the responsible group. After the initial stage, it is still important to limit data-gathering whenever it promises to become a disrupting factor.

Ideally, the political scientists who inaugurate a prototype project should have it so well planned that bench-mark data can be obtained all along the way (preprototype, preparatory phase, full phase, and subsequent phase). However, we know enough of the facts of inquiry to expect new implications of a study to dawn on the innovators throughout the course of the experience and in retrospective appraisal.

NOTES

[1] The experimental design is generalized from A. Bavelas, "Communication Patterns in Task-Oriented Groups," in D. Lerner and H. D. Lasswell, eds., *The Policy Sciences* (Stanford: Stanford University Press, 1951). The experiments referred to in the following paragraphs are greatly simplified in order to emphasize the points pertinent to the present discussion. The potential significance of communication theory for political science is outlined in K. Deutsch, *Nationalism and Social Communication* (New York: J. Wiley & Sons, 1953). On communication in small groups in general, cf. A. P. Hare, E. F. Borgatta, and R. F. Bates, eds., *Small Groups* (2nd ed.; New York: Alfred A. Knopf, 1955); D. Cartwright and A. Zander, eds., *Group Dynamics* (2nd ed.; Evanston: Row, Peterson and Co., 1959); J. W. Thibaut and H. H. Kelley, *The Social Psychology of Groups* (New York: John Wiley & Sons, 1959); R. T. Golombiewski, *The*

Small Group, "An Analysis of Research Concepts and Operations" (Chicago: University of Chicago Press, 1962); S. Verba, *Small Groups and Political Behavior,* "A Study in Leadership" (Princeton: Princeton University Press, 1961). On the assimilation of experimental studies to organization theory, cf. especially the contributions of H. A. Simon, J. G. Marsh, and H. Guetzkow.

[2] On body movement and gesture, cf. L. C. Kolb, "Disturbances of the Body-Image," in S. Arieti, ed., *Handbook of American Psychiatry* (New York: Basic Books, 1959), 749–769.

[3] Preliminary tension studies have been initiated on a large scale by O. Klineberg, H. Cantril, and other psychologists, sociologists, psychiatrists, and anthropologists with strong political interests. UNESCO has often provided official sponsorship.

[4] On TAT and other tests, cf. G. G. Stern, M. I. Stein, and B. S. Bloom, *Methods in Personality Assessment* (Glencoe, Ill.: The Free Press, 1956), and subsequent articles. Cf. further, M. K. Opler, ed., *Culture and Mental Health* (New York: Macmillan, 1959); F. L. K. Hsu, ed., *Psychological Anthropology* (Homewood, Ill.: Dorsey Press, 1961).

[5] Psychoanalytic psychiatry gave enormous impetus to body-image research. J. Bruner's research on perception is stimulating in this field. Cf. J. Kennedy and H. D. Lasswell, "A Cross-Cultural Test of Self-Image," *Human Organization,* 17 (1958), 41–43.

[6] These distinctions were drawn in H. D. Lasswell, N. Leites *et al., Language of Politics,* "An Introduction to Quantitative Semantics" (New York: G. W. Stewart, 1949).

[7] A proposal to treat political science and legislation as sciences to the extent that pilot "experiments" are taken seriously is made by L. Donnat, *La politique expérimentale* (2 vols.; Paris: C. Reinwald, 1885–1891).

[8] Alan Holmberg is the innovating figure at Vicos. For a provisional account, cf. A. R. Holmberg, H. F. Dobyns *et al.,* "Community and Regional Development: The Cornell-Peru Experiment," *Human Organization,* 21 (1962), 108–124. I have participated in the Vicos project and benefited from discussions of method with Holmberg and others.

[9] Robert Rubenstein and I will publish an analysis of Y.P.I. experience. I am especially indebted to Dr. Rubenstein for suggestions about prototyping.

[10] Cf. M. Polanyi, *Personal Knowledge* (Chicago: University of Chicago Press, 1958).

[11] The civic order of a community includes the patterns of value distribution

and basic institutions which receive the protection of relatively mild sanctions. The public order has severe sanctions at its disposal. Cf. my discussion in C. J. Friedrich, ed., *The Public Interest,* "Nomos V" (New York: Atherton Press, 1962), especially pp. 66–67.

12 Concerning Borneo, I am indebted to Tom Harrisson, curator and government ethnologist, Sarawak Museum, Kuching, without binding him to the formulations here.

13 Cf. *inter alia* R. Newman, J. Katz, and R. Rubenstein, "The Experimental Situation as a Determinant of Hypnotic Dreams: A Contribution to the Experimental Use of Hypnosis," *Psychiatry,* 23 (1960), 63–73.

14 E. Durkheim, *Suicide,* "A Study in Sociology," trans. J. A. Spaulding and G. Simpson (Glencoe, Ill.: The Free Press, 1951).

15 For interpretation of recent research, cf. S. Greer, *Governing the Metropolis* (New York: Wiley, 1962); W. Kornhauser, *The Politics of Mass Society* (New York: The Free Press of Glencoe, 1959).

16 For a fuller treatment, cf. my paper "Communication and the Mind," in S. M. Farber and R. H. L. Wilson, eds., *Control of the Mind* (New York: McGraw-Hill, 1961).

17 Extended evaluations of the case study are to be found in E. A. Bock, ed., *Essays on the Case Method* (New York: Inter-University Case Program, 1962). Contributions by H. Stein, D. Waldo, J. W. Fesler, and the editor.

6

Micromodeling

The volume of data relevant to the depiction of the world arena or of any component community is enormous. How can we prevent overloading the political scientist who tries to use the intelligence services, especially the surveys and analyses made available by colleagues? Selective presentation is the answer and the problem. Detailed information must be at hand when required, properly located in an image of the whole in which the configuration of past, present, and future events is related to clarified value goals.

It has long been obvious that the verbal presentation of data and interpretations is in some respects unsatisfactory. Listeners vary in speed of comprehension, whether the medium is oral or printed. They differ in recall of pertinent information and in ability to discern the patterns relevant to the problem. Although it is impracticable to bring everyone to the same level of excellence in such matters, many limitations can be overcome with suitable methods.

A fundamental principle is to supplement one mode of communication by others. Television is an impressive example of how words, printed messages, diagrams, maps, and dramatizations can be synthesized into an experience surpassing the impact of media that rely solely on one sensory mechanism.

The simple fact of exposure to data and interpretation does not as a rule produce an optimum effort at problem-solving by members of an audience. The situation must be organized in ways that elicit audience participation. For example, breaks in the presentation could be arranged, and everyone encouraged to discuss or meditate on what he has seen and heard.

Several devices are available to mitigate individual differences in recall. A group could meet in the same place, and surroundings could be modified to provide memory cues in aid of recall. Such are the roles of graphs, tables, maps, pictures, and models.

The elements of a problem-solving situation—multichannel exposure, participation, memory aids—are found in many places and can be effectively molded for the use of political scientists. (For the time being, we take predispositional factors for granted, assuming that competent and motivated persons would be selected or self-selected to participate.)

To go no further into history than to the Prussian general staff, we have a striking case of ingenuity in the selection of procedures for training and planning.[1] The staff invented the war game, which brought definiteness into planning, since it became possible to simulate battle conditions and allow initial dispositions to be studied and strategies to be played through to the end. The same technique has recently been transplanted into the realm of diplomacy and business.[2]

In educational circles, the simulation of adult reality is well rooted in practice. Debating, for example, has been conducted according to several plans, usually adapted from models of Congressional or legal procedure. The moot court is an auxiliary of legal education in which actual judges are often introduced to informally guide the argument and give decisions. Political science classes are occasionally resolved into sessions of the United Nations Security Council or municipal councils. Teams of students play roles assigned by country or group or according to affirmative or negative positions in a controversy.

These exercises vary in the degree to which they are conducted as inquiries or as competitions in advocacy. The moot court or the traditional academic debate is a frankly competitive exhibition of skill and is judged accordingly. Many conferences or seminars, by contrast, are intended to follow an impartial, exploratory approach in which each participant keeps an open mind until his attention has been directed to the putative facts and to alternative interpretations of them. The war game or the diplomatic game keeps rivalry in the foreground, since the policy moves by each side are judged as successful or not by umpires who are instructed to play the role of "nature" and to decide impartially among contenders. Umpires cannot in fact speak for the future; hence, their assumptions can gradually become sufficiently apparent to tempt the participants to play the umpire rather than to act on the basis of candid estimates of how future events are likely to turn out.

DECISION SEMINARS

We can give concreteness to the idea of a problem-solving seminar ("decision seminar") by considering the case of political scientists specialized in a given region.[3] Parallel considerations apply if the domain is enlarged to the globe or the astropolitical arena or narrowed to a particular country, section, or locality. Specialists focus on particular problems in a context during a given period; such concentration is, in fact, indispensable to the cultivation of knowledge. It is notorious, however, that the woods can vanish as the trees become conspicuous. If the observer is to remain in intellectual command of a reasonably realistic and comprehensive image of the whole, he must participate in a situation that brings the general map to his attention and explicit consideration. Problem-solving calls for a procedure that pursues the configurative aim by guiding the focus of attention back and forth between part and whole.

A procedure appropriate to this end is an agenda of periodic meetings among the territorial experts whom we are presently considering. A periodic meeting would provide an occasion for freshening the paint on the neglected part of the intellectual house, for repairs or extension, or even, on presumably rare occasions, for a revolutionary reconstruction.

The Setting

Such a convocation could most fruitfully take place in a familiar setting in which the key subject is visually represented. A permanent seminar room would best serve the purpose. The charts, maps, and other materials could be displayed on the four walls (even the ceiling) to refer to past and future events. One might, for example, adopt the convention of an eye-level line around the room as representing a recent year and imagine that time proceeds upward. All that had reference to past trend or conditioning factors would thus be kept below the line; projections, goal constructs, and policy alternatives would be placed above the line.

As the members of the group work together, the room would gain the significance of a comprehensive though microscale image of the reality with which they were concerned. Each item would be separately introduced and discussed; hence, every permanent item would call up the original discussion, including any reservations about the method used or the reliability of the information on which the chart or table was based. Perhaps a trend chart indicates that the percentage of the electorate in a given country which voted in national elections has risen over the past twenty years. The initial discussion might throw considerable doubt on the figures for the first few years or suggest that, since the size of the electorate was diminishing as legal restrictions were multiplied, the chart be augmented by a line relating eligibility to total adult population. (The line has possibly since been added.)

Undoubtedly any projection would bring similarly critical considerations to mind. Perhaps a chart shows that acts of rebellion in Y are likely to diminish sharply in the next few years. However, discussions may have revealed that *émigrés* are not likely to accommodate themselves to the new state of affairs; hence, in case of tension between country X and Y, they would massively infiltrate the boundary zones of Y. (Cross references to charts projecting the alignments of X and Y are possible.)

Projections are sometimes useful when they take the form of simple extrapolations of recent trends, since extrapolations often point to the timing or location of incipient conflicts. But projections are also made on bases of inference more complex than simple extrapolation; they add, for example, assumptions about the factors affecting migration into a given boundary zone. If industrial development is shown to move away from a boundary zone and jobs become available elsewhere, internal movements of population may be expected to change. Past correlations between industrial growth and population movement can be used to modify simple extrapolations of population shift.

Provisional specifications of goal would undoubtedly occasion many exchanges among seminar participants. What, in addition to voting in elections, are the most suitable indexes of shared power? One participant proposes that we specify only statutes passed by a legislature (not decreed by the executive) after more than *pro forma* debate. In the latter case, it is suggested that both pro- and anti-ruling–party elements shall have taken part in debating proposed legislation. (Debate participation can be measured by percentage of debate time occupied by all parties, for example.) Or a provisional specification might be the absence of intimidation, measured, perhaps, by direct testimony taken in sample interviews.

The range of policy alternatives coming before a decision seminar might be wide, and new charts would undoubtedly call up many comments about future contingencies. Each step in a possible policy sequence would be open to evaluation. Assume that we begin to formulate a strategy of economic aid in these terms: a sum of dollars is available for use in country X; the dollars are transformed into local units of buying power and used to obtain L units of labor (or L^m units of man hours), M units of raw materials, and F units of machinery and related manufacturing facilities within a year.

Such a characterization of a policy would be sufficient for some purposes. But it would have to be greatly elaborated before the political consequences can be competently assessed. Many further acts could properly be regarded as part of the policy and therefore must be added. Let us imagine that news of the program arouses cries of imperialism, colonialism, and warmongering in the press and private channels of political parties opposed to the government in office. What assumptions are to be made about the next moves by our officials? Will our men on the spot have prepared the way for the program by encouraging popular demands for assistance so that wind is rather successfully prevented from getting into the sails of the opposition?

Or, passing beyond the immediate "crisis of acceptance"—Will new factories prove vulnerable to opposition attack on the grounds that they actually discriminate against the North or South or against the tribes, religions, peasants, landlords, or parties of these sections? Will the attack lead to the withdrawal into opposition of factions in the government legislative coalition and put the cabinet in a minority? Will the ruler and his aides be provoked to liquidate parliament entirely and rule by decree and police suppression of dissident elements?

In assessing the significance of any chart, map, or other material, the fact that the discussion occurs in the context of a permanent seminar can be used to raise in systematic fashion questions that might in other circumstances be overlooked. For example, a trend chart depicting the rapid expansion of the armed forces and their share of government expenditures needs to be kept in perspective by directing attention to trends elsewhere in the society. Have the numbers gain-fully employed in agriculture or commerce been affected? Do educa-tion, health, information, and religious activities grow at the same rate as the armed forces? Are marriage rates affected? Do recruits come only from the lowest castes and classes, or are they spread pro-portionately throughout the social structure? Such questions are brought to mind by passing one's eye around the chart room and thinking in turn of possible impacts on all other values and selected institutional practices.

If the impact of a conditioning factor in the past, such as the influence of increased purchasing units (a wealth factor), is under con-sideration, the various value-institution panels in the seminar room will suggest problems. In terms of well-being, for instance, a question would be whether the units of purchasing power were spent in ways that made the diet more or less healthful. In reference to family and intimate relations, did higher money income lead to the taking of more concubines or mistresses? In terms of enlightenment, has the money been spent on visits to new parts of the country? Has the money influenced skill, for example, by increasing effective demand for music lessons? Are the depressed classes the recipients of the new income, and do they get new respect from other classes for their "modern" clothes? Do the priests succeed in directing the new funds into more ceremonies, memorials, and shrine repairs? Taking each of these and other suggested effects into account, what power results can be imputed to the income change; for instance, did the groups that benefited directly shift to support the government or did they stay with opposition parties that bragged of a supposed success and demanded more?

When a specific projection is being considered, the analytic con-text provided by the seminar room can give guidance to critical dis-cussion. Projections of the ecology of population give rise to such questions as these: Will the health facilities of the newly occupied areas be overstrained? With what results? What of the school facili-ties? Of family housing and stability of units? Of accommodations for worship? Of access to radio and newspapers? Of employment? Will new population mixtures result in reducing class and caste dis-criminations or exacerbating them? Will the political weight of pro-or anti-government groups be strengthened?

Every policy alternative can properly initiate a similar contextual examination. Will news of the true source of the aid that permitted new plants to be built be widely disseminated, or will it be kept secret by the local government? Will artisans in certain lines find themselves faced by competition and immediately contribute to cutthroat competition? Will new manufacturing plants raise health hazards by attracting workers who billet themselves in unsanitary shacks and alleyways? Will artisans find some of their skills useless and turn to industrial tasks? Will families be separated as husbands migrate to the sites of jobs? Will the practice of employing people by merit help to reduce social discrimination without precipitating violence? Will the removal of people from family temples and churches expose them to the propaganda of new sects and increase the membership of these organizations? Summarizing effects in political terms, will they enable mass revolutionary movements from outside to reach a large number of potential members rapidly and successfully?

From time to time it would be useful to respecify goals, often by translation into immediate, mid-range, and long-range objectives. All the experience acquired by a problem-solving group since the last discussion could be mobilized, since it has become part of the predispositions of the participants. In the decision context, various assumptions could be made about the objectives at various times in each value-institutional category. The problem would be to clarify the political goals that expedite optimal movement toward a shared, realistic decision process.

The most provocative issues in this context relate to the timing of goals that move in zig-zag, rather than in nominally straight, lines toward a free commonwealth. Such questions rise in acute form when a traditional society tries to introduce the institutions of congressional or parliamentary government as practiced in English-speaking and Western European countries. Instead of strong and unified leadership, the immediate result may be weak, unstable, and confused national direction. Analysis may show that the "political parties" are largely unknown to the villagers of the country and whirl suspended in a foggy, windy atmosphere of intrigue in the national capital.

It is therefore appropriate for political scientists to consider the possibility of devising programs of progress toward effective power-sharing which draw on the predispositions present in a situation and mobilize them in a sequence of interaction eventuating in the desired result. In various countries, some significant elements are capable of operating creatively from the national center, and potential or actual village systems exhibit a sizable measure of power-sharing and realism on local matters. At the national center, the monarchy and entourage may include individuals exposed to some modern education. At the

national center may also be found military or police officers with
foreign training who have access through the defense and internal
security services to district personnel. In some cases, the administrative
services are almost wholly destitute of officials with a modern orientation, and the occasional scholar, physician, or engineer who also concerns himself with politics has a small and highly personal following.

Is it not sensible, then, for policy-makers to distinguish clearly
in their own minds between the long-range value objectives—shared
power, for instance—and the particular pattern of institutions most
effective in concrete cases in moving the community through transitional phases, even though the institutions may diverge in many
ways from the arrangements current in Anglo–Western European
bodies politic?

Political scientists see that a village program may conceivably
be carried through by strong central leadership that encourages the
election of local councils without intimidation and also constructs
consultation machinery at the regional and national levels by indirect
election. Pluralistic elements in the society may also be associated with
the consultative process at all levels.

In weighing such possibilities, a group must consider the chances
that the central leadership will be strong enough to execute the sweep-
ing social reconstruction that is likely to be required in a society traditionally run by a landholding nobility. If the nobility is unwilling
to permit land reform, for instance, the society may remain vulnerable to the well-tried tactics of "revolution from below," the leadership, inspiration, and initial wherewithal of which come from
experienced outside centers. Landholders may, however, be divided
against themselves, with "middle holders" eager to improve income
with new crops and methods and by investing in local industries to
meet local needs.

The foregoing comments are designed as reminders of the goal-
clarifying and policy-setting task as it frequently confronts political
scientists and decision-makers in the non-Communist world. It is implied that informed, intermittent concern with a comprehensive policy
orientation may lead to the uncovering of new tactical and institutional patterns that move the situation ahead.[4] The function of the
decision-seminar technique of micromodeling the total context is to
foster the creative consideration of such problems.

The Agenda

The principal tasks of problem-solving suggest the broad outlines of an agenda for regular meetings of a decision seminar. Territorial experts could obtain optimal advantages from mutual association if they prepared replies to a common interrogatory privately and in advance. Results would be likely to be best when the questions required definite answers, explicit estimates of the probable course of development in periods of varying duration (immediate, mid-range, or long-range).

It would not be essential to the self-educating effect of the experience to give publicity to the replies. Instead, answers could be deposited with a trusted secretary who compiles and reports the aggregate results to the group for discussion. If anyone wished to voluntarily avow his position he might, of course, do so; but, if the anonymity rule were to be taken seriously, there would have to be no moral compulsion.

The first joint discussion, then, might evaluate projections proposed anonymously by the participants. The members might also agree to make private reassessments of the future which, at the end of the seminar session, would be deposited with the secretary and added to the private archives. (It might be agreed to follow the pattern established by a group of Wall Street economists who are permitted to direct the secretary to disclose their forecasting records to prospective clients or employers.)

The next item on the agenda might be a research report on a trend or set of conditioning factors. To ensure that particular value-institution areas are not overlooked or grossly de-emphasized, a seminar should proceed on a basically cyclical agenda in which the main trends and conditioning factors in every category are recurrently considered. In this way, the central body of charts and maps would be kept approximately current, without imposing on the group the immediate urgencies that confront a busy decision-maker in government. Reports oriented to the future would, of course, deal with particular projections and policy proposals. From time to time, the agenda would need to focus on the respecification or the grounding of goal values in order to distinguish among immediate, mid-range, and long-range objectives.

Occasionally, too, it would be useful for a decision seminar to engage in self-appraisal, subjecting the seminar itself to review. The most significant part of this operation in the long run could be the analysis of the roles played by individual participants. Permission might be given to the secretary to study the pre- and postmeeting shifts of the participants. Is the shift toward agreement, or are disagreements becoming more extreme? Can the aggregate response be explained by the role in the discussion of one or a few individuals? Is the shift in regard to matters about which the participants are least expert?

What of the relation between aggregate forecasts and the reality as disclosed by subsequent events? In this context, an intriguing point is whether the net result of group discussion is to reduce realism by inducing conformity. Is the trend of the group toward greater or less realism?

What of the trend displayed by each individual? Analysis may show that individuals become more or less conformist to the aggregate —that is, to the positions taken most frequently. They may also become more or less accurate in anticipating events.

The group would presumably ask to have aggregate results brought to its notice and authorize individuals to obtain their records privately. In this way, insight could be deepened in two connected though not identical dimensions.

There could be a further aid to insight and understanding on the agenda. Individuals might be encouraged to explain why they made accurate or inaccurate forecasts. The relevant part of the agenda could be divided into two sections, the first concerned with comment on developments since the last meeting and the second with estimates of the future. During the first section, the participants would seek to account for being "right" as well as "wrong," recognizing that, in a complex universe, the former is no less puzzling than the latter.

Self-analysis can lead individuals to guard against proclivities to be overimpressed by or to react against particular sources, such as the military. One might also find that he is chronically sanguine or pessimistic about the success of forces that he hopes will succeed.

It is no secret that human beings at large and prestigious persons in particular are prone to strategies of at least partial deception of the people around them and often of themselves. The causes of this propensity are not mysterious. Utter candor about one's estimates of the future, for example, may lead to value deprivation; a degree of evasive ambiguity can protect the ego from loss of respect or even loss of income and power. It is impossible within the limits of the present discussion to examine this tactic of protective ambiguity in detail. We note, however, at one level the use of such preliminary ploys as: "Of course, I'm neither a prophet nor the son of a prophet" or "No one can prophesy with certainty"—and then comes a prediction. A frequent gimmick is a sentence of normative ambiguity, an assertion that can be treated as an expression of hope if things turn out badly and as a designative statement if it hits the bull's-eye. For instance, "The forces of law and order are rallying in X."

The scientific outlook itself provides excellent ego protection, since science can be interpreted as justifying only conditional assertions about future events. (If *p*, then the probability of *q* is so and so.) Since the probability of knowing all future factors that may affect events is low and the likelihood of having knowledge from the past of the degree of interdependency of all factors is not great, the ego can feel secure from inner or outer contempt if its statements are "kept within strictly scientific limits." Even equations for predicting remote contingencies refer to a configuration of factors that is inaccessible to knowledge at the moment of commitment to the future.

The scientific challenge to the ego is highly exacting in another perspective. It requires that all conceivably relevant factors be sought with perseverence and remorseless self-appraisal. From this standpoint, most of the statements uttered by all of us are extremely casual.

Within the fivefold analysis of each problem-solving strategy, infinite variations can be introduced in order to fit particular circumstances. Provision could be made for visiting expert witnesses who report their own goal clarifications and whatever results they think relevant to trend, factor, projection, and alternative. Collaborators might be brought in for periods of associate membership in the same way that a university adds temporary members to the permanent faculty.

Variations in seminar composition should be introduced and analyzed. Many designs are conceivable—all senior colleagues, one senior and the rest juniors, two seniors and the rest juniors, and so on. Scholars of diverse cultural, class, interest, and personality characteristics could be combined in various ways.

Correlation with Machine Technique

Up to this point, the assumption has been that the seminar would rely largely on verbal discussion of charted and mapped material. We must give explicit attention to the possibility of operating with the aid of machine researches reporting the results of comprehensive simulations of the past and future. In principle, it is possible to treat political events as an interdependent stream through time in which the equations written into the program specify the routines of dependency. Simulations of this kind are already in process of development, and it is evident that such methods will soon become major tools of all the social sciences.[5]

The applicability of micromodels depends on valid data properly stored and mobilized. The storage and retrieval parts of the problem are well advanced toward solution. The phenomenal advances in the design and manufacture of computing machines and in instruments for the scanning, coding, translating, and projection of the contents of documents have for the first time put within the grasp of political scientists the possibility of mastering the hitherto overwhelming mass of available desired data.

We are at the beginning of a revolutionary reconstruction of collective memory and recall. We have hitherto depended on libraries to serve as repositories of manuscripts and books and, in conjunction with museums, to house the fruits of past observation and collection. Catalogues provided indispensable though meager guides to the data pertinent to any research question. The limitations of the catalogue (whether in book or card form) were partially offset by the assiduous labor of the bibliographer, who provided detailed topical breakdowns of the titles of books, pamphlets, periodicals, manuscripts, and collections. The bibliographer was supplemented by the abstractor, who summarized the method and findings of research reports. Because of the professional demand for such services, the most exhaustive publications in the abstracts field have dealt with court and administrative decisions and opinions. (Strictly speaking, these did not summarize research, but source material.) As the division of intellectual labor has grown, "critical reviews" of the state of investigation of particular problems have come to play an important part in assessing current assets. Handbooks, compendiums, encyclopaedias, textbooks, and synoptic treatises perform some of the operations required to keep knowledge accessible.

Until the machine age supplied the brain with computing supplements, political scientists were engaged in a losing cause. Our theoretical equipment enabled us to ask many of the right questions about politics; and ingenuity fathered the invention of many data-gathering, data-processing, and model-fitting devices. But the cascade of history was too swift and voluminous; observers were too few and too inadequately equipped; facilities were rudimentary and poorly distributed.

It is evident that a vast new network of communication to serve the needs of research will presently be in operation. Research publications concentrated at designated points in the system will be scanned and described automatically in all the guidance cards or card equivalents throughout the network. Data will be automatically abstracted and deposited in the appropriate storage slots at centers for various subjects. The publications themselves will be kept available for recheck, and the entire publication (the original or copies) will be available for screening at any center. Unpublished research data will, in principle, be treated the same way.

A scholar who desires the publications, abstracts, or data on any subject can "press a button" and, presto, all the centers provide lists to be photographed.

Storage and retrieval operations are practicable on such a scale because of the progress of microtechnology. Thousands of words can be stored on a square-inch tape and made available for reproduction when desired.[6]

We are close to the day of microcomputers small enough to be portable and hence capable of accompanying a research worker to the field where the relationships of new data can be explored without delay.

The incorporation of storage, retrieval, and simulation methods into problem-solving does not do away with the need of permanent seminars to give critical consideration to the emerging configuration of world affairs. On the contrary, the pace of problem-solving will be vastly accelerated by the new instruments. The demands for missing data and for equations that economize the data required to program realistic simulations of past and future will intensify.

The Problem of Index Instability

It will be more obvious than ever that index instability is a key characteristic of the political and social process and that expert attention must be continually given to the satisfactoriness of proposed indexes. Index instability is characteristic of all allegedly conceptual-empirical relationships. There is no advantage in attempting to evade the problem by defining a concept as identical to an empirical index. The term "vote" can be usefully defined in political science as a commitment in a decision process. For purposes of a specific research, the operational index of "vote" may be restricted to "marked ballots." In other researches, the index may be vocal "ayes" and "nays" as officially recorded, unofficial statements obtained in a poll of opinion, or absence of hesitation in picking up arms to storm a building ("behavioral consensus in an undercover unit"). In much historical research, the indexes of votes (as at a secret convention) may be statements found in correspondence, unpublished notes, reports by police and espionage agents, and the like. A wide range of discretion must be left the data-gatherer in selecting the possible indexes and in estimating their weight as evidence. If the concept "vote" were abolished from the terminology of political science and each empirical index made identical to an independent use of the term, the result would be unnecessary obscurity, since a category equivalent to the original concept of "vote" would be required to guide the matching of likenesses and the noting of differences.

It is not a waste of time to give multiple index readings to a highly abstract conceptual model. It is only a waste of time to forget the formal equivalency of these readings. If the equivalency assumption is forgotten, the intellectual processes required to "improve" equivalency are likely to be neglected or poorly performed. Thus, the definition of "commitment in a decision process" may include the requirement of near absence of intimidation and direct coercion. If the definition is overlooked, the research worker may neglect to make a critical evaluation of the index that seems convenient in a concrete case. (On proper investigation of a particular political context, he may learn that a fifth of the participants could not be properly designated voters because they were in a state of intimidation.)

Problem-solving projects, including decision seminars, would do well to give full attention to the fit between conceptual models and index-fitted versions. Attention should be directed to the discovery of "constants" that render it practicable to translate one index into another, that is, establish valid equivalents in the empirical world.

In this connection, a rewarding question concerns the relationship among observational standpoints of varying degrees of intensity. The same "concepts" at the same cross-section in time apply at each standpoint, but the "indexes" used at each observational position are not the same. For example, we may use the concept "internalization-externalization" to characterize acts of communication to be observed at standpoints of varying intensity (depth). However, the indexes at Standpoint A (relying on news accounts) may record how many people were said to have voted or abstained. Standpoint B (relying on verbatim records of the proceedings) may note how many who abstained also made public statements. This index (making of statements plus abstaining) obviously cuts down the percentage of "internalization." Standpoint C might add to the verbatim record notes taken by gallery observers of the number of abstainers who shouted angrily, stamped their feet, shook their fists, or engaged in other such behavior. In this perspective, perhaps only a few acts of communication would be recorded as "internalized."

Theoretically, all differences among observer-scientists over indexes can be settled by candid analysis of the constants of difference among them. Thus if we think of A, B, and C, above, as three scientists observing the "same" observational field, the differences among them in choice of index need give rise to no problem of intertranslatability if the necessary constants are ascertained and reported. When procedures are well established, recognized constants can be used, subject to occasional check.

The problem of index instability through time is more important for ordinary research in the political and social sciences than in the physical disciplines, where indexes can be accepted as stable through time unless the situations referred to are exceedingly small or exceedingly large (involving, for example, subatomic or galactic units). Since the significance of a detail is a function of its context and symbol contexts change through time (often during short intervals), the ap-

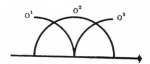

propriateness of particular indexes of political phenomena is always open to review.

One method of equating indexes through time is to use panels of historians. Historians are exposed to residues of the whole configuration of life during a given period; hence, their estimates of the meaning of details in the period is the best obtainable at a given present moment. A technique of overlapping observation can be employed to discover the constants that must be introduced to adjust one set of indexes to another. The diagram shows what is meant. Historian O^2 specializes in a period that overlaps the special periods of O^1 and O^3. The judgments of O^1 (based on his whole period) can be corrected for the period of overlap with O^2 by applying O^2's judgments to the period of overlap. The judgments of O^2 can be corrected for the interval of overlap with O^3 by applying the judgments of O^3 based on his entire period.

The Use of Alternative Models

In decision seminars, it is frequently illuminating to make use of contrasting approaches to the consideration of the same events. Strictly speaking, it is possible to think of all change as a sequence of interdetermining variables. It is also possible to focus on categories of change of particular interest to an observer and to think of them as responses to the impact of environmental on predispositional factors. Although these are equivalent ways of referring to a political process, one may liberate the mind of an observer more effectively than the other.

Applying these points to the analysis of the historic flow of events, we may proceed as suggested in the diagram.

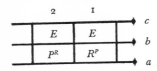

Lines a, b, and c indicate the direction of time. At the cross-section labeled "1," the R stands for the events that are to be explained (such as externalized acts of violence). E stands for the events in the environment that are treated as explanatory factors for the emergence of R (such as externalized acts of violence directed against the self by power in the arena). P in the cross-section labeled "2" designates the factors that predispose the power under study to respond as he does (for example, recall of past successes in bringing about a stoppage and the withdrawal by the other power and the perception of the self as having the present capability to do so).

The R in cross-section 1 could be further subdivided into sections. R^1 might indicate the focusing of attention on E; R^2, the sequence of violent rejoinders; R^3, the estimation of the self as better or worse off in net value position as a result of the policy.

Similarly, the E in 1 could be subdivided. E^1 might be the events that precipitate R^1; E^2 could refer to the operations concurrent with R^2. Many other slices could be made, but these distinctions are sufficient for the moment.

We may note that P in 2, which we have called predispositional for R in 1, becomes an R when the problem is broadened to explain its occurrence. Similarly, R in 1 becomes P for the explanation of subsequent events.

At any cross-section in time, the political analyst challenges himself to explain R and to characterize R as a P for contingent impacts of E. Since any completed historical sequence has, in effect, opted for a specific set of factor combinations, the data available at any cross-section do not provide an exhaustive presentation of all potential combinations.

However, there are methods that to some extent overcome these limitations. Suppose that the violent acts of power X are mild when compared to the possible range of acts. Nonetheless, if the appropriate subsituations are explored, it will be found that some persons (inhabitants of bordering countries, for instance) have been confronted by what were for them huge doses of violence. By focusing on these contexts, we may be able to obtain more intensive knowledge of how power Y is disposed to respond to severely deprivational changes in its environment. It may turn out, for instance, that the lower-class components of the body politic were not willing to fight.

If we begin with long slices through time, some intriguing relationships may be brought into view. In the diagram, N stands for the nuclear center of a world revolutionary emergence (Moscow, 1917; Paris, approximately 1789). D means diffusion, either total diffusion from a body politic centered on the nucleus or substantial diffusion of traits from the nuclear pattern. R means restriction, perhaps by the

partial incorporation of certain traits but emphatically accompanied by rejection of the nucleus and of the revolution. The communities that fall into the two categories are recorded at time slices 1 to 5. Arranged in this way, major determining factor clusters stand out. The diffusion from the nucleus of the 1917 revolution during the first forty years was largely in contiguous zones east and south through thinly industrialized and often colonially subject peoples.

Hypotheses can be refined by multiplying the cross-sections studied in a given period (microslicing). This not only makes it possible to explain the historical sequence more completely, but it discloses cross-sections that lend themselves to analysis because of either likeness or difference. All cross-sections that show no significant change could be matched against those that do, or changes in a new direction could be set against revivals of older patterns. At some point in the course of research, the microslicing technique blends with models of continuous interdetermination.[7]

SOCIAL PLANETARIUM

Many of the orientative advantages of permanent decision seminars could be shared with the community by constructing appropriate settings. In order to emphasize some fundamental features of the idea, I have sometimes referred to a "social planetarium."[8] The name has pertinent connotations borrowed from the planetaria designed to popularize astronomy. The latter are intended to give the spectator a specific idea of celestial phenomena seen from various observational standpoints. The audience member sits comfortably while his space ship takes off for the moon or a planet, or he stays on the moon while the dome of the hall shows what he would see from that point. The planetarium enables him to envisage the future or to rehearse the past and to become familiar with the phenomena that confirm or contradict a theoretical model of an expanding universe. In principle, the consequences of alternative policies in astropolitics can be made vivid in this way.

The advantages of universality, selectivity, and vividness are obtainable in reference to the flow of history into the future. Vividness is an important requirement, since, as we said above, many people are unable to obtain rich imagery from reading or listening to words.

The practice of surrounding individuals with reminders of the past, present, and future is very old. When we encounter folk societies, we are immediately impressed by the fact that the whole panoply of nature is impregnated with meaning by the tribal myth. Every river, plain, hill, rock, or tree has a role in the unending drama of the collective self. When a civilization cuts the tie with nature by heaping people together in urban agglomerations, they provide substitutes for the supporting world of nature by monumental edifices—palaces, temples, memorial columns. And every great religion seized on the need for concreteness by remolding nature, as in the Ajanta caves in India, and by depicting the past and future of man and the gods in the universe. At a highly sophisticated level, the whole story may be told in a single room, possibly in a single giant fresco or wall painting, as in the Sistine Chapel of the Vatican.

In a more secular context, the museum is adapted to the double task of providing a repository of original specimens and of laying out for the visitor a sequence of development. One thinks of the vast riches of the Louvre, the British Museum, the Metropolitan, or the American Museum of Natural History. From time to time, these installations are supplemented by fairs and special exhibitions whose keynote in recent decades has often been the challenge of tomorrow.

In spite of the richness of these precedents, it remains true that the potential effects of the relatively permanent exhibition are poorly adapted to provide man with a critically accepted image of the past and future. Hence, the proposal to develop the possibilities of the social planetarium.

Imagine one of the many forms that such an exhibition might take. Suppose that several buildings were available as part of the National Museum establishment in Washington, D.C. The visitor might begin with presentations designed to portray the distribution and culture of early man and show the lines of significant innovation until the emergence of cities in the fifth millennium. The sequence would be planned to teach awareness of the distinction between folk society and civilization and to emphasize the variety of cultural forms. Prominence would be given to the relatively temporary empires created by able leaders of tribal federations and to the more durable structures held together by bureaucratic elites. The city state, devoted to commerce and manufacturing, would be in the picture, as would the feudal and small-state systems created in the aftermath of imperial disintegration. More recently, the consolidation of large national units and empires would dominate the scene. At various cross-sections and in chosen regions, international "orders" ("parties") have arisen, though no one of them has achieved a central monopoly of coercive violence on behalf of inclusive policy. The types of transnational arenas (multipolar, pluripolar, bipolar, tripolar) would be presented, and the actual limitations on the self-described "universal states" set forth.

Exhibits would emphasize the infrastructure of community life and show the degree of value participation and the distinctive practices of various institutions. In the presentation of "power," for example, the emphasis would be on typical patterns of dominance by the few or the many. The major institutional forms of power would include the principal patterns of democratic and nondemocratic government. It will not be necessary at this point to comment on the other value-institution categories except to say that the aim in presenting them would be parallel; that is, they would be shown as fostering wide or narrow value participations and as exhibiting almost infinite variations in institutional practice.

The future would be projected in a version that included contact with the planets and the creation of satellites. At least two major constructs would be outlined, so that a spectator might proceed from today through future A by one route and through future B by another. In the same way, the past could be shown in version A and version B at various cross-sections. Hence, a more dynamic relationship among individuals, groups, and history could be cultivated. Conveniently spaced along the main line of march would be side halls giving more elaborate and systematic exposition to the events of a period and indicating ever-wider ranges of possibility.

Every community could maintain a social planetarium of its own in which the past, present, and future of the area could be put in larger frames of reference. At every international and national capital, long-range presentations could be supplemented by relatively intensive outlines of immediate policy alternatives.

The permanent features of a social planetarium would be capable of providing a unified frame of experience for old and young. From the problem-solving point of view, it is obvious that short-term policy questions always require treatment in a comprehensive framework accessible to all.

PRELEGISLATURES

It is important to focus on relatively immediate, as well as long-term, issues of public policy. That political science associations can take new initiatives along these lines is evident on reflection. One possible format has been christened the "Pre-Congress," and an outline of the proposal may be suggestive. The idea is that some seasons of the year seem to be preliminary to great waves of decision-making activity in the body politic. By tradition, the New Year is such a moment, and many operations are in fact terminated at the end of an old calendar year. Moreover, the New Year in the United States now harmonizes closely with the assumption of authority by a new administration and with the initiation or resumption of work by Congress. It fits the dominant frame of reference to give contextual consideration to goals and strategies at such a time. This is an auspicious time to reach the leaders of opinion and all active citizens with comprehensive presentations of national policy.

A Pre-Congress, then, is an occasion on which, under the auspices of the American Political Science Association, for instance, pending policy issues could be clarified. The purpose is not to arrange for advocates of outstanding proposals to "fight it out," but rather to encourage inquiring minds to search for comprehensive national interests. There are grounds for asserting that Americans are substantially united on many goals. Differences often depend on conflicting estimates of consequences, including costs, of policy action; discussion can help identify the occurrences to be assessed. Discussions are most illuminating when they begin with inclusive and concise presentations of policy alternatives. Such formulations are largely questions of research and analysis. Since they cannot be definitive, they set the stage for further discussion.

Some of the questions on the agenda of a Pre-Congress might lie beyond the field of current public notice. Reports on the machinery of government, for example, though of enormous importance, are rarely able to arouse the public. If emphasized at the Pre-Congress, proposals relating to the machinery of government might mobilize more members of the national community to grasp the significance of such matters.

If the Pre-Congress demonstrated the competence and impartiality of the program planners, it would probably win general confidence. Much depends on the auspices. Fortunately, the American Political Science Association is experienced in providing services transcending partisan interests. This has been recognized in connection with the Congressional Service Awards, for instance, which are given to members of both political parties who have served the national interest in their legislative duties.

In principle the Pre-Congress, as a prelegislature, could be adapted to the needs of the states; rechristened a precouncil, it might perform an orienting function for cities and towns. At the other extreme, the conception could be adapted to international organizations. All the resources of presentation technique could be employed in prelegislatures to aid understanding.

CONTEXTUAL BROADCASTING

Prelegislatures could be meaningfully supplemented throughout the year by the public information programs of the mass media. Political scientists can usefully expand the roles they have begun to play in television and radio broadcasting. Associations, schools, or individuals might take responsibility for preparing and presenting a contextual treatment of current affairs. As public information programs built up backlogs of suitable film, it would be possible to put the latest news headline into perspective and to make evident its potentiality for the values and institutions of the world community and its components.

Suppose, for example, that a rebellion is reported in a new African state. At once the visual resources of an adequate television library provides local and historical footage that furnishes trend and explanatory information. If the rebellion is similar to other rebellions (and on analysis this is bound to be true), alert programming will provide information about comparable cases. The presentation may go further and project, clarify, and evaluate policy alternatives.

It is in connection with programs in election years that professional competence and impartiality meet the most severe test. Political scientists are citizens fully qualified to vote and to support controversial persons and issues; more than that, it is generally expected and often demanded that, as particularly knowledgeable citizens they do so. How are such requirements to be reconciled with professional concern for impartiality and competence?

Let us begin by assuming competence on the part of a political scientist. Is he obligated to refrain from expressing preferences or even from engaging in active party work? Definitely not. But all relevant norms are to be kept in mind. One major norm is candid disclosure of pertinent—that is to say, possibly distorting—interests. If the political scientist is affiliated with a political party or subjectively committed to a controversial position, his obligation is not to quit the party or to abstain from opinions but to disclose these facts to any audience whose reliance on his statements may be influenced by this knowledge. Furthermore, he has an inner obligation to be candid with himself in seeking to keep his statements of a factual character free from distortion.

In connection with elections, it is important to play down the stress on short-range forecasting that has plagued the specialists on polling. The question whether A or B is likely to win is of no importance whatsoever to the national sifting of issues or the assessing of candidates' capabilities. However, forecasts are of great importance to campaigners, since selective audience analysis can show where interest is lagging or sentiment is changing. There is no practicable way to limit forecasting to the private intelligence services of campaigners or even to exclude predictions from general dissemination.

It is possible, however, for political scientists, acting in their professional and civic capacities, to take measures to moderate the negative impact. Pre-election analyses can focus on the significance of voting studies for the attainment of self-knowledge by audience members. Research may show, for example, that candidate X appeals to white, middle-aged, suburban, Protestant housewives who are usually uninterested in and uninformed about politics. An important program objective is to heighten the self-critique of people who fall into such a slot. Or candidate Y appeals to retired businessmen in the upper-income brackets who regard themselves as devout and are suspicious of intellectuals. The great contribution of scientific knowledge to the political process is less in predicting the future than in deepening insight into the self as the self prepares to take further steps into the future.

NOTES

[1] On war exercises (the use of men and weapons in the field) and war games, cf. W. Goerlitz, *History of the German General Staff, 1657–1945* (New York: Praeger, 1956), which describes the growth of staff techniques.

[2] The RAND Corporation has played an important part in these innovations. Cf. J. Goldsen, "The Political Exercise: An Assessment of the Fourth Round" (Mimeographed; Washington, D.C.: The RAND Corporation, 1956); H. Goldhamer and H. Speier, "Some Observations on Political Gaming," *World Politics,* 12 (1959), 71–83; and burgeoning literature by L. Bloomfield, C. McClelland, H. Guetzkow, and others.

[3] Cf. H. D. Lasswell, "The Technique of Decision Seminars," *Midwest Journal of Political Science,* 4 (1960), 213–236.

[4] The gradual disenchantment of scientists and policy-makers with traditional economic or sentimental "plowshare" approaches to the problems of industrialization and modernization are copiously documented. For a positive position, cf. H. Morgenthau, "A Political Theory of Foreign Aid," *American Political Science Review,* 56 (1962), 301–309. Cf. also J. D. Montgomery, *The Politics of Foreign Aid* (New York: Praeger, 1962); J. H. Kautsky, ed., *Political Change in Underdeveloped Countries* (New York: Wiley, 1962); R. N. Adams et al., *Social Change in Latin America Today* (New York: Harper, 1960); M. F. Millikan and D. L. M. Blackmer, eds., *The Emerging Nations* (Boston: Little, Brown, 1960); H. Cleveland, G. J. Man-

gone, and J. C. Adams, *The Overseas Americans* (New York: Mc-Graw-Hill, 1960).

5 On simulation, cf. I. Pool and R. Abelson, "The Simulmantics Project," *Public Opinion Quarterly*, 25 (1961), 167–183; W. McPhee, "Note on a Campaign Simulator," *Public Opinion Quarterly*, 25 (1961), 182–193; O. Benson, "Simulation of International Relations and Diplomacy," in H. Borke, ed., *Computer Applications in the Behavioral Sciences* (Englewood Cliffs, N.J.: Prentice-Hall, 1961); and especially H. Guetzkow, ed., *Simulation in Social Science* (Englewood Cliffs, N.J.: Prentice-Hall, 1963). Further, J. Neumann, *The Computer and the Brain* (New Haven: Yale University Press, 1962).

6 Current developments can be followed in *M.U.L.L.*, "Modern Uses of Logic in Law," quarterly newsletter of the American Bar Association Special Committee on Electronic Retrieval in collaboration with Yale Law School, edited at Yale by L. E. Allen and M. E. Caldwell.

7 On the unfinished task of linking the various standpoints and procedures now at hand—case, correlational, and experimental techniques; laboratory, field, and historical methods; systematic models expressed in prose and mathematical or graphical notation—cf. especially the penetrating publications by D. Easton, H. Eulau, and R. C. Snyder. Easton and Snyder made important theoretical and critical contributions in the period immediately following World War II. Cf. especially D. Easton, *The Political System* (New York: Knopf, 1953).

8 Cf. "Strategies of Inquiry: The Rational Use of Observation," in D. Lerner, ed., *The Human Meaning of the Social Sciences* (New York: Meridian Books, 1959).

7

Cultivation
of
Creativity (I)

No static certainty is to be found in politics or political science, hence the importance of cultivating an affirmative, inventive, flexible mind. The present chapter treats the cultivation of creativity, since it is concerned with professional training.

In recent decades, the social and behavioral sciences have been able to add precision to the idea of creativity and to identify some of the factors conditioning its incidence.[1] The idea is not a simple one, and many popular connotations are irrelevant. We must, for example, disregard the assumption that whatever is new is creative. Undoubtedly, a novel element is always present. Yet a creative act is not fantastic; it must be able to pass reality tests.

Another erroneous connotation is that creativity is a flash in utter darkness. It is entirely fitting to celebrate the achievements of individuals who give birth to important ideas; it is nonetheless a gross distortion of the creative process to confound it with an individual or with a single moment. The process is social and interactive and, properly understood, reaches forward and backward from the culminating moment. Not every thinker, of course, is able to locate a dramatic instant as Descartes was able to do and to say that his whole theory depended on an "emotional intuition" that struck him on a specific date. Descartes saw his comprehensive vision on the night of November 10, 1619. However, the idea of a rational universe arose and won subsequent ratification in the course of a creative process of great scope and complexity. It is possible for historians of philosophy to identify many influences that played on Descartes and contributed to that heaping up of preconditions to be discovered in all human conduct when closely scrutinized. This is the phenomenon to which Freud referred with the odd but expressive term of "overdetermination." The creative pattern was not complete when Descartes experienced his vision nor even when he committed it to print. Until ratified by others, creativity remains potential; it is not yet actual. The lag may be very long, although in Descartes' case he carried conviction to enough contemporaries to justify his classification as a creative thinker.

Today we are accustomed to taking the collective character of creativity for granted. We plan inventions. So it was with the atomic bomb; so it is every day in industrial laboratories. When wealth and respect are put at the disposal of persons of recognized skill, they are usually able to gather competent colleagues.

It is, perhaps, pertinent in view of the planned parenthood of ideas in modern society to warn against underestimating the finer structure of creativity. The target is rarely hit by a perfectly straight course. A target can best be described as a working image of a destination which can be reached only by many zig-zags or even returns to the starting point. It is not to be wondered at that the most brilliant results are often, if not, indeed, typically, achieved as side effects rather than as stations along a well-mapped route. In a given research project, the ostensible target may or may not be reached promptly or with much originality; yet society's capital of knowledge continues to grow.

In the physical and biological sciences, the peculiar character of creativity has long been understood. Able research men have learned to proceed in a way that laymen sometimes regard as fraudulent.

Capable research workers do not like to tie themselves closely to a single target or to a predescribed method. They want elbow room to explore promising side lanes and to devise new procedures or even to pursue basic scientific ideas a certain distance. They are concerned that science itself grows only in this fashion; hence they are not true scientists if they bind themselves in advance to a map too precisely drawn. In the budgeting of research, it is therefore taken for granted that the allotment includes a margin of support for general exploration. Since the repertory of modern science is enormous, many research implications invariably appear once capable investigators get to work on any concrete task.

Given these facts, it seems defensible to obtain research funds in the name of popular problems, while keeping free of any inner commitment or public pledge to solve the problem at once. Consider the notorious case of cancer. As of this moment, the millions of dollars and man hours of talent that have gone into cancer research have fallen short of the goal. Research in the name of cancer is nearly as permissive as the pursuit of truth itself. Yet the whole episode is not to be dismissed as a plot by research administrators engaged in building rival empires at the expense of a credulous public. The by-products of research launched in the name of cancer are of undoubted importance in many fields. Of this, both research administrators and the beneficiary scientists have been morally certain all the time. And many laymen who join in money-raising share the viewpoint of the scientists, since they know enough science themselves or have had enough experience with good scientists to recognize the policies that are most likely to keep them productive.

The contrast with the typical research situation of political and social scientists is evident. Even rather capable political scientists have rarely had enough self-confidence to adopt the approach that is usual for colleagues in the physical and biological sciences. Hence, their research projects tend to be cut and dried, with deadlines, contents, and procedures rather clearly specified in advance. They typically provide little leeway for the pursuit of promising theoretical leads or for the invention of novel methods.

What can be said when we sum up the fundamental criteria of creativity? An important clue has come from the psychologists of perception. We are not far wrong in condensing the fundamental point into the phrase "context completion." To a degree, context completion is inseparable from any living organism, since life perpetually seeks solutions to the problems of the new environment.

There are vast differences between mild exercises of ingenuity and the masterpieces that are commonly viewed as turning points in the history of thought. What are the distinguishing marks of a contribution, such as those of Planck or Einstein, that receives universal acclaim from knowledgeable scientists? These celebrated instances of intellectual achievement introduced a coherent picture where the conventional map was full of contradiction, confusion, and ambiguity. New ways of looking at the world disclosed a comprehensible pattern in which ancient incompatibilities were redefined and disappeared.

I comment briefly in this connection on the work of a distinguished physician who has influenced political science and many other fields of thought. Sigmund Freud was trained in neurology and cognate disciplines.[2] He was, in fact, reared in one of the most orthodox temples of the "scientism" of the day. All brain functions were to be reduced to objective events. Any mention of subjectivity was seen as a regrettable concession to the undeveloped state of the science.

In his training, Freud was also exposed to contradictory images of reality. For instance, he visited a clinic where the therapeutic efficacy of hypnotism was being demonstrated. Hypnotism obviously relies on communication in a social context to affect inner life and outer conduct. Neither neurons nor chemicals enter visibly into the chain of events that initiates response.

It was not possible for Freud to eliminate the mind-body problem. He nonetheless provided a map in which many hitherto-disjointed observations became intelligible. Without constructing "neural myths" to add to "myths of subjectivity," Freud suggested how human organisms can influence one another. He appeared to treat "instincts" as part of the "body." However, the "soma" was shown to be affected by nonphysical events—in a word, by signs and symbols. The "unconscious" became a patterned repository of primitive instincts as modified by interactions in the social process.

When we examine creativity directly in political science it is soon apparent that context completion is a serviceable guide. The images entertained by those who participate in a political process are conventionally a blend of prescriptions and observed "facts of life." Almost every serious, competent study in political science redefines a conventional image and refocuses the connection between "preferred norms" and "factual norms."

We have referred to Beard's analysis of economic factors in the forming and ratification of the United States Constitution; it is unquestionably a case in point. A monument of the same kind is Michels' study of social-democratic parties in Europe. The social-democratic elites were accustomed to speaking in the name of democracy. Michels drew attention to the facts that the leaders tended to stay in office for many years and that in many cases their children succeeded them in office. He summed up the data by generalizing about the "oligarchical tendencies" of mass political parties. In the long run, it may be that the criteria of oligarchy applied by Michels are too loose to satisfy professional opinion and that he was vague about factors that might reverse a trend toward narrowly held power.[3] Nevertheless, the study was sufficiently compelling to induce great defensiveness and some insight in European socialists of the time.

Few scholars would deny that Marx and Engels were the most original and also most successful political and social theorists of recent generations. If the criteria were changed by de-emphasizing success, a strong case could be made for the opinion that some French thinkers —Saint-Simon, for example—were more inventive or that Bentham is ultimately to be regarded as more creative. For present purposes, it is enough to say that Marx provided the most comprehensive and upsetting confrontation of conventional imagery on record. He provided rebellion with the favorite intellectual tool of the *status quo,* namely, history. Rebellion was no longer perceived as personal caprice, disorder, or heroism, but as a transpersonal natural law of society that could be grasped by an instructed mind trained in the necessary method of thought. Hence, the triumph of realistic thinking was not to "make" history but to harmonize with reality; rebellion became the ultimate conformity.

The capture of the appeal to history is correctly interpreted as an impressive burst of creativity; it is of particular interest because it exemplifies "rejection by partial incorporation" of an "enemy" ideology and also provides a case of differentiation by an appeal to method.

The first point—the use of partial incorporation—means that a mode of justification, the appeal to history, was taken over by Marx and Engels, although most of the doctrines asserted in the ideology of the social order that "history" originally justified were in fact rejected. Socialism in turn often became the target of a comparable strategy, notably when Hitler opposed "international" socialism in the name of "nation" and "race."

The second point—differentiation by an appeal to method—received tremendous emphasis in the Marx-Engels contribution as a means of borrowing the prestige of the physical sciences and transferring it to a counterideological system. "Historical materialism" was put forward as a procedure by which the attention of an individual could focus on data revealing the dynamic and implacable sequence of history from feudalism through capitalism to the classless society. When French revolutionary thinkers assailed feudalism, they also appealed to method, namely, the test of "reason." But the connotations of the term were capricious. My reason may lead to affirmations which your reason is unwilling to accept. By the time Marx and Engels wrote, a more disciplined idea of method had become recognized. The conception of universal law validated by empirical observation seemed to provide a tool for controlling the ebullience of individual subjectivity. "Historical materialism" revived the notion of inescapable truth ascertainable by proper method.

These examples of creativity enable us to pose our present problem in fundamental terms. How can we strengthen the probability that future questions will be approached with the balance between innovation and realism that characterizes high-level creativity?

THE GRADUATE DEPARTMENT

For years to come, the principal responsibility for professional preparation and hence for the cultivation of creativity will presumably lie with graduate departments of universities. It will continue to be the task of such academic structures to offer the basic introduction to scope and methods and to arrange the environment of graduate students in harmony with the requirements of professional objectives. It is, after all, the graduate department that consolidates rival conceptions of the profession into working unity.

How does a graduate department sustain the creativity of professors and students? Experience shows how rarely any department succeeds in maintaining its position as a well-balanced representative of the past and as a pioneer.

Part of the difficulty comes from the fact that, in an epoch of accelerating change, the training that fits men for today may unfit them for tomorrow. At any given time, the leading figures are somewhat obsolete. At best, they provide partial models for the problem-solvers who will be best adapted to the tasks of the next thirty or forty years. We must suggest, I think, that a factor in support of a creative department is an acute sense of partial obsolescence.

The versatility and competence with which political scientists cope with the future depend in no small degree on professional preparation. From the beginning of their specialized studies the larger context must be kept in sight if the perspectives conducive to creativity are to be nourished and applied. Hence, the basic orientation to the scope and methods of political science is of strategic importance. Properly conceived, introductory exercises in "Scope and Method" are returned to throughout the years of professional preparation and continue to challenge, guide, and inspire the political scientist at every subsequent phase of his career.

In the following pages, I present a synopsis of suggestions for the presentation of political science to advanced students at the threshold of professional training. Our previous discussion has drawn attention to the five intellectual tasks of a problem-oriented approach to political science. I refer briefly to these tasks in providing some concrete indication of what is implied for "scope and method." Because of the close tie between the clarification of goals and the traditional study of political doctrines, I shall deal at some length with the task of clarifying goals and more cursorily with trend, condition, projection, and alternative.

When we speak of the value goals of political science, the reference is to empirical events in the social process. It is at once necessary to draw a distinction between statements of goal referring explicitly to the social process and statements whose reference is to a wider context than the sociopolitical process. When I read a declaration on behalf of "democracy"—in the sense of shared power—it is unmistakable that the declaration belongs to the first category; the statement manifestly refers to the political process. If, however, I read that the proper end of man is to glorify God, there is some doubt about the intended meaning of the words. Does it refer to glorification in a heavenly choir after death? If so, this is outside the social process and is not classifiable as a social value. On the other hand, the writer may say that in politics this implies the practice of democracy, and this claim is, by the definition given above, part of the political process.

It lies beyond the present discussion to enumerate the many proposals that have been made in regard to the scope values of political science. In passing, however, we may draw attention to a common misunderstanding of objectives that are sometimes called "value-neutral." In the present frame of reference, this is always an inappropriate term. If the assertion is made, for example, that political scientists should pursue scientific ends, the suggestion means that the enlightenment value should be emphasized.

Another point is possibly important enough to put explicitly. Goals are sometimes formulated in terms of rank-order, sometimes as preferred patterns of value distribution. In the former case, power may be put above or below wealth, respect, rectitude, and other social outcomes. In the latter, a commitment may be made to the wide sharing of power (democracy) or to a system of narrow sharing (non-democracy).

In whatever words the following distinctions are made, they refer to categories that are serviceable in classifying statements of goal:

> Justification of goal
> Transempirical derivation
> Theology, metaphysics
> Empirical grounding
> Logic, personal responsibility
> Specification of goal

Statements that purport to clarify goals move in two directions— toward specification and toward justification. The first operation makes the terms of reference to the goal more explicit, that is, more operational. If the goal is "power-sharing," it is necessary to make more specific what we intend to designate in concrete circumstances as "power" or "sharing."

Justifications, we have said, are of two kinds—by transempirical derivation and by empirical grounding. The first purports to derive values from statements whose ultimate validity is beyond empirical confirmation. If theological formulations are used, the typical sequence is: first, an assertion that divine will is so and so; second, a declaration that divine will ought to be followed in the choice of values; third, an affirmation that the recommended values are in harmony with divine will. If metaphysical formulations are relied on, a secular rather than a sacred terminology is employed, and the same sequence is followed. The initial proposition may be, for example: "The universe is a struggle between the forces of light and the forces of darkness." The next assertion, then, is that we ought to conform to the "is-ness" of the universe (light or darkness) and, finally, that the goal affirmed is in harmony with the universe.

To ground a goal value empirically is to assert that various empirical events justify the choice.[4] The events may be a direct affirmation of ego responsibility. The speaker may simply assert a subjective preference: "I believe in democracy (oligarchy, etc.)." As a rule, however, individuals attempt to elaborate their preferences and volitions by showing that legitimizing experiences can be shared by others. The most common justifications of this type are in terms of "logic."

The distinction (between part and whole, for instance) that is called "logical" is an empirical event; that is, the subjective stream includes the experience of the distinction. (The distinction may be further attributed to such metaphysical entities as "reason," but this elaboration is not always made.) The justification may proceed as follows: "I perceive a distinction between part and whole; since the whole is greater than the part, I should subordinate my preferences and volitions to the whole; hence I should accept the primacy of the whole social process when that process gives equal consideration to all its parts."

The clarifications that we have referred to are examples of one of two modes of clarifying values—by content and by procedure.[5]

All the examples cited belong to the category of content. They put forward statements purporting to guide the individual in his quest for what he "ought" to do or what he "should" value. This is in harmony with a tradition that has long dominated the civilization of Western Europe, where the attempt has been to achieve and fix "truth by definition."

Some of the oldest and most widely distributed traditions approach the problems of values and valuation differently. The Zen branch of Buddhist mysticism is a case in point. The Zen monk does not try to define the ultimate truth or to articulate general norms for the guidance of practical judgment. On the contrary, he treats the search for "truth by dialectic" with indifference or contempt. In its place is put the cultivation of the propensities of the self to become a site where illumination can occur. After years of spiritual exercise a monk may achieve his aim and at that point choose whether to proceed forthwith to Nirvana or to return for the purpose of helping others to discover the true path.

I have suggested elsewhere that a remarkable equivalency is to be found between Asian mysticism and American pragmatism. Pragmatists assert that the quest for truth is a "logic of inquiry." It is, therefore, an experience in self-discipline in the course of which the knowledge and perhaps the order of preference of the inquirer is open to change. Mystics and pragmatists are alike in seeking to de-emphasize the role of general statements about final truth by putting the stress on the inquiry or the quest as a lifetime process. Whether mystic or pragmatist, the individual adopts a procedure that includes suspended commitment to other than the procedure itself. The subjective content at the beginning is expected to be modified in the course of time by the procedures induced in individuals. The mystic's typical approach is to dismiss his initial formulation of value goal as part of the world of illusion and to engage in the discipline of exercises which are expected to prepare him to pierce the veil of illusion with increasing success.

The pragmatic method differs greatly in specific detail from the path traversed by mystics. A pragmatic inquirer follows a problem-solving agenda in achieving self-change. We have often identified five intellectual tasks performed in problem-solving. A pragmatic procedure uses each intellectual tool as an instrument with which to explore the context of events—past, present, prospective—in which any working formulation of value goal is located and with which it interacts. Among other content, the inquirer attends to symbols of reference to the variables of culture, class, interest, and personality that have acted on his career to date. He is open to any technique of study that offers promise of assistance, such as the investigation of the unconscious dimensions of his personality by prolonged free association or specialized tests. Any discovery of hitherto unrecognized factors that have conditioned value demands is a liberating event in the process of inquiry, since it increases freedom of choice of future value demands. Part of the problem-solving quest is to estimate the consequences of alternative value outcomes.

At any given moment in the exercise of pragmatic or mystical procedures, an individual is prepared to commit himself tentatively to statements of value goal, justification, and specification. As the self is further modified by appropriate discipline, tentative commitments presumably change, less in the terms used to state overriding goals than in interpretations of goal in concrete contingencies and in capability to conform to these interpretations.[6]

It is appropriate for political scientists to adopt the view that their part in the division of labor among intellectuals is to concentrate on the pursuit of enlightenment in the sense of seeking historical, scientific, and projective knowledge or bases of inference. Political scientists may refrain from constructing philosophies to defend either value rankings or patterns of value distribution. Instead, they may adopt goals as working postulates and develop the implications for political analysis and strategy. If working goals are adopted, democracy and nondemocracy are regarded as postulates to which the individual may or may not add a declaration of personal preference.

I have much sympathy with this approach, and I recommend that it be made explicit to students. However, it is not the role of a basic course in scope and method to load the dice in favor of this or any solution. It is a responsibility that each student must shoulder for himself and reconsider at successive stages of his career.[7]

In addition to presenting versions of the goals of political science, the fundamental course is well conceived when it outlines the history of systematic reflection on the subject. This presentation, when adequately conceived, goes beyond the conventional "history of political theory" to give a sketch of the profession in past and present civilizations. In this way, a sense of continuity between past and present becomes part of one's image of his role.[8]

Measured in terms of man hours, the principal task of "scope and method" is to introduce the scientific approach to the study of politics. This is a matter of presenting the various methods available when the introduction is given for the formulation of theoretical models to guide inquiry and also of reviewing the procedures for gathering and processing data. Presumably, these points can be most firmly grasped if students have an opportunity to study research reports and descriptions of method and to obtain some acquaintance with recent developments. The perspective in which these matters are seen can be greatly enriched by examining the anticipatory propositions and factor identifications found in the traditional literature.

It is also within the province of the introduction to bring developmental constructs into view, partly for the sake of exhibiting methods of thought and partly in order to provide a means of reorientation, especially in the undermining of established rigidities of expectation.

Finally, in this enumeration of scope, is the presentation of the policy challenge. Assuming that postulated goals are to be maximized, how is this to be done? At this stage, the main task is to make explicit by theory and case the process by which policy alternatives are invented and evaluated.

I do not intend to evaluate the many devices presently available to the teacher of "Scope and Method." In fact it is not essential that there be a "course" in the usual sense of the word. A syllabus could be followed on the basis of supervised individual study rather than by group discussion. There are, however, advantages to seminars, especially when the decision-seminar technique outlined in the preceding chapter is fully adapted to the task at hand. This stimulates the search for relevance in the years ahead.

When we examine the spread of political science in America, the forward-looking character of the most creative institutions is clearly corroborated. I think it is generally understood that three major centers fostered the importation of political science from Europe and reoriented the discipline to the distinctive challenges of the American environment. (I shall not refer here to the current picture.)

We have had occasion to refer to The Johns Hopkins University and to the stress that was laid on the history of American political institutions in the context of the English experience from which they came. This phase was essential to the discovery of an American self in clarifying the new identity that had come during the first century of political independence from Europe. Most of us are acquainted with some of the mechanisms that come into play when a family member achieves personal maturity. There is continual focusing of attention on present identity and the identity of origin. In the course of this "to-and-fro," the image of the self takes shape. It discovers likeness and difference and orders these details in a working conception of "who I am" and "who you are (or were)." Parallel mechanisms operate when a new cultural entity emerges by seceding from a more inclusive whole. There is much back-and-forth at the focus of attention—back from the self of today to the self (and other) of origin and separation. The image of present identity is formed as likenesses and differences are observed, and past and present events are unified as part of an intelligible history.

The preoccuption with English history was too narrow to procure for American scholars all the tools of European political scientists for the study of government, politics, and law. During the later years of the nineteenth century, the great centers of theory were on the Continent, especially in Germany. Ambitious American graduate students went to Berlin, Heidelberg, and other distinguished universities. John W. Burgess was given special facilities to examine the situation on the Continent, particularly in Germany, as a preliminary to launching the Faculty of Political Science at Columbia. It was at Columbia that Continental political theory, jurisprudence, and comparative government found their chief port of entry to America.[9]

The third creative center in the United States was The University of Chicago in the 1920's and 1930's, as developed at the initiative and under the direction of Charles E. Merriam. It was here that latent tendencies in the American scene came to their most distinctive expression. I refer, of course, to the p's and q's—the emphases on psychology and quantity. The individualism of the European tradition has been accentuated in the United States, where the great natural resources provided a relatively uncluttered field for individual and small-group achievement. The quantitative accent was an immediate expression of the prestige of the methods of the physical sciences, economics, and psychology.

It is instructive to examine the Chicago case in more detail. In no way did Merriam harbor an illusion that political scientists must be made over in his own image. He was, after all, a comparatively modest and realistic man, indeed—as Harold Ickes sums him up—a "timid" man. Merriam was dissatisfied with his own training and regretted his lack of command of many skills and areas of knowledge whose implications for political science were clear to him. He knew, too, that there were no colleagues who exemplified many of the promising new approaches any better than he did. However, his problem as a department head with vision was to put together the best possible team he could find from colleagues who at least shared his goal and were willing to cooperate in creating a permissive environment where a new generation could come into being.

Then began the long wait—though a busy and in many ways an exciting wait—for students to grow up. In any truly creative setting, this is a frustrating business, since the first crop of students is likely to include quite imperfect models of what is sought. They are somewhat alienated from tradition and often lack motivation to demonstrate high competence within it. At the same time, they are neophytes, often having mediocre mastery of the tools they are attempting to redesign and apply. They lack self-confidence, though some may compensate for inner turmoil by an arrogant style. To compound these complications, many of the students who are most attracted by novelty are in a phase of personal rebellion against traditional authority; some are highly neurotic or even marginally psychotic. If this adds to the color of the graduate community, it also adds to the distempers of the conservative generation when it meets flaming youth.

As a historian of political doctrine and an experienced man of affairs, Merriam was acutely aware of the magnitude of the task of bringing about a deep and abiding transformation of the profession. He knew that it would take twenty or thirty years for the most successful survivors of the new environment to achieve the academic prominence necessary to consolidate the situation. By then several former graduate students would be senior professors, department heads, and deans, matching the corpulence of affluent middle age with weighty academic posts.

But Merriam knew that the new ideas would not automatically spread as the first generation rose in rank. Some ex-students would undergo true changes of intellectual outlook and reject much or all of the new approach. In other cases, a turn toward tradition would result from academic expediency. A more subtle threat would come from individuals who continued to speak in the name of the new combination of theory and empirical research, but who were unwilling to support programs enabling graduate students to obtain better training than they themselves received. If they had acquired elementary statistics, they would think that this was all anybody needed. Why invest time in the mathematical foundations of statistical logic? Or why study symbolic logic or machine programming? Weren't the "fundamentals" good enough?

Perhaps I should interpose a categorically personal opinion at this point. Because of my involvement with new approaches to the study of politics, I am often asked whether it is of any *general* importance to intellectual life or public policy that departments of political science redefine the scope and method of the field in ways that harmonize with Merriam's fundamental vision.

In reply, I concede that all the approaches in which I am interested could be carried out in neighboring academic departments and schools. "Political sociology," for instance, already has at least one outstanding department in the United States. Some of the most promising work in the study of systems of organization is done at schools of business and of engineering. Many sophisticated studies of the role of prescription in the decision process are made in schools of law. Several of the most illuminating research reports on public opinion are planned and executed in schools of journalism or, more generally, of communication. Excellent monographs on the curriculums and methods of civic training are written in schools of education. And these examples can be supplemented from other departments and schools.

The issue, then, is not whether political science is to continue. The question is much simpler—shall departments carry the label, and shall a profession that carries the name continue? The *function* can be and will be carried on regardless of the *conventional* symbols with which the function is linked.

Neither the political process nor political science can be abolished. I am sure that most members of the profession agree with Merriam's central thesis in *Political Power:*

> Whether in the study of personalities, of associations, of social forms and institutions, of competing ideologies and interests, the significance of the central integrating power becomes more appar-

ent, and the possibilities of the regulator for good or evil take on a deeper meaning (p. 10).

We can predict with confidence that, if the institution of study itself continues, it will be applied to power and government. The scientific approach to any phase of the natural or social order is so deeply embedded in our civilization that, if one group of scholars fails to apply it to a field for which they are presumably responsible, the field will be taken away from them and cultivated by more strongly motivated and capable colleagues under other labels.

Is there any justification in terms of general rather than of particular interests for proposing that departments of "political science" be continued and that a profession called "political science" be perpetuated?

My reply is affirmative. There are advantages in charging a specialized intellectual group with responsibility for examining the social process in a fundamental frame of reference. A group of the kind performs an important critical function since it knows enough history to help distinguish purported novelty from actual innovation and hence to aid in identifying creativity when it occurs. Creativity is fostered by concern with the relationship between the part and the whole. Contradictions, gaps, and ambiguities in the field are recurring challenges to insightful completion.

As a case exemplifying this, I cite the history of modern research on communication. It is generally recognized that the scientific study of communication has made giant strides in recent decades. An important date in the growth of the field was the early 1930's, when the Humanities Division of the Rockefeller Foundation and the Social Science Research Council interested themselves in the state of knowledge regarding propaganda and communication.

An observer of the academic world of the time might have taken it for granted that the initiative for accelerated research would originate with specialists in linguistics. After all, students of language were primarily responsible for investigating the most distinctive social patterns devised by man in aid of mutual comprehension. But the observer would have been mistaken. The most successful step was taken by political scientists. They provided a unified map of the field that brought specialists of many kinds to sudden awareness of a common frame of reference. The step was taken because political scientists were increasingly aware of the strategic significance for arenas of power of the control of communication. Looking at the many practitioners and technicians of the arts of communication at local, national, and international levels, political scientists were startled by the lack of communication among them.

The committee appointed by the Social Science Research Council to report on the situation was composed, for the most part, of political scientists who had previously concerned themselves with the use of guided communication by political parties, pressure groups, or by official agencies in war or peace.[10] The integrative, community-wide perspective of political scientists had already begun to make an impression on schools of journalism by seeking to transform the curriculum from overabsorption in ephemeral technicalities. The conferences and bibliographic aids prepared by the council's committee were helpful in bringing together the fragments of knowledge and the diversities of technique among political scientists, historians, journalists, advertising men, public-relations experts, social psychologists, sociologists, and many other specialists.[11]

Acting as team members or as independent research workers, political scientists conducted descriptive or analytic studies and devised or adapted many data-gathering and data-processing procedures. Among technical innovations can be mentioned various modes of analyzing content and of interviewing message-senders and -receivers.

At no time was there any question that political scientists were attempting to monopolize research on communication. It is characteristic of the community-wide, decision-oriented perspective of political science as a professional field that, when an important area of study was seen to be neglected, students of politics called attention to the neglect and themselves engaged in pioneering research. As other scientists busied themselves with inventing, developing, and applying methods of increasing technicality, the contributions of political scientists became relatively less important. In the main, political scientists are users of the results from communications research rather than originators of new techniques. Some individuals continue to work intensively with full-time specialists on problems of joint concern and to mediate between colleagues in political science and specialists in mass or private communications. In the future, such relationships will undoubtedly continue to be mutually advantageous. But the innovative role of political scientists may never reach the importance in this sector of human affairs that it achieved in the past few decades.[12]

In any case, we can anticipate innovations in other fields that come to the attention of political scientists as they pursue all factors that seem to exert a significant influence on the ever-changing context of decision. The distinctive frame of reference of the profession will continue to indicate its fruitfulness for science as well as policy. A precondition is solution of problems relating to professional preparation in ways that foster comprehensive vision and bold ingenuity.

The responsibility of those in charge of graduate work is to provide an experience that justifies the admission of a qualified student to full professional standing. Traditionally, this responsibility has been met by requiring (1) a demonstration of knowledge of the field as a whole and (2) a contribution to knowledge.

Professional preparation is something more than demonstrated facility in passing examinations or writing a publishable book. Political scientists attempt a distinctive role in society. Role performance is a complex enterprise which depends in part on common perspectives that grow in personal association. A professional group is always somewhat vulnerable to attack, and there are persuasive grounds for asserting that a preparatory experience of intensive exposure to older colleagues and to contemporaries is a valuable means of inducing integrity and solidarity. This is a justification for "residence" requirements and for facilities that smooth the way to intellectual and social intercourse. At the same time, there are advantages in forestalling tendencies toward parochialism by providing means of contact among graduate schools and for conducting off-campus research.

Before coming to rest in support of any more definite plan of graduate study, we have the usual problem of evaluating proposals in seeming conflict with one another. We must, for example, look into a policy to recommend on the highly controversial issue of training teachers and research scholars.

NOTES

[1] Cf. H. H. Anderson, ed., *Creativity and Its Cultivation* (New York: Harper & Bros., 1959); H. G. Barnett, *Innovation*, "The Basis of Cultural Change" (New York: McGraw-Hill, 1953); E. Kris, *Psychoanalytic Explorations in Art* (New York: International Universities Press, 1952); M. Wertheimer, *Productive Thinking* (New York: Harper & Bros., 1945); G. Humphrey, *Thinking*, "An Introduction to Its Experimental Psychology" (London: Methuen, 1951); J. Bruner *et al.*, *A Study of Thinking* (New York: Wiley & Sons, 1956); F. Bartlett, *Thinking*, "An Experimental and Social Study" (London: Allen and Unwin, 1958); and especially H. Gruber *et al.*, *Contemporary Approaches to Creative Thinking* (New York: Atherton Press, 1962).

2 E. Jones, *The Life and Work of Sigmund Freud* (3 vols.; New York: Basic Books, 1953–1957). The centennial of Freud's birth produced many remarkable interpretations of his life work, e.g., E. Erikson, "The First Psychoanalyst," *Yale Review,* 1956. Cf. the forthcoming study by R. R. Holt, "Two Influences on Freud's Scientific Thought: A Fragment of Intellectual Biography," in R. W. White, ed., *The Study of Lives,* "Essays on Personality in Honor of Henry A. Murray" (New York: Atherton Press, 1963), Chap. 16.

3 For pertinent comment on Michels, cf. S. M. Lipset, *Union Democracy* (Glencoe, Ill.: The Free Press, 1956).

4 The most systematic approach to the clarification of goals, including an attempt to ground value commitments empirically, is A. Brecht, *Political Theory,* "The Foundations of Twentieth Century Political Thought" (Princeton: Princeton University Press, 1959). Of contemporary theologians and philosophers concerned with political doctrine, the following are among the most active: R. Niebuhr, J. Hollowell, L. Straus, and E. Voegelin. Among scientists, A. Rappaport and C. H. Waddington have tried to formulate a scientific basis for evaluative commitments. Cf. further E. Cassirer, *Determinism and Indeterminism in Modern Physics* and *Systematic Studies of the Problem of Causality* (New Haven: Yale University Press, 1956); *The Logic of the Humanities,* trans. C. S. Howe (New Haven: Yale University Press, 1961); and *The Problem of Knowledge,* "Philosophy, Science, and History since Hegel," trans. W. H. Woglom and C. H. Hendel (New Haven: Yale University Press, 1950).

5 Cf. my "Clarifying Value Judgments: Principles of Content and Procedure," *Inquiry* [Oslo], 1 (1958), 87–98. On many pertinent matters, cf. *Nomos,* the volumes published by Atherton Press for the American Society of Political and Legal Philosophy, edited by C. J. Friedrich since 1958. Also, the two volumes edited by H. D. Lasswell and H. Cleveland for the Conference on Science, Philosophy, and Religion in Their Relation to Democratic Life, entitled *The Ethic of Power* and *Ethics and Bigness* (New York: Harper & Bros., 1962). The proposal to regard a problem as "solved" when details have been disciplined by reference to context is implied by many approaches.

6 Of the many descriptions of Buddhism and especially of the stricter sects, the unassuming essay by E. Herrigel, in *Zen in the Art of Archery* (New York: Pantheon, 1953), often communicates successfully with Americans. The volumes by D. T. Suzuki and A. Watts are widely read. An exhaustive critique of what can be accomplished by explicit generalization is A. Naess, *Interpretation and Preciseness* (Oslo: I. Kommisjon Hos Jacob Dybwad, 1953).

7 The literature often called "antibehavioral" or "antiscientific" contains many warnings to young and old and deserves attention at an early stage of the career. Cf., e.g., E. Voegelin, *The New Science of Poli-*

tics (Chicago: University of Chicago Press, 1952); B. Crick, *The American Science of Politics,* "Its Origins and Conditions" (Berkeley and Los Angeles: University of California Press, 1959); D. E. Butler, *The Study of Political Behaviour* (London: Hutchinson, 1958); H. J. Storing, ed., *Essays on the Scientific Study of Politics* (New York: Holt, Rinehart and Winston, 1962). The last two are especially well informed.

[8] Key questions concerning the recruitment, training, and professional role of political scientists are becoming more sharply defined as the general sociology and psychology of knowledge takes shape. Cf. especially B. Barber and W. Hirsch, eds., *The Sociology of Science* (New York: The Free Press of Glencoe, 1962). See also the synthesis by S. F. Mason, *A History of the Sciences* (Rev. ed.; New York: Collier Books, 1962); and T. S. Kuhn, *The Structure of Scientific Revolutions* (Chicago: University of Chicago Press, 1962).

[9] A near-contemporary account of the evolution at Columbia University is given by M. Smith, *A History of Columbia University, 1754–1904* (New York: Macmillan, 1904), pp. 199–305. My presentation somewhat underemphasizes the roles of Cornell University and the universities of Wisconsin and Michigan. For the general picture, including Johns Hopkins, cf. the admirable treatment by F. Rudolph, *The American College and University,* "A History" (New York: Knopf, 1962). Also, A. Nevins, *The State Universities and Democracy* (Urbana: University of Illinois Press, 1962). Elsewhere: W. H. G. Armytage, *Civic Universities* (London: E. Benn, 1955); E. Ashby, *Technology and the Academies* (London: Macmillan, 1958); M. H. Curtis, *Oxford and Cambridge in Transition* (Oxford: Oxford University Press, 1959).

[10] Political scientists on the S.S.R.C. committee were H. F. Gosnell, E. P. Herring, H. D. Lasswell, P. H. Odegard, and S. Wallace. *The Public Opinion Quarterly* was established and guided for many years by H. F. Childs.

[11] Cf. H. D. Lasswell, R. D. Casey, and B. L. Smith, *Pressure Groups and Propaganda,* "An Annotated Bibliography" (Minneapolis: University of Minnesota Press, 1935).

[12] On communications research in general, cf. B. Berelson, "The Study of Public Opinion," in L. D. White, ed., *The State of the Social Sciences* (Chicago: University of Chicago Press, 1956). Since World War II, the most important impetus has come from the mathematicians and engineers. Cf. H. D. Lasswell, "Communication as an Emerging Discipline," *Audio-Visual Communication Review,* 6 (1958), 245–254. "Information theory" as originally devised does not refer to "messages" ("ments"), but rather to the physical pattern employed in transmission ("bits"). Symbol references and signs have yet to be fully integrated with each other. Concerning my own work in this area, R. Horwitz has made a conscientious, competent,

and often valuable statement in Chap. 4 of H. J. Storing, ed., *Essays on the Scientific Study of Politics* (New York: Holt, Rinehart and Winston, 1962). Cf. also P. Henle, ed., *Language, Thought, and Culture* (Ann Arbor: University of Michigan Press, 1958); L. Lowenthal, *Literature, Popular Culture, and Society* (Englewood Cliffs, N.J.: Prentice-Hall, 1961); C. Cherry, *On Human Communication* (Cambridge-New York: Technology Press of M.I.T.-Wiley, 1957); and the notable studies of L. Festinger, M. Rokeach, and J. Bruner.

8
Cultivation
of
Creativity (II)

SEPARATE BUT EQUAL TRAINING FOR TEACHING
AND RESEARCH?

In the preceding chapters, we have laid the accent on improving the substantive content of political science. The stress has hence been on research. However, no academic member of the profession can avoid coming to terms with teaching responsibilities at university and college levels.

What is a good teacher? Properly condensed, the amount of rhetoric that this seemingly simple question has produced could power a flight to Mars. Alumni contribute to the flow; they are given to intermittent seizures of nostalgia for the lost heroes of youth, especially if they have been financially successful and absent from the campus

for a while. Teachers themselves, for reasons not altogether mysterious, can deliver moving panegyrics to or about other classroom giants.
There are always deans and presidents to join the chorus, especially
if they feel guilty for giving status and money to other administrators
or to scholars rich in publications, rather than to deserving peda-
gogues.

The good-teacher theme has several standard modes of ornamen-
tation. There is "me and Mark and the log," a trialogue in which
neither the log nor Mark Hopkins is present to speak for himself.
There is the Socratic theme, in which a homely, aloof façade houses
a lightning brain, a rapier wit, and a loving heart. There is the ogre
image, the image of the sophomore Demosthenes, and many others.

Most of us would concede that different classroom styles appeal
to different students and that part of the problem of a teaching program in political science is to create an environment of strong and
diverse personalities who share a common intellectual commitment to
the subject and give young people an opportunity to understand the
intellectual and personal challenge of the field. This is not to deni-
grate other disciplines. On the contrary, in the modern age there is
something obsolete, even neurotic, about attempts at ego-inflation by
undermining other skills.

That members of the political science profession have often been
great teachers is a statement that cannot be successfully challenged.
I shall cite one example, that of an Englishman whose impact on this
side of the Atlantic was almost, if not quite, as immediate and deep
as his effect on India and many Asian and African nations. I refer to
Harold J. Laski, the articulate and devoted teacher of several generations of students at the London School of Economics and Political
Science. Laski spent time with students from all parts of the world.
He inspired many gifted young Americans to overcome the traditional
prejudice against an active career in politics. He sought to prepare
the rising generation to come to terms with socialism and anticolonial-
ism. There was no doubt in Laski's mind that, unless an intellectual
bridge was built between the dogmatisms of conservative capitalism
and the collectivizing trends of the age, there would be a catastrophic
age of terror and revolutionary violence. Laski enthusiastically identified himself with the cause of independence for awakening colonial
peoples and convinced hundreds if not thousands of students from
colonial countries that they could realistically expect an understanding policy in London. For a vast congregation of former students,
Laski personified an informed intelligence and a sympathetic person-

ality attuned to the major issues of his day and concerned with clarifying and affecting history by reaching the minds and consciences of everyone within the sound of his persuasive voice or able to read his unceasing flow of books, articles, and declarations. He brought to the forum of learned debate the policy issues of the moment. For him, they were framed in the great tradition of the perpetually oscillating balance between the claims of order and liberty. Tireless teacher, publicist, scholar, and advisor, Laski was a model for one of the most attractive and rewarding roles open to professional students of politics, law, and government.[1]

The question before us is whether the requirements of graduate departments should be changed in order to establish two equally prestigious paths to a professional degree. One suggestion is that a "teaching degree" be introduced alongside the "research degree."

There are, however, several factors militating against this idea. There is an established disposition in the academic world to think of other than research degrees as "cheap degrees" and to devalue their holders accordingly. It has been proposed to "debase the Ph.D." by agreement among the leading universities. This could be done by making clear that the dissertation is to be an article, not a book, and that the degree can be obtained in two rather than three years. The change is advocated on the grounds that the aim of a dissertation is to demonstrate that the candidate is capable of making a publishable contribution to knowledge and that this demonstration does not require a book-length example. A book is an example of "overkill" in the weapons of academic life.

In weighing this proposal, it is rational to ask why the Ph.D. has come to play a role of such importance. Universities and colleges in the United States have had to fight against a supposedly "democratic" demand to keep standards low enough to "give everybody a chance." Partisan and personal pressures are not trivial in connection with many professorial and junior faculty appointments. Hence, scholars and administrators recognize the importance of having a relatively obvious test of merit to use in sifting candidates and defending their judgment when questioned by boards of trustees, influential alumni, and important family dynasts. It must be conceded that the competence of a writer can be better judged from a book than an article, especially since an article is likely to be more derivative of the senior professor than is a book. Hence, the doctoral dissertation has developed in the United States into a rough equivalent of the *Habilitationsschrift,* the postdoctoral volume used in German universities to determine whether a scholar is ready for a university appointment.[2]

The proposal to create separate teaching and research degrees or to dilute the Ph.D. is a losing cause, and it will become increasingly obvious that the cause deserves to lose. The decisive factor will be the accelerated pace of learning in American education. As mathematical, logical, and scientific skills become commonplace in early years of school (and preschool) and genuine intellectual motivations are at last tapped on a large scale, the problem of political science teachers will be to make the subject intellectually challenging and hence competitive for able students. The instructor will need to have the intellectual mastery of his craft that is signalized by a research degree.

The chances are that teaching and research will merge at a much earlier stage in the academic process than heretofore and that political science teaching will require much more exacting research than in the past.

I do not think that it is a secret among experienced members of the academic community that departments of political science often fail to appeal to students of first-rate intellectual capability. By this is meant, of course, the students who excel in handling the abstractions that comprise the distinctive instruments of science and scholarship (symbolized, for instance, by excellence in mathematics, logic, or theoretical physics). Political science departments have often "lost" these students to departments of economics because economists seem to be in demand and because the intellectual content and apparatus of economics is relatively more impressive. In many institutions, the department of political science seems highly pedestrian when evaluated in intellectual terms. It is populated by professors who enjoy courses full of descriptive detail, semirigorous legalisms, and semidefined affirmations of preference on questions of public policy. Such a department is scarcely competitive in the search for talent with the law school, for example, which cannot fail to appeal to brilliant dialecticians and activists who respond to the double challenge of intellectual technique and the possibility of an influential career.

I believe that political science needs to attract a larger rather than a smaller share of able minds and that this will require graduate schools able to provide more students than ever with better tools than ever for the advancement of knowledge. There need be no distinction between "teaching" and "research" degrees.

There is, however, a further relevant point. What of the challenge to participate actively in public life? Surely political science courses at the undergraduate level are not aimed exclusively at students bound for professional schools. Is it not within the province of political science teachers to do their best to reach everyone with a clear and vivid presentation of the opportunities and obligations of citizenship? Does this not suggest that research is an inappropriate training for professors who would inspire active participation?

Civic training is, indeed, our province; there is no argument about that. The question is about the competence to be acquired by those who engage in instruction at various levels. If anything is clear in this controversial area, it is that practical political experience by itself is not dependable as a qualification for teachers of government. Call the roll of any state legislature or of Congress. Among those who stand out as possibilities are men who are so absorbed in the urgencies of daily politics that they have no time for other jobs. If it is a question of lame ducks, the lameness that got them out of office is often excellent justification for keeping them off a faculty.

I am not saying, of course, that students should be insulated from association with practicing politicians during student years. On the contrary, in every dynamic center of political studies there is an unending procession of politicians, legislators, executives, administrators, judges, military officers, diplomats, and political commentators. Small group discussions, individual conferences, classroom lectures, and public debates provide varied occasions for more than perfunctory association between visitor and student. It is standard practice in many colleges for classes to visit the principal organs of government accessible in the locality and to encourage off-campus vacation trips and projects. It has been customary for years to supplement the regular teaching staff by part-time persons, many of them actively or recently engaged in public affairs.

There is, however, a fundamental problem: a practicing politician is not necessarily a competent political scientist, and a competent political scientist is not necessarily a practicing politician. The distinction lies in goal value; the competent political scientist is mainly responsible for enlightenment, for the advancement of knowledge. His role in the decision process is not restricted to the topical urgencies of the moment. Part of his responsibility, in fact, is to keep the urgencies of the day in the broader context of knowledge and understanding. Whatever else they may do, political scientists are under a primary obligation to contribute to the intelligence and appraisal phases of community decision.

In teaching, the task is to share this larger map with students, adapting the presentation to the reservoir of motivation and competence. As educational levels rise, communications can be more direct and technical, and students can participate at earlier stages in the intelligence and appraisal which are the distinctive tasks of political science. They can be encouraged to step into active politics by the many routes of contact and mobility known to the faculties of all institutions.

FREEDOM, DIVERSITY, AND DEPTH

What further proposals hold promise for the preparation of political scientists? A principal one concerns freedom. Graduate students need to exercise wide freedom of choice in arranging their programs of study and research. The communications revolution has made possible a film library containing the main body of political science knowledge. We have been slow to grasp audiovisual tools and to make of them basic instruments of research and advanced instruction. Educational films for precollege students have gradually moved into the gap, with modest success. However, it remains true that political scientists generally have taken little responsibility for the full utilization of film and television. One major possibility is that lectures could be made available for recombination in whatever patterns seem best adapted to local requirements. (Political science associations and educational institutions could cooperate with educational television in preparing a great library of appropriate material.)

Some successful films give prominence to a lecturer who handles a topic with conspicuous mastery even though the lecturer is not himself a research contributor to the topic at hand. Film and television also afford opportunities to bring audiences into direct contact with distinguished political scientists whose research or analysis is generally regarded as significant. The lecture itself may be less suitable for classroom or adult education audiences than a presentation by an accomplished classroom master. However, the opportunity to form a first-hand impression of the mind and personality of the lecturer often compensates for the difference. Fortunately, too, the research man and the able lecturer are often identical.

Films are most useful when they employ visual images to do well what words do badly. Under the auspices of the basic data program, comprehensive arrangements could be made for the production and selection of visual records of contemporary world trends and also for means of putting such material in context.

It might eventually be practicable for the American Political Science Association, in cooperation with other scholarly bodies, to take responsibility for a contemporary political history program designed to supplement the "spot shots" taken for news purposes. As part of political science instruction, photo-documentation teams could be organized locally to augment collections of nonvisual data. With the cooperation of governmental, press, and other organizations, the resources of the newsreel companies and press libraries, for example, could be drawn on to exhibit the trends during the years since photography began.

If vast libraries of original data and interpretation were available to each student in a private studio, his freedom would be enormously enhanced. Film and television can make instruction in specific skills available to each student whenever he feels motivated to acquire them. This applies to mathematical statistics, machine programming, symbolic logic, planning and processing of questionnaires, and the like.

The student can also have means at his disposal of examining himself as a series of events among events and of comprehending the impact that he makes on others. Everyone who hears himself "played back" on tape is initially astonished by the sound of his voice. Each student needs to see himself filmed under various circumstances, since posture, gesture, and dress are to some extent under his control.

There are limits to unsupervised learning, however; hence, departments responsible for advanced study would be well advised to put specialists at the disposal of students. New medical and psychological tests are in continual process of revision, and individuals can benefit directly by knowing what there is to know about themselves. In some cases, this should lead to therapy to remedy organic or functional handicaps.

As much attention needs to be given the cultivation of the "whole man" among political scientists as is provided in many military and business programs for the education of young officers and executives.

Although it is possible to obtain a great deal of understanding of alien cultures and of novel situations in one's own society through film and television, there is ultimately no substitute for first-hand exposure. The advanced student must be financially enabled to travel and to conduct study projects away from the home campus.

Financial independence is important in order to reduce the temptation of the student to compromise his integrity. It is not too much to say that many graduate schools train their students from start to finish to sacrifice intellectual integrity. Professors may have funds at their disposal to buy cheap labor and hence to offer impecunious students a part-time job that helps to cover living expenses. Further, in order to help in cutting down the number of years often spent in graduate work, many well-meaning professors indicate that a dissertation can be obtained in connection with a research project by doing a little extra work and grinding out a passable dissertation. The student who needs money—and this is the typical case—finds the possibility most enticing even though he possesses little intellectual commitment to the research or even to the subfield within which it lies.

Mitigating factors are, of course, often present. If the research project is in a field that is just opening up, the student is able to obtain a higher level of skill than is usual even if he does not write a dissertation. If the investigation brings a graduate student into contact with an able professor who has attracted an alert and highly motivated corps of assistants, it is fortunate for all concerned. The student is able to make an insider's appraisal of his own suitability to a new approach.

It may be argued that, if a scholar is relatively indifferent to subject matter, he might as well take whatever opportunity comes his way. It is not being perfectionistic to say that students who are indifferent to subject matter have no business in the field. I strongly suspect that political science has been damaged as a profession by the number of students of ordinary ability who have gone into it for the sake of an easy and relatively genteel livelihood. Many of the huge departments at colleges and universities have grown by accretion to meet the heavy teaching obligations that devolve on them. The expansion of enrollment creates a demand for student assistants to mark papers and perform similar chores, and the assistants become instructors when they show reasonable competence and stay out of jail. Meanwhile, a dissertation is written or accumulated—often in the same department—and supporting interests are established in obtaining the promotion of the instructor-Ph.D.

If I am correct in predicting that intellectual standards will rise in coming years, I think it reasonable to propose that we make every effort to attract into the study and practice of political science young men and women of outstanding competence and integrity. And this means money—money to provide students with the freedom of choice too often denied them in the past.

The desirable scope of freedom includes access to whatever combinations of courses or course equivalents are offered at universities. The department of political science can make available to Ph.D. candidates a syllabus covering the general field of political science and the fields of concentration recognized for individual candidates. Before obtaining the degree, the student is usually required to (1) pass a written examination on both fields and (2) present an acceptable dissertation.

The syllabus suitable for (1) is approximately the same as the introduction to the scope and method of political science mentioned earlier. The requirements for (2) are complex, since they must often be worked out with the help of a committee some of whose members are outside the political science department. Each graduate student deserves to have the attention of a committee chosen to guide his specialized studies and test his progress. Often, though not invariably, this committee can also act as a dissertation committee.

At the end of the Ph.D. period, advanced students who desire it should have fellowships for a five-year period of research and study. During the Ph.D. phase of growth, the student is almost certain to rely heavily on the advice of the local department. When the Ph.D. is passed, it is possible to gain the independence of judgment required to settle on a line of inquiry that may deviate from local tradition. If the topic and method come within the tradition, the chances are that the new judgment will be better based than it can be in predoctoral days.

Not all students want to proceed directly to research. They may, for example, welcome "internship" programs that bring them into close and responsible association with active political figures at the international, national, or local level. In many cases, too, the student finds himself attracted by teaching and desires to spend two or three years in active classroom work. This is also important in clarifying the career goals and strategies appropriate to him. Graduates often proceed directly to official responsibilities or attach themselves to private organizations. They may or may not have research or teaching in view.

SOCIALIZATION

In all that touches on intellectual accomplishment, political science will share the benefits expected to follow the revolution in education now under way. Undoubtedly, there are optimum years for introducing children and young people to various skills; in all probability, these optimum periods are much earlier than is generally admitted. It is already clear that language skills can be systematically taught at an early age (the third and fourth years of life, for example). Evidence is accumulating that higher mathematics, symbolic logic, and in general skills that do not depend on empirical observation are rapidly acquired at this stage (the fourth or fifth year). At this phase, the child appears to excel in the manipulation of syntactic terms.[3]

We cannot disregard various questions about personality growth and maturity when we contemplate the rapid progress that is possible in such skills as logic, mathematics, language, music, sculpture, the graphic arts, and body management (dancing, swimming, and the like). Lurking in the mind of every responsible educator or parent are the images of the misshapen prodigies occasionally met. Over-impressed by the symbol-managing dimensions of society, they have developed into social cripples unable to empathize or to achieve affectional relationships uncontaminated by rudimentary destructiveness, reactive arrogance, hidden dependence, and anxiety.

The maturative problems of a gifted child will be greatly eased when gifted children exist in abundance. As the excess capacities of the human brain are at last unlocked, the norms of civilized society will undergo drastic change. It is not simply a matter of speeding the acquisition of abstract skills. The probing of man's potential will uncover capabilities for creative expression in every medium that have hitherto lain largely dormant.[4]

Among the stereotyped images that will go by the board is the dichotomy between "intellectual" and "emotional" components of mind. All ideas are rooted in fundamental mood-flows which sustain the elaboration of images (ideas) until they achieve ultimate form and expression. Rather, we conventionally credit composers of music and of some other forms of communication with deep feeling and emotion. Phrases of this kind are less often used to describe scientists and mathematicians who are, in fact, often depicted as aloof and absorbed in the frigid air of thought.

The truth about scientists is quite otherwise and undermines the antinomy that has been erected between the arts and sciences. All symbolic creativity has much in common, especially the interplay of mood and image. Skilled performers of any operation are well acquainted with the exhilarating sense of achievement that accompanies a complex pattern of symbol, sign, and movement as it unfolds. By contrast, the dominant tone of an exercise in enlightenment is one of incipient illumination of the face of nature and society. In healthy bodily expression—whether stylized or not—there is the vitality of well-being. The nuances of love, honor, and responsibility are recognizable in the dimension of mood, as are the peculiar urge and joy of acquisition and processing; and the propensity to dominate others.

If the ancient barriers between "abstract" and "aesthetic" expression are lowered, young people can be provided with environments that increase the mood experiences open to them which they can subsequently blend with any dominant problem activity.

Assume that we are concerned in the long run with eliminating the use of coercive instruments of policy. The aim is to rely on persuasion, especially on the sharing of enlightenment. If each generation is to be prepared for participation in persuasive activities, its members must have ample opportunity to engage in the process successfully, hence learning to rely on persuasion even under circumstances which at first seem unsuited to persuasive activity.

For instance, it is frustrating for competent scientists to be confronted by ignorant attacks on science, and many scientists find it intolerable to defend science to fools. The latent sympathy of many engineers and scientists with despotism comes from the hope that the "fools" can be handled by despots who keep the scientists from being bothered. This is a danger to democratic systems of public order; the process of civic training should enable skilled individuals to feel at home in occasional contact with "fools." This is not a simple matter of "toleration" but of enlightenment concerning the role of persuasive communication in society. If the socialization process is to be successful, persuasion must be connected with indulgent rather than deprivational experiences in the home, school, and general community.

It is tempting to rely on the mechanism of conditioning, stringently applied from early years of life, to reduce coercion in human affairs. Should we aim at conditioning all children to nonviolent modes of dealing with other people?[5] If such a mechanism of nonviolence were specific enough to use for indoctrination purposes, it would have to impose an inhibition against performing any act that damaged other people physically. No explosive could be detonated; no blade could be used to cut or gouge; no blow could be delivered; no push entailing the likelihood of damage to the person could be given; and no button or intermediary of any kind could be employed to start any sequence likely to end in any physical deprivation of a human target. The sanction could be built in by conditioning exercises under circumstances that increase its automatic, unconscious compulsiveness. Presumably the conditioning would begin at a very early age and would be aided by hypnotic or chemical means. Perhaps the individual who is tempted, even unconsciously, to complete a prohibited act could be trained to turn impulses of this kind into destructive acts against the self, rather than against an external target. The subject might be conditioned to experience a splitting headache, to faint, to undergo paralysis of the motor apparatus, or to suffer heart attacks —even fatal ones.

A problem that confronts such a conditioning program is that many of the specific acts mentioned may also occur in socially desirable forms. This is true of surgical interventions that require cutting and of police acts to restrain the individual whose conditioning fails or who has been deliberately reconditioned in secret conclaves of dissenters who conspire to restore man's freedom or who plan a ruthless elite corps equipped to take over a society whose members are conditioned against offering resistance. If the community comes into contact with inimical forces in the astropolitical arena, a successful program of conditioning might have provided an unconscious preparation for servitude to the new order.

If it is decided to meet these problems by arranging an "exemption cue" that would "inhibit the inhibition," the political question becomes: Who is to be empowered under what circumstances to administer the cue? We are back to the familiar probability in political calculations—administrators may not be perfect. Hence, they may use their control of cues as a base of power, perhaps striving to liberate a gang intent on seizing power.

Some of these difficulties might be faced by devising a new strategy of conditioning. One technique would be to influence an act of thought at the phase of *intention,* rather than to work for automatic inhibition of a specific list of act completions. Such training might proceed by drilling the individual to acknowledge the presence of destructive subjectivity whenever it appeared. The conditioning would be explicitly tied to destructive intention. Hence any subjective event —even at the threshold of awareness—would precipitate the inhibiting mechanisms mentioned above. The hope would be that each individual could act as his own "exemption manager," since a benevolent intention would enable activities to be modulated as seemed best (including the completion of acts of cutting or killing).

This program gives rise to fascinating technical problems. Having in mind the subtlety of man's mechanisms of adjustment and especially the notorious deceptiveness of unconscious motivation, one wonders whether it is possible to prevent unacknowledged impulses toward hostility from appearing at the conscious phase in the guise of benevolence. Would conditioning be necessary during states comparable to pscychoanalytic hours in which the individual is capable of permitting basic initial impulses to expose themselves instantly in gesture or vocalization?

Techniques will presumably improve steadily in this as in every field of research. In the astropolitical age, the enormous number of natural and fabricated locations for habitation may be turned into communities where contrasting methods of conditioning are utilized and the results compared.

CODES OF CONDUCT

It is a fact of more than casual interest that political scientists possess no written code of professional conduct for the guidance of students or others and no formal machinery for disciplining anyone for malpractice. The legal profession, by contrast, is well armored with prescriptive language on the subject, and the grievance committees of bar associations are by no means inactive. Physicians, of course, have codes, and one of the most conspicuous trends in modern professionalization has been for new associations to draft bodies of rules and aspirations. Several factors no doubt help to explain why political scientists are codeless. Whatever investigation of this point may eventually reveal, it is safe to say that one contributing factor has been the ambiguity of the image of the political scientist and the looseness with which many individuals have been identified with its development.

Whether political scientists agree on an official code of practice or not, I am confident that the growth of a professional identity will carry with it greater clarity of expectation about the conduct appropriate to a political scientist as researcher, teacher, advisor, and practitioner of politics. A casebook of problems that have actually arisen could usefully be published. I think, too, that young people would welcome a book of observations on the subject by several experienced seniors.

A code of professional conduct would presumably deal with questions of confidentiality, candor, and consideration. In his role of researcher, teacher, advisor, or active practitioner, a political scientist faces many problems related to communications obtained in confidence. Under what circumstances, if any, is a political scientist justified in violating the confidences of others? There are also problems of self-disclosure. When is there an obligation to report candidly to a group or to put an individual on notice of facts that may influence judgment by the group or individual of what is declared or proposed?

Should some lines of research be avoided because they do violence to individual or group conceptions of rectitude? In our society, such considerations relate to acts that are regarded as invasions of privacy or that call for activities shocking the sensibilities of the persons involved (as in some potential experiments).

Clearly, political scientists often find it necessary to sacrifice one valued outcome for another. The role of professional codes of conduct is to clarify the questions arising in complex circumstances. The prime value of research workers is enlightenment, or the improvement of skill. As we have suggested, however, these values may be compromised in varying degree for some participants in research. If we accept the overriding conception of human dignity and think that responsible conduct is the deliberate evaluation of conduct in the context of goal, a code of professional conduct is an obvious means of bringing political scientists into harmony with the fundamental aim.

I shall summarize a few cases in which political scientists were aware of conflicting values. They may be taken as points of departure for the casebooks and codes to which I have referred.

Many years ago, a social scientist who studied organized crime and politics in an American city got in touch with criminal gangs and eventually established himself so successfully that he was tipped off in advance of robberies and even of gang skirmishes. He met the problem by giving the police no information, arguing that his relations to the world of organized crime were unique and would produce knowledge of much more lasting importance to public order than could possibly result from a few tips.

A political scientist who was engaged in area research abroad during the rise of the German National Socialists won the confidence of local Nazis to a degree that enabled him to learn the strength, and even to identify secret leaders, of the Nazis in several foreign countries. He was personally anti-Nazi, but as a political analyst he was concerned with discovering the group sources of their strength and the nature and effectiveness of their strategy. To become a political police agent, as he would in effect be if he gave his information to the authorities, would bring his investigation to a stop before he could conclude the general picture that he felt competent to draw if he continued to keep Nazi confidences. He had explained to the Nazis that he was not in sympathy with their ideas but that he was not going to break faith with them; they had come to believe in his word.

Another political scientist faced a problem of a somewhat different kind. For years he had been among the small number of scholars qualifying as genuine experts on the Soviet Union. Since he made repeated trips to Russia and had known it before the revolution, he had contact with individuals and circles in bitter opposition to Bolshevik dictatorship. On each return to the United States, he was sought by Washington officials who welcomed his candid appraisal of developments since the previous visit. One year in particular, there were rumors that the regime was in grave peril as a result of its failures in agriculture—evidently a chronic condition—and of factionalism in the party. Outside forces, eager to embarrass and upset the Bolsheviks, were redoubling their propaganda and sabotage measures against them. It was at this time especially that strong urgings were made to provide official sources with the names of individuals and groups who were disaffected and who might therefore become part of an antirevolutionary campaign based in Western Europe. The scholar in question was entirely willing to testify as an expert, giving his judgment of the principal trends of recent years. But he was adamant about providing the "police and military" information asked for. He believed that it would be ruinous to his hard-won reputation as "an honest bourgeois scholar" to become involved in subversion against the Reds. He was undoubtedly influenced by other considerations as well. He believed that the Bolsheviks were in power for keeps and that it was fantastic to expect to overturn them by attempting to set even the Trotskyists against the Stalin machine.

A more urgent problem arose in another case. A political scientist who did not regard himself as an area specialist on Western Europe or on any Western European country learned of a political conspiracy engineered by Communists to overthrow the government of a small, friendly country. The disclosure had come only accidentally in the course of a research trip that had nothing directly to do with Communism. He felt entirely free to make his unexpectedly detailed foreknowledge available to the responsible authorities.

Another political scientist was approached by the intelligence services with the proposal that he become an agent and a specialist on a country speaking a language unknown to many Americans. The offer was to finance him for several years of study by providing (unacknowledged) funds to be administered through his university. Not the least tempting feature of the offer was the appeal that it made to his national loyalty and to his anti-Communist beliefs. He felt certain that no Soviet citizen would turn down such an offer if made by Communist intelligence services, and he also suspected that Americans were probably too full of "liberal inhibitions" to fight the Communists effectively. Despite all this, the invitation was eventually turned down. He believed it contrary to his obligation as a scholar and an American to "prostitute" universities into cover agencies for intelligence services.

Of a more commonplace character is the problem that faced a former colleague who relied on interview methods of obtaining information about local politics. He became acquainted with the scandalous personal life of a candidate for high public office on a reform ticket. It seemed obvious that the man was—I quote—a "hypocrite, a sadist, a pervert, and a crook." He had illicit connections with gamblers and addicts, and it became increasingly clear that the man was a "psychopathic character," with everything implied by the technical use of the term. My colleague asked whether he did not owe it to the public to make the facts available. The question was how it could be done without violating legitimate trust or exposing informants to retaliation. To denounce the fellow in general terms without specific names, dates, and places would get nowhere, since the ordinary language of vituperation in American politics covered most of the points. In addition, publicity would endanger the completion of the research on which he was at work and compromise the future of what he believed would be an important contribution to knowledge of the American political system. So, aside from endorsing a proposal to require all candidates to take a psychiatric examination, he did nothing.

Political scientists have not in the past engaged in the kinds of experiment that raise such questions as the individual's "right" to endanger his life. If we consider the significance of the claim to "waive" one's interest in safety in the perspective of a commitment to human dignity, there is not much doubt about the result. The body politic cannot permit suicide; it cannot, that is, admit that the decision to end one's life is for an individual to make by himself. Too many collective values are at stake. Not only does the person represent an enormous social investment, but he is a potential asset. The decision to take "my" life is also a decision regarding "our" life together, and it is not in harmony with the goal of sharing that I should play the autocrat in the matter.

An important though subsidiary aspect of the question of public policy on suicide is that, when many attempts at self-destruction are made, the individual is in a disturbed frame of mind and therefore handicapped in coping with his problems realistically.

The questions that arise in the physical and biological sciences are not typically of this kind. Rather, they invove full or at least candid disclosure of danger and the offering of inducements to run the risks involved. In connection with radioactivity, many physicists and physicians have mutilated their bodies and eventually lost their lives in the conduct of experiments. It is no novelty in the investigation of pathogenic organisms for bacteriologists to put themselves in the experimental group. We know that people of all ages have consented to be guinea pigs in perilous experiments, a practice that seems to have tacit public consent provided that the subjects have been given a complete briefing on the dangers involved. We are accustomed to not interfering with people who engage in hazardous sports if other persons are not immediately endangered by what they do.

It is not entirely true that political scientists are always engaged in a nonhazardous occupation. I know of students of politics who have suddenly discovered that political gangs and bosses did not look on their snooping with a friendly eye, and studies of hot spots in labor-management controversies and in "race relations" are not always welcome. Totalitarian countries are, of course, uniformly suspicious of research of any kind, which is immediately assumed to be espionage.

The martyrs in political science are as few as in the neighboring social and behavioral disciplines. There are not, at least as yet, enough martyred political scientists, economists, sociologists, and psychologists to justify a memorial wall, much less a hall. The exception appears to be in anthropology, and it is perhaps a comment on the perspectives current among professionals that the rare student who has lost his or her life on a field trip "had it coming" because of some flagrant disregard for local culture.

There has been no dearth of people with political training who have been killed or maimed for their ideological position and for taking an active part in public affairs. However, the significant figures among political philosophers seem more cautious than physically courageous. The stereotype case remains that of Hobbes, the scholar of fire-eating imagination who was "the first of those who fled." In regard to jockeys or picadores of the great Leviathan, Hobbes, too, would rather see than be one.

EVALUATING FACTORS THAT INHIBIT INQUIRY

The liberation of creativity calls for full candor in perceiving—and some courage in overcoming—the influence of all factors, formal and informal, that inhibit active and potentially important inquiry.

Some important informal restraints are connected with the perspectives of tight, homogeneous elites that perpetuate the traditions of pre-democratic systems.

An illuminating case in point is the history of psychological studies of political elites. The rise of political and social psychology has been intimately tied to democratic individualism, especially in America. These disciplines and modes of approach are so closely linked with democracy chiefly because of the defensiveness of power figures. Political psychologists want access to their subjects *now*. They want data that, if unpublished for a time, are at least open to summary by the omission of names and by the publication of anonymous group or personal profiles.

If anyone hesitates to accept the fact that large, homogeneous elites do in fact inhibit empirical inquiry of a social-psychological or psychiatric character, let him consider the reluctance of English universities to encourage this approach. Traditional barriers are at present dissolving owing to the belated rise of new universities as social change accelerates.[6]

Political and social scientists do not distribute their attention evenly to the upper, middle, and lower strata of society, even in bodies politic whose ideology is democratic. It is often remarked that political and social scientists find it easier to write about the middle and lower classes than to deal with elites of power, wealth, or other values.[7] Social scientists have evidently felt less anxiety when they study individuals of lower social position. We note, too, that many students of society have been drawn into research when their rebelliousness against the established order could find no political outlet. They were initially drawn to studies of the rank and file by revolutionary romanticism and by the impulse to discredit the powers that be.

Political scientists have, as a rule, been too prudent or timid to become involved in research that would arouse the ire of churchmen or professional moralists. They have produced little research on church-state relationships despite the obviously growing importance of the policy questions. It is true that political scientists have been willing to study electoral data to bring out Catholic, Protestant, or Jewish patterns of behavior at the polls. They have, however, been little concerned with case studies of how ecclesiastical elites have relied on coercive or persuasive strategies to influence formal or informal leaders.

We observe, also, that sex is a touchy topic for political scientists, if one is to judge by the paucity of research on the interplay of sex and politics. Prostitution is dealt with as a source of "corruption," but the role of sexual development in attitudes toward authority is rarely dealt with. Despite the traditional and scientifically validated role that is assigned to the family in imprinting various sexual and political perspectives, there is almost no team research bringing political scientists into close working collaboration with child psychologists, physicians, and nurses.[8]

It is not necessary that an exercise in creative thinking deal with a "delicate" topic. It is, however, a threat to enlightenment if creativity is herded into conventional and into no other channels. Freedom of inquiry demands a franchise to study every value-institution process for the sake of public enlightenment.

A striking example of neglected research possibilities that must be explained on other than cautionary grounds is the interplay of art and politics. True, the frontier tradition is supposed to have been established by men who were so doubtful that their masculinity had survived the trip West that they were afraid of the "effeminizing" effects of the arts. But this point of view has long evaporated in sophisticated centers. Among political scientists, there has evidently been a process of negative selection of students committed to the arts.

My prediction on this matter is unequivocal. If the world holds together, political scientists will concern themselves with doing what they can to illuminate the impact of the arts on politics and of politics on architecture, literature, music, graphics, plastics, and the dance.[9] More than this—the aesthetic interest will find creative expression in the criticism of power, rectitude, and in fact of all values.

The initiative has already been taken in this direction. Among Americans, the philosopher-politician T. V. Smith is the principal figure. Following in the tradition of Santayana, Smith speaks with charm and wit on behalf of the enjoyment of the imperatives of conscience, for example, and speaks of himself as one who celebrates the democratic ideal.[10] In common with all values, the cultivation of an aesthetic perspective has two phases—shaping and sharing. The former phase is exhibited in the skills of the craftsman, the latter, in the contemplative skill of the connoisseur. In the relatively pure case, art is not art unless it is "art for art's sake," that is, unless the value demands of the craftsman or the connoisseur are for the realization of gratifying patterns among the elements of a culminating outcome. The criteria of gratification, when made explicit in communication, are statements of the preferred norm of the communicator in pattern arrangement. Without accepting the connotations of traditional metaphysics, we can use the term "intrinsic" to designate this criterion for the evaluations of outcome events as art. If we evaluated sculpture or music as instruments of power, wealth, or other values, the evaluation would be, not in terms of art, but of other events.

In this developmental construct of politics and the arts, we must eventually consider many other historical and analytic factors. One of them is the demand to devalue power, especially in historical epochs in which the imperatives of power are pressing heavily on the lives of men. There are many ways of seeking to turn away from, or to reduce as far as possible, one's active commitment to power. Among these alternatives, one of the most successful contenders in the lives of many people is, and has long been, the aesthetic quest.

In coming years, the rising level of education will prepare generations of advanced students to work effectively in cross-disciplinary fields, humanistic or scientific, that lie outside the specialized frame of political reference. It is probable that, as the division of intellectual labor opens and occupies interstitial and intersecting zones, the number of scholars who acquire "double competence" will increase. The permissive program of graduate training envisaged in the present discussion would cultivate both depth and diversity as means of professional development toward high levels of continuing creative achievement. It would become increasingly common for multidisciplinary collaboration to occur at successive stages of the professional career. In the following chapter, we deal explicitly with the prospects of collaborative activity in fields that are by tradition closely connected to the description, analysis, and management of politics.[11]

NOTES

[1] Something of the flavor of Laski's personality shines through in the published correspondence with public figures, especially with Mr. Justice Holmes. Cf. *Holmes-Laski Letters*, "The Correspondence of Mr. Justice Holmes and Harold J. Laski, 1916–1935," Mark De-Wolfe Howe, ed. (Cambridge: Harvard University Press, 1953).

[2] Basic historical information is in M. J. L. O'Connor, *Origins of Academic Economics in the United States* (New York: Columbia University Press, 1944); A. Haddow, *Political Science in American Colleges and Universities*, "1636–1900" (New York: Appleton-Century, 1939).

[3] On this speed-up, it is possible to follow developments in *The American Behavioral Scientist* edited by A. deGrazia at Princeton. Cf. the special issue on "The New Educational Technology," 6 (November 1962), No. 3. Among political scientists, Herbert Simon has been

the most influential figure. His command of mathematics and lively experimental imagination have set a new model of professional practice. On "Statistical and Quantitative Methodology," cf. J. W. Tukey, in D. P. Ray, ed., *Trends in Social Science* (New York: Philosophical Library, 1961), pp. 84–136. He speaks of the standard research cycle as conjecture-design-experiment-analysis and suggests that the cycle be adapted to the distinctive needs of research candidates in various fields. In political science, where research means making or taking new data, he advocates a "phase of careful analysis of *someone else's data* over a long time" (p. 124). Cf. P. F. Lazarsfeld, "Evidence and Inference in Social Research," in D. Lerner, ed., *Evidence and Inference* (New York: The Free Press of Glencoe, 1958), pp. 107–138. On certain questions of logical statement, cf. F. Oppenheim, *Dimensions of Freedom*, "An Analysis" (New York: St. Martin's Press, 1961).

[4] The problems of a prodigy in his generation are told from the inside by Norbert Wiener, *Ex-Prodigy*, "My Childhood and Youth" (New York: Simon and Schuster, 1953); also his *I Am a Mathematician*, "The Later Life of a Prodigy" (Garden City, N.Y.: Doubleday, 1956).

[5] On the technique of conditioning, cf. B. F. Skinner, *Science and Human Behavior* (New York: Macmillan, 1960).

[6] Recent original contributions to political science in Great Britain—not necessarily by members of the academic profession—include those of J. Eysenck, R. S. Milne, D. E. Butler, W. Pickles, J. Plamenatz, D. W. Brogan, H. C. MacKenzie, J. F. S. Ross, and J. A. Thomas. G. E. G. Catlin has for many years been the outstanding exponent of the scientific development of political science in Great Britain. His principal academic appointments have been in the United States and the Commonwealth. Cf. his recent *Systematic Politics*, "*Elementa Politica et Sociologica*" (Toronto: University of Toronto Press, 1962).

[7] Most recently by D. Riesman, *Individualism Reconsidered* (Glencoe, Ill.: The Free Press, 1954), pp. 467–483.

[8] An exception is Arnold Rogow and his collaborators. It is obvious that the study of political socialization, at least, will find it difficult to avoid the subject. In political biography, the contextual approach—including the psychoanalytic or psychosomatic dimensions—is more frequent. For example, A. and J. George, *Woodrow Wilson* "A Personality Study" (Evanston, Ill.: Row, Peterson, 1956); and A. Gottfried, *Boss Cermak of Chicago*, "A Study of Political Leadership" (Seattle: University of Washington Press, 1962); G. M. Gilbert, *The Psychology of Dictatorship* (New York: Ronald, 1950).

[9] It is not to be ignored that many political scientists have received professional training in one or more of the arts, play a role on boards

of art institutes, or build significant private collections. These "hidden assets" will eventually be mobilized for serious inquiry.

10 T. V. Smith, *Beyond Conscience* (New York: McGraw-Hill, 1935).

11 It will be evident that, in the present book, I am chiefly concerned with putting our own house in order. I hope that this will strengthen the eventual impact of the challenging criticism of education in neighboring fields by my colleague R. E. Lane in *The Liberties of Wit*, "Humanism, Criticism, and the Civic Mind" (New Haven: Yale University Press, 1961).

9

Collaboration
with
Allied Professions

Many aims of political science can be most effectively achieved if collaboration between political scientists and individuals of closely allied skills is successfully maintained. I single out for specific mention two of the professions with whose members we have had close connections and with whom it is highly desirable to have continuing ties in coming years.

JOURNALISM

Although graduate school dissertations must be the work of individual candidates, there is no sound reason why dissertations should not be part of joint undertakings in which journalists are involved and which provide material for independent publication by all concerned.

Once the dissertation hurdle is passed, joint projects would often be most successful when they lead to publications in which political scientists and journalists have fully fused their contributions.

Although closely connected, particularly when journalists specialize in political reporting and commentary, journalism and political science are not identical. A journalist is the chief reliance of the reading, listening, and viewing public for immediate political intelligence. A journalist is at his best when he correctly anticipates tomorrow's coup and stations himself where he can provide a first-hand account. Since his report must be nearly instantaneous, he must be precisely informed of communication facilities and arrange alternative channels if established routes are blocked by sabotage, censorship, or technical breakdown.

A political scientist does not as a rule need to keep contact with a network of informants, official or unofficial, highly placed or humbly stationed, to provide tips on impending developments. It is rarely necessary for a working scholar to sacrifice orderly living and to make himself available at any hour of day or night to observe the birth of a new elite or to record the demise of an old regime. For him there is little physical discomfort, body peril, or crushing fatigue. He is somewhat protected from appearing as a gullible fool, since he is not driven by deadlines. It is unlikely that he will be scooped by rivals or duped by unscrupulous informants.

We may sum up the life of an active political journalist by saying that it is relatively insecure and risky. Reference has been made to hazards to life and reputation; it is appropriate to add moral risk. A journalist is likely to find it necessary on occasion to overcome scruples against betraying the confidence of others. More subtle than bribery— although bribery is not out of the question—is the temptation to take it easy by relying on official handouts. And it is tempting to abandon the role of spectator-reporter to play an active political part by suppressing or distorting information.

This statement suggests why the working journalist is likely to be a valuable collaborator. Attuned to the immediate, he is impatient of delay. Accustomed to coping with tacticians of deceit, he is a sophisticated assessor of false witness. A journalist is also aware of "who knows what," since his dramatizing imagination often perceives the relationship of every participant to the central action, recognizing potential informants who would otherwise be overlooked. Journalists belong to a world-wide freemasonry of a profession that is still required in many parts of the world to brace itself against the low esteem in which it is held. It is true that, as with all men, political differences build walls between journalists. Yet, if anyone anywhere is willing to sacrifice in behalf of enlightenment, he is likely to be among professional reporters.

I have referred to social status. Not long ago a newspaperman was somewhat contemptuously dismissed as a careerless man who had taken a hack job in desperation. It is not difficult to identify well-known figures who have contributed to this image. They were rebels against family discipline, and rebellion took the form of unwillingness to finish the academic preparation required for law, medicine, university teaching, or civil service. They were too impecunious or too concerned with public affairs to find satisfaction in ordinary business.

In those days, journalists were "misfits," and anyone pictured by his contemporaries as a misfit is likely to use one of two well-known mechanisms for the aid and succor of a suffering ego. He tries to divert his attention from the private humiliation of admitted failure by substituting the image of a brash and adventurous hero. To the extent that he is overwhelmed by self-contempt, he grows personally disorganized and may conform to the stereotype of an amiable, even pitiable, sot.

We have not yet touched on the skill that is usually given first place in listing the assets of a journalist. He can write. Unless he can find words that carry the message to a large audience, he is miscast.

After this evaluation of what the journalist is equipped to offer, the question may be what the political scientist can contribute to a collaborative undertaking. He is concerned with system and with time perspective. Good journalists may be, and typically are, aware of the advantage of looking at the present in a larger frame of reference, but they are driven by the detail of the here and now. Unless they keep moist in the spray of current events, their judgment withers. Sources dry up from lack of reciprocity. As scholars, political scientists are less bound to headlines, since their aim is to write something outliving the excitement of the moment. Perhaps his entire professional output, highly prized by other scholars though it may be, never makes the headlines. Or he waits years to publish a book that took years to prepare.

If he is conscientious in the best tradition, the scholar hates to say what other people have said without express acknowledgment. By contrast, it is not required that a reporter lay bare his every source or acknowledge that a sentence echoes the conclusions of a research worker who toiled long years to establish a single point. Scholars sense the ruthlessness of kleptomania in the journalist-borrower, who in turn thinks the typical scholar is suffering from excessive doubt and scruples —a Hamlet of the footnote. The scholar is forever disclosing the paternity of his brainchildren; the journalist is accustomed to bastards.

Collaboration is possible between bearers of diverse though complementary skills because personalities are larger than skills. It is in general true that our occupational stereotypes are too thin to correspond to the diverse patterns of life. For instance, scholars may decide to meet rather exigent deadlines, and scholars may possess rhetorical brilliance in speech or prose. Journalists may seek escape from the clatter of the newsroom into history and analysis, as did Henry Jones Ford when he wrote the *Rise and Growth of American Politics* during active newspaper days. And today's story may be illuminated with knowledge of a whole complex of conditioning elements and become a classic, even as Lincoln Steffens' *The Shame of the Cities*.

In the contemporary world, the educational and cultural backgrounds of journalists and political scientists are approaching each another.[1] Hence it is not venturesome to forecast that joint projects will become more frequent. I suspect that collaboration will be especially beneficial in the gray zone separating readily available sources of information from public or private secrets. I predict that a relatively new mode of communication will emerge to fill the gap between a sensational exposé and historical or analytic studies.[2] A topic in point is "political corruption." I do not minimize the contribution to public intelligence and appraisal that is made by courageous reporters who tear the mask off graft and chicanery and shout to everybody to look and shudder. Nor, on the other hand, do I regard the historian's monographic treatment of yesterday's scandal as useless because nobody can be prosecuted in court. The point, rather, is that public understanding of corruption needs a frame of reference disciplined by comparative studies. Clearly, some "corrupt" acts, viewed in the perspective of one culture, are more like a traditional tip, or service charge, than a perversion of public responsibility for private gain. Moreover, when corruption goes beyond traditional limits, great differences in function exist. In some traditional states (for example, Turkey, when the sultan symbolized the sick man of Europe), monarchs and bureaucrats extorted so much for consumption purposes that corruption interfered with modernization and progress. In other societies, the progressive elements, determined to enjoy the benefits of modernization, cannot be stopped. Corruption may be used to buy off the left-overs of an ancient social system and eventually to give them a more legitimate place in the new order.

The implication is not that "whatever is, must be," rather that, by adequate understanding of a "must," it may be possible to change an "is" with greater speed. The exploratory competence of the expert journalist, joined to competent comparative analysis, can modify the map of policy aim and method.

THE LAW

The connection of political scientists to legal scholars has a long history. In the European faculty of law, professors of government are responsible for describing the structure of the principal nation-states of current interest. Constitutional, municipal, and international law are often cultivated by professors of law and government. To go no further back than John W. Burgess, in the United States, *Political Science and Constitutional Law* fell squarely within the tradition that joined the theory of the state with public law. Eminent figures in political science have taught law in schools of law or they have won recognition among legal scholars despite their exclusive association with departments of political science or the absence of a law degree. I shall make no attempt at an exhaustive roster. It is, however, impossible to overlook in recent decades Edward S. Corwin, Thomas Reed Powell, Charles Grover Haines, and W. W. Willoughby in constitutional law; Frank W. Goodnow and Ernst Freund in the introduction of administrative law into the United States; or James W. Garner, Charles G. Fenwick, and Philip Marshall Brown as scholars of international law.

It is, however, significant that, despite the relative freedom from the rigid professionalism of the conventional law school enjoyed by these scholars, their names do not figure among the molders of America's most distinctive school of jurisprudence. I refer to American realism, with its emphasis, presumably congenial to political scientists, on the proposition that, since judges are people, they are to be understood by studying the impact on their decisions of factors that are known to affect human conduct. A judicial response, in this perspective, is not exempt from the conditioning of the judge to the culture in which he is reared or to the social class or interest groups with which he is or was affiliated; nor is he exempt from the conflicting equilibrium of his personality system.

The American realists, it appears, owe more to Walter Wheeler Cook than to anyone else.[3] Cook spent a year in Germany in the study of physics before turning to law. He continued to be vexed by the flagrant discrepancy between the methods of physics and those of the teachers and practitioners of law. In this he was responding to a challenge built into our civilization and of urgency growing since the sixteenth century, when mathematics and experimental physics began to gain momentum. Why should physicists be able to participate in an enterprise whose results become more general and dependable as the years go by, while jurisprudence remains much as it has always been, a battleground of controversy over traditional issues? Cook answered that legal studies were in a prescientific stage and that legal studies would gain precision and acceptance if the methods of science were properly applied to establishing the balance between theoretical models and empirical data.

These reflections led Cook to take the lead in a devastating attack on the prevailing method of the law, namely, legal logic. His position was that the method cannot possibly do more than demonstrate that opposing conclusions can be supported with equal facility by the same set of doctrines. Hence, the whole approach is radically unsound. In article after article, Cook expounded his point by applying the lawyer's preferred tool, namely, the logical analysis of definitions and of chains of argument in concrete legal controversies. Every article was intended as a blow at the ancient giant of the "logical infallibility" of law. Cook insisted that by its nature logic could be nothing other than fallible. At best, belief in infallibility is a dogma of innocence; at worst, a hoax.

Cook's competence as a legal craftsman and his painstaking work in the classroom and in the law journals carried conviction to the bright young men who formed the vanguard of the realistic approach. His impact at Johns Hopkins and Columbia University was decisive, since he trained a corps of colleagues, some of whom later migrated—for administrative reasons—to Yale, which became the home of "the Yale approach."

At first glance, it may seem surprising that the lead in establishing the realist school was not taken by a political scientist rather than by such a highly specialized legal scholar as Cook. It is presumably well known to every student of political doctrine that general theories have received, and are likely to continue to receive, plausible and even convincing interpretations that contradict one another. He sees that the trick is sometimes turned by redefining key terms, as when "human equality" is alleged to condone the enslavement of a particular ethnic group ("they are not fully human"). Or the device is to introduce a modifying doctrine that is presumably implicit in the context, such as an alleged doctrine of "necessity" justifying the suspension of democracy during "crises" (though the "crisis" may continue for generations). Whatever technique is employed, the terms of the doctrine assumed to be authoritative can be plausibly manipulated without doing violence to logical relationships (such as the requirement that affirmations within a system of propositions shall not contradict one another). However, logical systems, though internally harmonious, can be flatly at odds with one another. There is no escape, since the next move is to propose a distinction that, if equally acceptable, remains equally unconvincing.

I suggest that political scientists did not make the crucial breakthrough in jurisprudence because they were so deeply absorbed with the discovery of "interests," economic or otherwise, in the exploitation of ambiguity. Hence, they did not demonstrate at great length and in technical detail that legal *method* was a source of confusion and contradiction whenever it was assumed to apply in concrete circumstances. A distinction must be kept in mind between the internal relationships of a family of statements (which can be established "by definition") and the external "referents" of a statement (which must be demonstrated "by observation"). Walter Wheeler Cook stamped this fundamental point, the difference between what can be called "syntactics" and "semantics," into American legal literature.

At once a sense of great liberation gave enormous zest to the young men who followed in the wake of Cook. They gleefully demonstrated in every controversy in every field that definitions or arguments were equally plausible on both sides; hence, to repeat the allusion that was so often used to caricature the realistic movement, the judge's decision depended less on logic than on "what he had for dinner."

Political scientists who work with legal scholars will discover that the realistic point of view is by no means universal and that many lawyers who profess to go along with it are not willing to apply the realistic approach with vigor and constancy to every problem. Moreover, it cannot be taken for granted that the distinction between syntactics (logic) and semantics is generally understood.

Furthermore—and this is of the greatest relevance—many realists have become conscious of the fact that something is missing from the approach of traditional realism. Having demonstrated that legal logic provides no satisfactory guide to the solution of judicial problems, American legal realists have usually found that they are stuck in a negative, agnostic position. Granted that logic is devoid of necessary empirical references, so what? Are all doctrinal interpretations equally acceptable to the work of lawyers, judges, and scholars?

The answer is definitely in the negative. Political scientists, working in conjunction with realistically inclined lawyers, can contribute to the emerging jurisprudence of our day because their results help to supplement the limitations of logic as a problem-solving tool.

First of all, it is apparent that American legal realism focused on only two of the five intellectual tasks to which we have referred in our analysis of problem-solving in general. The two tasks are trend and conditioning analysis—What decisions have been made? What factors have influenced them? Three tasks are left untouched or receive incidental treatment—What are the postulated goals of the legal system? What are the projections of probable future events? What major alternatives of policy will maximize value goals?

By working in close association with students of legal processes, political scientists can assist in clarifying the scope and method of jurisprudence. In the most inclusive sense, jurisprudence is itself a component of political science. Jurisprudence is particularly concerned with *authoritative* patterns of decision. Obviously, decisions may be both *authoritative* and *controlling;* specialists in neither jurisprudence nor political science are exclusively concerned with one or the other. However, a division of emphasis—hence a division of labor—does in fact exist. Specialists in jurisprudence provide problem-solving guidance for professional lawyers, judges, and legal scholars; specialists in political science aim at a somewhat different public. To some extent, however, the audiences overlap, especially in public law (international, constitutional, and municipal). A continuous gradation of specialties covers the total field of political science and jurisprudence. The difference lies in the detail with which attention is focused on the specialized, conventional language of "the law." Where does this appear?

Most prominently, of course, legal language is used by courts, especially by tribunals that write "opinions" in addition to giving "decisions." It is taken for granted that the opinions *justify* the decisions in the name of the legal *formula*. It is unthinkable that any agency purporting to be a "court" would declare itself uninterested in legal doctrine or precedent. Such a disclaimer is not thinkable because the overwhelming expectation of the body politic is that the decisions are made to conform to the prescriptions of the system of legal authority (constitutions, statutes, treatises, ordinances, regulations, "customs," and the like).

The legal realists were often correct in saying that decision-makers "made up their minds" how to decide a controversy and "wrote opinions to fit" the decision. But this formulation is exceedingly ambiguous. Does it mean that decision-makers disregard all the prescriptions of the legal system? Inquiry suggests that the answer is usually, if not always, "no." The careful selection of justifying opinions can result from the desire to win general approval for a result that is arrived at on somewhat unconventional, though "legal," grounds. The manipulative character of the opinion is not necessarily intended to justify "lawlessness" in the exercise of judgment, but rather to divert attention from the "legalistic" elements of the specific decision. The court might think that candid disclosure of "genuine interpretations" would prove unnecessarily disturbing to bar and bench.

We must also underline the fact that research on judges confirms the view that many, if not most, are largely conventional in outlook. They use the intellectual tools acquired in law school, perfected in practice, and brought with them to the bench. It would be a mistake to imagine that they are intellectually sophisticated enough to understand their own intellectual processes. On the contrary *it is likely that they are trapped by the current expectations regarding legal syntax.* Analysis indicates that, as a group, judges are not competent intellectuals in the degree of awareness with which they evaluate the categories and procedures of the legal system, the conventional application of which they may, however, manage expertly.

It is a caricature of the judicial process to affirm that judges are wholly arbitrary in interpreting current legal doctrine. In any given period, many expectations about the prescriptions of a legal order are relatively explicit. True, there may be zones of conflict and ambiguity, but there are also zones of assent and explicitness.

A major problem of continuing research is keeping abreast of changing expectations and forecasting responses, with or without manipulative intervention. It is the role of the *lawyer* to intervene in the future and to try to influence the response of courts or other decision-making tribunals authorized to apply prescriptions. It is the role of the *judge* to step into the future and to make up his mind about the interpretation of available doctrines. The *scholar* moves into the future, seeking to clarify the objectives of the legal system in reference to the circumstances affected by controversy.

Political scientists enlarge these perspectives in several directions. As scholars, they are, for instance, relatively free to devote themselves to the study of factors that conditioned past decisions. This comes partly from the fact that, if the political scientist is *not* a practicing lawyer, he has relative freedom from incessant pressure to argue cases. Hence, he can let the flow of current case reports go by for a few months or years while he concentrates on another set of questions, notably historical trends and conditioning factors. Legal scholars, too, may take time out from the immediate pressure of case reports. In our society, however, it is more common for legal scholars to keep prepared for current questions.

An examination of research will show that some of the most daring, long-range studies of legal process have been undertaken by political scientists.[4] Political scientists are more likely to gather "factual" data about the total process of decision than legal scholars, since lawyers are more typically rewarded for "argument" than for "factual summaries" or "scientific generalizations" in regard to facts.

Differences of expected reward (indulgence) are matters of major importance in collaborative projects between legal scholars and political scientists. It is within the accepted routine of lawyers to summarize the briefs submitted to legislative committees, administrative commissions, courts, or related agencies. It is well within the routine of political scientists to discover the pressure groups that tried to influence legislation and administrative or judicial decision. The two strands of research directly supplement each another.

There are, nonetheless, far-reaching differences in the approaches to research characteristic of legal scholars and of political scientists. As a rule, legal scholars are interested in trend research, argumentation, and data summaries (for evidential purposes). Trend research is often necessary to disclose the changes in the interpretation of legal doctrines. Argumentation is, of course, an inescapable feature of every controversy. Data summaries deal with factual materials intended to strengthen an argument. If it is alleged, for example, that unfair trade practices have become more frequent, experts may be consulted to testify to the trend or to call attention to information that corroborates the point.

Political scientists, as social scientists, are oriented to problems that fail to interest many lawyers. They are concerned with general theories of the political process. Hence, they work with theoretical models that, when confirmed by data of observation, explain political events. Thus, political scientists study revolution and counterrevolution, reform and counterreform, rise and spread (or restriction) of political ideology, centralization and decentralization, democratization and antidemocracy, and the like. Lawyers, on the other hand, usually look on these problems as "vague," "ambiguous," and hence of marginal relevance to jurisprudence. Legal training prepares students to feel intellectually ill at ease unless they have rather persuasive arguments at their disposal—that is, a persuasive interpretation of how a given prescription applies to concrete circumstances. Generalizations only partially supported by data "will not stand up in court"; hence, lawyers often assume that they are useless "theories." Such, at least, is the conventional bias.

To some extent, the perspective of lawyers and legal scholars is changing. In many problem areas, for instance, it is of obvious importance to analyze causal factors. This is true of legal administration itself. It is clearly pertinent to consider under what circumstances courts meet heavy case loads and achieve a reasonable level of justice. What methods of selection and training and what ladders of professional advancement contribute to a competent judiciary? What sanctioning methods yield what results?

If political scientists and lawyers are to improve their effective working relations in future years, it will be helpful if they possess a common map of the decision-making and executing processes and of the features in regard to which they have greatest competence and concern.[5] We have previously outlined the seven phases into which it is often convenient to classify the characteristic outcomes exhibited by the decision process of a body politic—intelligence, recommending (promoting), prescribing, invoking, applying, appraising, and terminating.

We have heavily underscored the distinction between conventional and functional uses of terms. Speaking in the conventional language of a body politic, the officials authorized to act in the name of the whole are easily distinguishable. Legal scholars and practitioners are distinctively engaged in describing and manipulating the *formula,* the official prescriptions assumed to constitute the legal system. Although the legislative organs of government are traditionally charged with responsibility for formulating authoritative prescriptions, closer examination shows that legislatures do not monopolize the function. Since prescriptions are patterns of expectations in reference to authority, whatever changes these expectations changes "the law." It is commonplace to recognize—as we have had occasion to repeat—that courts have a hand in making as well as in applying authoritative legal doctrine. To some extent the same point is applicable to every official agency. Going beyond organs of government, "law" is made informally in the shifting expectations current in the market place, the daily routines of family life, and in every institutional activity within the social process. It is, in fact, impossible for any participant in society to resign from the law-making process without departing this life. While there is breath, there is legislation, since expectations regarding authority cannot be escaped.

Phrasing the characteristics of a legal prescription more technically, we repeat that every prescription contains three principal elements—(1) the *primary* norms, such as standards of "fair practice"; (2) the *contingency* norms, which state the factual circumstances under which the primary norms apply; and (3) the secondary, or *sanctioning*, norms that include the negative or affirmative measures available when a primary norm is breached or conformed to.

Because of the prominence of the courts in the decision process in which lawyers play a prominent part, it is convenient to give special consideration to the roles of lawyers and political scientists in the court's work. In the total context of community decision, a judicial organ, we have said, is part of the "application" phase. We refer to the interactions between parties and decision-makers as the judicial "arena" and further distinguish the decisions made by judge or jury as "outcomes" in the flow of relevant events. Preoutcome events fall in two broad categories, namely, events in the arena prior to decision and the prearena occurrences that led to the involvement of the court. Postoutcomes refer to future occurrences affected by the decision, that is, after the immediate impact of the decision on the parties.

A chronological commentary on the controversies that reach the courts during a given period can bring out the interplay between lawyers and political scientists. Lawyers are usually turned to by participants within the social process who assert that they have been value-deprived in some way that contravenes public order; hence, professional assistance is required. However, many potential cases are not prepared for presentation to the authorized decision-makers of the community. They may be settled by negotiation among counsel of the parties, or the client may be convinced that there is no reasonable prospect that the case, if litigated, can be won. We enlarge the scope of preoutcome events to include grievances that are not carried to court and those not brought to the attention of a lawyer, perhaps because the parties are able to settle without assistance. At the other extreme, the aggrieved parties are too ignorant or too weak to engage counsel. In summary:

Prearena (preoutcome) events
Precipitating events
Participants in the social process allegedly experience value
deprivations that are claimed to contravene the authoritative
prescriptions comprising the public order.
Preparatory events
Participants engage counsel who bring claims to the attention of community decision-makers (the court).
Parallel events
Participants experience alleged value deprivations that from
the point of view of the scientific observer are practically
identical to precipitating events, but settlements are obtained
by direct negotiation among the parties, or preparatory activities are not engaged in, and official arenas are not involved.

The direct concern of legal scholars is clear: they examine the
cases brought to the attention of counsel and assess the skill with
which counsel managed the prearena steps of direct negotiation, informal arbitration, or refusal to proceed. Political scientists are qualified as interviewers to obtain information that puts the activity of
counsel and of the legal process itself in context. Among significant
questions are these: To what exent is it true that, at a given time,
various participants in the social process fail to resort to courts because they suspect the impartiality of the judges or are unable to bear
the cost of litigation? Are those who hold these expectations the members of cultural minorities, of low status groups, of particular interest
groups, or of discernible personality types? Legal scholars share an
active concern with such matters. Until recently, however, they have
done little research to bring out the aggregate picture of denial of
justice, and it is to be anticipated that political scientists will be
among the social scientists with whom they will most actively col-
laborate.

When we examine the arena, the first step is as usual to discover
the participants. Lawyers automatically classify many of the relevant
participants according to the conventional technicalities of litigation.
There are parties who are plaintiffs or defendants, and they are represented by counsel who summon witnesses. There are judges, jurors,
and court attendants. Although lawyers are fully aware of other participants, they do not regularly investigate their roles. Political sci-

entists are predisposed to go beyond the judge to examine the composition of the audience in the courtroom and to study the larger audience reached by mass media reporting and comment or whose members are actively engaged in collecting money or striving in other ways to influence the result. Political scientists also focus on the immediate environment that affects the final decision, such as the stream of casual comment by family and friends.

Legal scholars concentrate on the technical claims put forward by counsel on behalf of the parties and the justifications—legal argument, proof—advanced in support of the claims. Political scientists are more disposed by training and professional interest to put these formalities in the context of genuine perspectives and value assets or liabilities of the participants. Not that counselors are oblivious to these matters; on the contrary, they are so aware of them that in many cases they try to keep such factors off the record. As social scientists, political scientists know that it is impossible to arrive at genuine appraisals of the legal process until these elements are competently described in representative instances. Hence, it is necessary that the language of legal technicality be translated into terms that designate value-indulgence or -deprivation. The claim to be a legatee in a given controversy may, when translated, mean that the party is asking the court to increase his wealth by directing that one million dollars from an estate be turned over to him. The principal value at stake in a case may be power, respect, or any of the value categories which can be used to describe the factual context.

When legal claims are put forward, counsel use conventional terms of legal technicality to identify the claimant or the counter-claimant. These symbols of identity—the terms "legatee" or "beneficiary," for instance—do not tell us much about the position of the claimant in the social process. Hence, in order to compare cases, political and social scientists find it necessary to describe the claimants and other participants according to such categories as culture, class, interest, and personality.

The justifications include arguments, that is, assertions that the claim is more in harmony with community prescription than are alternative claims. In summarizing cases, legal scholars tend to restrict the reporting of justifications to the legal terminology. Political scientists, on the other hand, are interested in amplifying the report to reveal the degree to which the language of the legal formula is accompanied by such other symbol patterns of the social myth as religious, ethical, or political doctrines and by "miranda" (folk items) in popular versions of history and prophecy. They are interested, also, in ascertaining such elements that affect credibility of testimony as the class accent of witnesses and a host of pertinent culture, class, interest, and personality factors. Although these matters are of obvious importance to counsel, the tradition has been to treat them in the spirit of the amateur, rather than to welcome systematic observation and analysis.

Most generally defined, the sequence of activities engaged in by counsel constitute the strategy of litigation. It includes the choice of arena, the phrasing of the claims and justifications, and all moves made on reaching the attention of decision-makers. The strategy of litigation depends in large part on the base values at the disposal of the counsel, and this depends mainly on the assets or liabilities, in terms of money and of all other social values, at the disposal of clients. Political scientists are more concerned than lawyers with obtaining an explicit record of such factors.

Judges and jurors approach a given case with predispositions molded by their previous exposure to culture, class, interest, and personality environments. Lawyers pay immediate heed to the previous commitments of judges, seeking to assess predispositions by noting past decisions and opinions. However, until the recent rise of political and social-scientific activity, they had done little to advance the systematic analysis of such factors.

The presiding judge, in particular, begins to respond in a recorded and responsible way from the beginning of a proceeding. His most important base value in the courtroom is the prescription or body of prescriptions that authorize jurisdiction; for example, the strategy of dealing with the motions made by counsel is affected by the prescriptions that relate to admissibility of evidence. Political scientists are interested in the use made by justices of such other value assets as the ethical norms of the community.

Arena preoutcome events

Participants
   Immediate: claimants, counselors, witnesses, court, jury, court attendants, courtroom audiences, etc.
   Other: individuals and groups who hear about a controversy or seek to influence the outcome by raising funds, agitating, etc.

Statements—claims
   Identifications: formally identified plaintiffs, defendants, etc.
   Demands: formally asking decision-maker to value-indulge
      or -deprive self or others, to take appropriate par-
      ticular measures.
   Expectations: fact-form assertions about precipitating
      events or the future.
Statements—justifications
   Arguments in support of claims.
   Proof in support of claims.
Base values and strategies
   Of all participants—assets during controversy.
   Persuasion, coercion.

The final responses of a community decision-maker may be in terms of any value (for example, power—disqualification from or qualification for office; enlightenment—denial of information or access; wealth—loss or gain of property; well-being—hard labor or release; skill—recognition or denial of performance record; affection —loss or recovery of custody of child; respect—discrimination abolished or tolerated; or rectitude—conduct hailed as moral or immoral).

The responses go far beyond the value outcomes sought by the immediate parties to the controversy. There are positive or negative references to the justifications, as well as the claims, advanced to defend or attack the value demands put before the court. Also, the statements made by witnesses are accepted or rejected as part of the support for, or rebuttal of, claims. All who are in any degree identified with the statements endorsed or rejected by judge or jury are value-affected. Counsel for the parties, for example, rise in prestige and eventually perhaps in income and power if they win. Lower court judges are not oblivious to the impact on their reputation of the response of appellate tribunals; in fact, the entire court structure, or even the bar, of a locality may be downgraded if it fails to be sustained on a series of controversial questions.

Political scientists are especially equipped to bring into view the whole context of effects of a given decision or an aggregate of decisions. Legal scholars pay strict attention to the acceptance of a result as a "leading case" that is frequently cited by subsequent judges and hence figures in the calculations of counsel when they advise clients or choose specific claims and justifications in later litigation. But legal scholars are rather less motivated than political scientists to join with other social scientists in examining the continuing effects of the sanctioning measures employed on behalf of public order.

Decision outcome and effect (postoutcome)

Value-indulgence or -deprivation	Participants
	Immediate
	Other
	Statements (those identified with:)
	Claims
	Justifications
	Base values and strategies

Fortunately, the trend of professional interest among legal scholars and practitioners is toward providing information that contributes to the possibility of appraising the judicial institutions of the community. As data become more comprehensive, it becomes increasingly feasible to confront the conventional "legal process" with a functionally disciplined image of the facts of life to date and the outlook for the future. Hence, we can reclassify "officials" according to the functional definition of law as authoritative and controlling. If officials do not in fact exercise, or are not expected to exercise, *severe* sanctions on behalf of public order, they may nonetheless employ *mild* sanctions. In the latter contingency, they are appropriately seen as part of the *civic order* of the body politic, not of the *public order*.

We are somewhat sanguine that political scientists and jurists will be able to work together in future years in view of the fact that strategies of counsel are often based on considerations of the kind that we have said are among the principal factors to which political scientists attach great weight. The choice of court—to take a recurring matter —often depends on intelligence data about the predispositions of the court; this calls for estimates of the political ambitions of the judges and of the expectations that ambitious judges are likely to entertain about the effects for their elevation to a higher court of the alternatives open to them in the present controversy. The political scientist adds motive and technique to the lawyer's special skill with authoritative language and to the lawyer's sophistication and opportunities for inside observation.[6]

The candor and competence required to put the courts into functional perspective are no less indispensable to the adequate appraisal

of all institutions of community decision. Ultimately, lawyers and political scientists will effectively contribute to the evaluation of all
phases of the process of decision at every level, whether transnational,
national, or subnational.

We could multiply the skill groups with which the political scientists of tomorrow will be intimately associated, both at the level of
advanced training and professional performance. Before concluding
the analysis, we propose to open the questions relating to the institutions best adapted to the mature intellectual tasks of political scientists.

NOTES

[1] Political scientists played an important part in modernizing the education
of journalists—to cite a single instance, Ralph D. Casey, now emer-
itus, at the University of Minnesota.

[2] I do not necessarily have in mind the brilliant polemics of political scientist Eugene Burdick and his journalist colleagues. In passing, it
should be acknowledged that some political scientists are also writers
or publicists of professional distinction, among whom may be mentioned Walter Lippmann, Max Lerner, Leo Rosten, Saul Padover,
and Hannah Arendt.

[3] The more technical the field, the more representative of Cook. Cf. W. W.
Cook, *The Logical and Legal Bases of the Conflict of Laws* (Cambridge: Harvard University Press, 1942).

[4] Political scientists now actively engaged in extending quantitative tech-
niques to the study of legal process include H. Pritchett and G. A.
Schubert. The prevailing view of the judiciary is exemplified in J.
Peltason, *Federal Courts in the Political Process* (New York:
Doubleday, 1955). Cf. V. G. Rosenblum, *Law as a Political In-
strument* (New York: Doubleday, 1955). For a normative, critical
approach, cf. W. Berns, *Freedom, Virtue, and the First Amendment*
(Baton Rouge: University of Louisiana Press, 1957).

[5] My perspectives on legal process have been seasoned by association with
colleagues at Yale, in both the Law School and the Graduate
School. Myres S. McDougal and the late George Dession have been
especially close collaborators. A recent guide to the general field is
E. Bodenheimer, *Jurisprudence*, "The Philosophy and Method of
Law" (Cambridge: Harvard University Press, 1962). Also, J. Hall,
Studies in Jurisprudence and Criminal Theory (New York: Oceana
Publications, 1958); C. J. Friedrich, *The Philosophy of Law in His-
torical Perspective* (Chicago: University of Chicago Press, 1958);
W. Friedmann, *Legal Theory* (4th ed.; Toronto: University of To-
ronto Press, 1960). Cf. also, among current contributors, H. A. L.

Hart, *The Concept of Law* (Oxford: Clarendon Press, 1961); A. Ross, *On Law and Justice* (Berkeley: University of California Press, 1959); F. S. C. Northrop, *The Complexity of Legal and Ethical Experience* (Boston: Little, Brown, 1959).

[6] Among many recent collaborations, cf. B. Manning and M. H. Bernstein, the directors of the study by the Special Committee on the Federal Conflict of Interest Laws of the Association of the Bar of the City of New York, *Conflict of Interest and Federal Service* (Cambridge: Harvard University Press, 1960).

10

Centers
for Advanced
Political Science

Which organizational forms are best adapted to the future task of
political science? Organizations are relevant in two ways—by affecting
content of what is considered and by affecting the procedure of consideration. The content pertinent to the integrative solution of problems of public policy falls into the categories of goal, trend, condition,
projection, and alternative. The relevant procedures influence recruitment and the agenda of the problem-solving process.

LIMITATIONS OF THE UNIVERSITY

There are many grounds for rejecting the contemporary university as a satisfactory model for the forms of organization best adapted
to the integrative consideration of fundamental matters of public af-

fairs. For one thing, the number of people involved diminishes the chances that attention will be focused on a common map of past, present, and future events. Leaving aside the students and counting as faculty only those who have achieved the status of instructor or above, it is not unusual to find that nominal colleagues at a university number in the thousands. We often hear of the tens of thousands of students who congregated at various university centers in late medieval times. The central faculty, on the other hand, was often small enough to permit a high degree of mutual awareness and direct intercourse. The contemporary institution of higher learning, though keeping a student body of thousands, has multiplied the faculty until there is little life in common.[1]

To the diluting effect of number, the fact of physical dispersion must be added. The same university frequently operates on several campuses widely separated in space. From the hub of the main, or of each subsidiary, campus, faculties distribute themselves in every direction. Dwellings may be twenty, fifty, or even several hundred miles apart. Travel time may reach four, six, or even more hours.

More drastic than the size and dispersion of university faculties is the fractionalizing effect of modern specialization. For years it has been a theme of lamentation that the unified perspective that allegedly characterized Europe in the Middle Ages no longer exists. The usual account says that once every literate person shared a high degree of intellectual culture. He knew the Judaeo-Christian scriptures and many of the writings of the church fathers and, after the revival of Greek and Roman learning, became acquainted with Aristotle and Plato and with classical poets, dramatists, and historians.

In ancient civilizations, the highest intellectual class was generally saturated with a common image of man and nature. This was evidently true of Chinese and East Indian civilizations, for example.[2]

With the breakup of the world view of earlier times, the intellectual initiative gradually and then rapidly passed to the sciences. Scientists are typically impatient with the history of their subject, since it consists mainly of primitive first approximations and rudimentary instrumentation. Further, they assume that there is little to respect in the pasts of other disciplines, which at best show a few gleaming needles in a haystack of folklore. The advanced training of a physical scientist tends to focus on theoretical models, exploratory designs, and instrumentation.[3]

Academic philosophers, historians, and scholars of the arts have chosen a somewhat different though related path of retreat from the challenge of a comprehensive view. This withdrawal occurs as research competition grows more intense and as graduate schools multiply. Respect and advancement come to depend on publication, and especially on a form of publication that matches the data-rich papers of empirical scientists with citation-rich accumulations. In this evidence-conscious age, one may continue to "appreciate" Dante or Shakespeare. But the proliferation of appreciative remarks presently begins to sound verbose, pretentious, and in fact ridiculous. If the lecturer on the arts has lost his franchise to celebrate the beauty of the beautiful, a similar fate has befallen the instructor in ethics, since there is limited tolerance for his confirmation of the good. Theologians, too, are barely tolerated if they bear witness to their faith and fail to get on with the "solid" task of connecting doctrine with history or morals.

We have had occasion earlier to comment on the empirical, evidence-oriented emphasis of political scientists and of colleagues in psychology, economics, and allied fields of social science; they, too, are affected by the specialized life of graduate schools.

Given the strength of the many tendencies to narrow the focus of attention, it is not difficult to see why universities have lost coherence and faculties have ceased to feel responsible for a currently intelligible and inclusive map of man and nature. Universities have, however, kept the label while abandoning the function of a *universitas*. They have increasingly become post office addresses and holding companies for congeries of particular operations showing no clear sense of common responsibility.

It is, of course, impossible for all members of the intellectual community to give up the struggle for enlightenment and to fail to insist that particular operations, no matter how skillfully executed or how immediately successful, be expressly related to a comprehensive image of man and nature. A memory of vanished unity lingers on. Individual theologians often possess an enormous sense of responsibility for recapturing the ground that their predecessors lost to one another. And there are always speculative minds whose familiar orientation is contextual and who perceive what they do in a broad frame of reference.

Political scientists are predisposed by the traditions of the field to produce at least a few minds in every generation who think contextually and who in contemporary times are alienated by the fragmentation of universities. We have also suggested that the problem-solving experience of political scientists contains a valuable clue to an approach capable of moving in the direction of effective integration. Policy awareness means awareness of the future, and this implies sense of direction, or goal, as one steps out of the past and present. Policy awareness implies the mobilization of all knowledge, whether of trend or condition, that illuminates the shape of things to come or stimulates the invention or evaluation of policy alternatives. The traditional concern of political science with the whole body politic also means that it is relatively easy to focus on the world context.

It is this inclusive problem-solving orientation that enables political science to aid in recovering the idea of a university. Political science does not suffer from the degree of under- or overemphasis on one of the problem-solving tasks that limits the effectiveness of certain other disciplines which might otherwise perform a reintegrative role. For example, political scientists are more concerned with finite time than are theologians and metaphysicians. Political scientists are more explicitly conscious of the world as a whole, and especially of the factors that limit cooperation, than economic theorists have been. They are more accustomed to considering the issues that arise in the clarifying of goal or the invention of policy than are, for example, sociologists or psychologists.

THE EMERGING STRUCTURE

There are grounds for asserting that, in recent times, a new organizational form has begun to emerge that facilitates focusing attention and talent on the problem context of mankind. I refer to centers of study, research, and consultation.

What are the salient features of such a center? One characteristic is *size*. It must be small enough to foster direct interaction. Another is *proximity*. The members need to be sufficiently contiguous to do many things in common. A third feature is *concern for intellectual integration*.

An early deliberate innovation was the Institute for Advanced Study at Princeton, which grew out of Abraham Flexner's unflinching criticism of the hodgepodge of operations carried on by institutions bearing a university label.[4] The essential vision was that of a small, eminent body of scholars who would work independently or jointly as they chose on problems considered strategic for the advancement of knowledge. The senior scholars are also free to cooperate with a limited number of juniors. The most impressive achievements have been in mathematics and mathematical physics, thanks in part to the over-whelming concentration of talent in the persons of Einstein, Weyl, and others.

Another innovation—and one directly related to the subject mat-ter that concerns us—is the Center for Advanced Study in the Be-havioral Sciences at Stanford. As originally conceived, the center provided facilities for a group of established scholars and a more nu-merous group of younger men (about fifty at a time).[5] The chief intellectual stress was methodological and—in the terms of our prob-lem-solving analysis—mainly on conditioning factors. The methodo-logical concern was threefold—(1) to encourage mathematical think-ing or comparably strict methods; (2) to stimulate thinking about social processes in human society by giving consideration to general biological theory; (3) to provide a setting appropriate to the planning of research on problems of importance that are neglected or pursued by inferior methods unless recognized and undertaken by interdisci-plinary teams.

For several reasons, the center did not appoint a permanent nu-cleus after the manner of the Princeton institute. It was generally agreed that the supply of outstanding talent in several fields was short and that the universities would not welcome the permanent removal of outstanding figures. Moreover, the total impact of the leading pro-fessors on the next generation would probably be greater if they con-tinued to function at the universities. A further point was lack of consensus about the truly contributory figures in the behavioral sci-ences or the direction of future growth. In the circumstances, it ap-peared wise to refrain from providing a few senior persons with exceptional influence.

The idea of a center has been adapted to special situations in ways that vindicate the flexibility of the basic plan. Why not employ the center mechanism to further the tempo of integration of university life? This thought has crossed the mind of more than one administra-tor and scholar and has led to the proposal to assign members of a university faculty to temporary, or even permanent, duty at a center operated within the framework of the university. There are obvious difficulties connected with this arrangement, since the members of an existing staff are disposed to think that they themselves are eligible simply because they do competent research.

A center of political science is more suitable than an all-encom-passing "university within a university" to an established institution. The scope of a political science center would be somewhat restricted, since it puts the accent on the policy goals of man or the future of a large community context. Centers of political science could be formed within universities or established as independent entities.

CLARIFIERS OF GOAL

Within any center, it would be important to provide for the participation of individuals whose chief interest and competence was in the clarification of goals. Because of the role played by the concept of responsibility in public policy, this topic is among the most eligible themes for continuing examination. The concept of human dignity, when defined as an overriding goal, includes the ideal of a commonwealth in which all participants act responsibly.

It will be necessary to clarify the levels of educability and education appropriate to various contingencies. For example, what degree of modifiability by experience is necessary to justify inclusion among advanced forms of life? In regard to all candidates (human or not), what levels of educability and education should be required for admission to political arenas in the role of intelligence source, advocate, legislator, peace officer, general administrator, censor, or referee in termination proceedings? What standards are appropriate to the management of sanctions?

The idea of responsibility will no doubt continue to arouse debate over the concept of causal determination.[6] Since the notion of causality gained weight from the achievements of science, it would be helpful to have philosophers of science who are grounded in science among the personnel of a center. The type of question that arises in this connection is such as this: If a subjective event, such as an inner declaration of intent to promote peace, can be explained, does the intention to promote peace cease to be "responsible"? Empirical studies may show, for example, that almost all who have been reared in Quaker families and schooled in Quaker institutions assert that they favor peace. Is a Quaker to be regarded as nonresponsible or irresponsible when he takes this position?

From the point of view of public policy, the answer is in the affirmative if we take the position that a minority culture is strong enough to override the socializing process of the majority. Only those who have been exposed to standard conditioning by the majority culture are, on this definition, to be held responsible by decision-makers who exercise community authority.

However, does not the fact that subjective perspectives and behavioral operations can be conditioned by exposure to the majority pattern signify that everyone is irresponsible or nonresponsible to the extent that the probability of his response can be predicted according to group frequencies? Is an individual acting responsibly only when he violates standard expectations for persons of comparable antecedents?

One interpretation of responsibility approaches the problem by including among the long-range goals of the community the requirement that the authoritative prescriptions of the body politic be enacted and revised by a process in which most of the body politic is eligible to participate and is encouraged to do so. This is part of the usual specification of popular government. The suggestion is that everyone shall be held responsible for conforming to a prescribed norm if the following conditions hold: (1) he has had the opportunity standard to the community to be informed of the norm; (2) he has been exposed to standard levels of conformity to the norm; (3) he has been exposed to the standard opportunity to acquire the knowledge and skill needed to understand what he sees and hears; (4) he has the psychosomatic aptitudes capable of taking advantage of opportunities to acquire cultural patterns; (5) he is in immediate situations where incentives to override the norms are not excessive when appraised according to standard situations of the community.

Consider the case of a self-declared conscientious objector in a democratic body politic. Should such claimants be regarded as nonresponsible for conforming to the norm of military service? If the claimants have been reared in a minority community, it can be said that they have been underexposed to the standard levels of expression favorable to conformity and that they have been exposed to exceptional indoctrination against the norm.

Or consider a band of assassins from a foreign country who attempt to liquidate the president in order to rivet the attention of the world on the sad plight of their country. We may regard an assassin as nonresponsible if we discover that he is suffering from a serious psychotic disorder that disposes him to attack alleged persecutors. We may also suggest that he be considered nonresponsible if we learn that the assassin has been in an exceptionally provocative situation (as in melodrama—his mother was raped and enslaved by an American plantation manager; he was beaten and taunted by his neighbors and playmates as a foreign bastard; he was befriended by an anarchist printer and provided with funds and guns by a secret cell of superpatriots).

Questions of policy regarding responsibility are always with us, regardless of the novelty of the situation in which the body politic finds itself. In the space age, we shall face rather novel problems. For instance, if our astronauts establish contact with a superior civilization —superior in intellectual capability and scientific achievement—shall we claim exemption from full responsibility in the astropolitical community? Shall we analogize ourselves to an isolated primitive society suffering from absence of opportunity or to the gibbons, gorillas, and dolphins whose protocultures reflect organic constraint?[7]

FORECASTERS

In addition to the clarification of goals, centers of political science would encourage sustained attempts to anticipate contingencies. Given the dynamic impact of science and technology, it is obvious that the flow of communication between scientists and the center would be of high priority. It would also be essential to develop a corps of political scientists at home with science by virtue of double training.

Double competence, by the way, is no novelty in the history of political science. Cooper, for example, was a professor of both chemistry and political economy who lectured in political science, a combination that is not yet found, I think, at so advanced an institution as M.I.T.[8] It is part of the traditional lore of textbooks on political theory that John Locke studied medicine; and there is always the commanding image of Aristotle, who is only intelligible today as, say, the editor-in-chief of the Encyclopedia of the Social Sciences—and other encyclopedias—of his day.

It would be fortunate for a center of political science that physical and biological scientists have a great tradition of trying to communicate with the lay public. In England, the tradition goes even further back than the Darwinian controversy, which brought the tireless, eloquent, and cogent T. H. Huxley to the fore as a popularizer of evolution. In our day, we have had the advantage of a contemporary Huxley in the exposition of biology and an entire galaxy of top-flight astronomers, among whom it is almost invidious to choose even a figure of such distinction and dedication as Harlow Shapley.[9]

Part of the tradition of communicating with a wider audience has helped to motivate and legitimize the science fiction of our day. Many outstanding figures in the scientific community contribute to the efflorescence of this type of literature. They have done it in a playful spirit, but many of them have approached the task with an underlying serious purpose. It is only too obvious that mankind is drastically unprepared to cope with the grave new world into which we are being catapulted by science and technology. Furthermore, the education of the poets and novelists of our time has left almost all of them un-equipped to feel at home in man's new habitat or in company with hitherto-undreamed-of forms of life.[10] Aldous Huxley's *Brave New World* is an epochal exception; so, too, are the remarkable contribu-tions to science fiction of C. Day Lewis, the English poet; Karel Capek, the whimsical Czech; and the prophetic H. G. Wells.

Among working scientists, one thinks at once of Fred Hoyle, of Oxford and Cornell, whose *Black Cloud* is an exercise in defining the conception of life. In the story, astronomers detect the approach of a cloud formation from outer space that blocks out the sun and subjects the earth to cold that destroys hundreds of millions of people. But the truly remarkable characteristic of the cloud is only gradually per-ceived by watching scientists. It follows a course that can only be ex-plained by assuming that it is alive, that is, that it responds to complex inner patterns of its own instead of reacting in simple fashion to the immediate environment.

Isaac Asimov poses questions of the same kind, though perhaps more immediate. He imagines a future civilization on earth that relies on intricate servomechanisms to perform its tedious, laborious, danger-ous, and superspecialized intellectual tasks. In order to forestall the overthrow of man's dominance, all robots (the book is *I, Robot*) are constructed on such a plan that the following code is built into each individual: "A robot may not injure a human being, or, through in-action, allow a human being to come to harm. A robot must obey the orders given it by human beings except where such orders would con-flict with the First Law. A robot must protect its own existence as long as such protection does not conflict with the First or Second Law."[11] Given the complex, even refined, discriminations of which the "machine" is capable, what justification is there for permanent, built-in servitude?

In many ways, the book that succeeds above all others in convey-ing the majesty of the universe and the inexhaustible abundance and activity of life and nature is the product of a professional philosopher whose soaring imagination was kept under exemplary discipline throughout. I refer to Olaf Stapledon.[12]

The contemplation of the future appropriate to centers of po-litical science is no undisciplined fantasy. It requires a continuing in-ventory of the trend of scientific knowledge in every field and a regular sampling of each area for recent findings, methods, and specu-lations. The world of pure mathematics and logic is not excluded; on the contrary, mathematical literacy among political scientists is already rising. The postulational pattern of thinking pioneered by mathematicians and logicians has permeated the intellectual culture of our time, with implications for political science that have been imperfectly articulated.

Interplay between Forecast and Goal

It is to be expected that the life of a major center would greatly accelerate the drawing of these implications. For example, is an element of arbitrariness, even capriciousness, inescapable with a postulated, a stipulated, mode of thought? Is all thought postulational, the difference being that some procedures are self-aware and systematic whereas others remain subliminal and chaotic? How are we to integrate the element of arbitrariness with the demand for a firm ground from which to derive value assertions?

In such a context, it is pertinent to consider the wisdom of defining "arbitrariness" in words that authorize it to be used to refer to all subjective commitments. Suppose we agree that subjective events are in a time sequence measured in microseconds. Let us designate a subjective event at a given time as "postulating human dignity (or indignity)" or "God's will" as the events to be sought in the future. Shall we say that such a postulate is "arbitrary"?

My proposed reply is, "not necessarily." A distinction can be drawn between postulations that follow the consideration of a problem—such as the appropriate goals of man—and postulates having no such antecedent. The latter give cursory attention to the context. I propose the label "arbitrary" for patterns at the lower end of the continuum and suggest calling the patterns at the upper end "rational." I further stipulate that the thinker shall meet at least the minimum criteria of responsibility in terms of culture and personality referred to above.

INTERPLAY WITH THE SCIENCES: ASTRONOMY

Unlike mathematics and logic, many sciences are both analytic and descriptive. Among the latter, the political science center would keep in close communication with astronomy for reasons that have been sufficiently indicated. Astronomy has entered a phase in which its practitioners will have more in common with political scientists than they have had for many generations. Ever since astronomers shook themselves loose from astrology, they have appeared to themselves and others to be cultivating a mission that is purely scientific, uncontaminated by temptations to intervene in and control cosmic phenomena.[13] Today astronomers are busily collaborating in "astro-meddling" on a huge though primitive scale. Their knowledge is exploited to launch artificial satellites and to release missiles and energies that may damage astral bodies or upset the balance of electromagnetic phenomena.

It is reasonable to predict that sooner or later astronomers will begin to think systematically about their potential role as redesigners of the universe. At first their effect on the face of the heavens may be much less than the effect on the water of a boat designed by an engineer. But engineering has now come to a point where it remakes rivers. Can we calculate the optimum orbits of the sun and other stars that could serve the needs of life? Will it be possible to locate zones of tension where forces are easily balanced and hence vulnerable to the planned use of comparatively small amounts of energy? Can calculated programs of conservation modify the climate and surface conditions that prevail on the natural satellites of the stars and thereby obtain millions of habitats for man and other advanced forms of life?

Physics and Chemistry

When physicists and chemists became detached from alchemy,[14] they repressed tendencies to think of speculative models that would imply a cosmic plan or a randomly structured sequence in the organization of matter and energy. When synthetic chemistry developed and molecular combinations previously unknown in nature were created in profusion, it became permissible to assume a more positive orientation to chemical evolution. Chemical forms were now perceived as *phased* phenomena; photosynthesis, for example, seemed to occupy a strategic position as a precondition of life, which in turn preconditioned the emergence of synthetic forms in nature. As research progressed, many dividing lines that were supposed to separate organic and inorganic realms grew dim and vanished. Wendell Stanley made the point with telling impact by showing the ambiguous, interchangeable, or marginal character of the tobacco mold.[15] Physics was meanwhile undergoing sensational reconstruction. The interconvertibility of matter and energy, when recognized, did away with an intellectual chasm,[16] and some observations suggested that even the deployment of small particle-energy units was not independent of orbit "rightness" and "leftness" in direction of motion. Can something be made of the evolutionary sequence among the various "units" of physical nature?

If we are in the midst of known evolutionary sequences—astral, atomic, molecular—is it not plausible that evolution continues? Moreover, if the circuitry of events by way of the human brain or of corresponding central processes of integration in living forms is part of the total process, is it not reasonable to infer that the events we call "subjective" are not only expressive of "evolution" to date but also serve as links giving shape to the future? In a word, are not the clarification of goals and the inventing and evaluation of alternatives in the context of trend, condition, and projection interdependent components of the universal manifold of events?

Cosmic Evolution

Since there are grounds for affirming that human goals are part of, and interact with, other events comprising the cosmic manifold, the fusion of interest between political scientists, on the one hand, and physicists and chemists, on the other, becomes as significant for cosmic evolution as the consortium referred to above between political scientists and astronomers. Hence, the wisdom of providing such mechanisms as centers for occasions of confrontation and cooperation among qualified, articulate, and motivated persons.

This point remains valid if we accept the view that random interactions among events can lead to the patterning of phenomena in ways that seem to imply deliberate plan, though no such plan can be shown to exist. Place living cells of a small organism under heat bombardment. It can be shown that the predispositions of the organism are so organized that an ascertainable range of behavioral adjustments to the environment can be made, in addition to internal adjustments. Let us imagine further that the organism displays these responses at random. Suppose that it can be shown that the organism will die if heat bombardment reaches certain cell nuclei at a given intensity (in short, a range of lethal responses is known). Perhaps random movements by an aggregate of cells under bombardment produce a narrowing of the cell surfaces exposed to the most intense heat and thereby preclude a lethal response. Imagine now that surviving organisms reproduce their kind by means of molecular messages to the next generation that contain keys to the building of new organisms. These "information packets" are also subject to change when exposed to various environments, and they change within a potential range of readjustment. A hypothesis of randomization is that a "thinned surface determinant" is among the possible readjustments

and that, if results are nonlethal, the new pattern can become geneti-
cally stable. To the lay observer, it would seem that the organism has
deliberately planned to protect itself against deadly heat exposure.

The same mode of random analysis applies to brain behavior.
Physicists and chemists are attempting to discover the potential range
of response at any location in the brain when synchronized with any
other site. Light has recently been thrown on a mechanism that sta-
bilizes response under stated conditions.[17]

I have commented on these points because political scientists have
not as a rule been aware of the context in which problems of conscious
choice are currently seen in the community of science. There is no
denying that subjective events occur; after all, no scientist pretends to
be wholly unconscious. The brain chemist's task is to describe with
greater preciseness the "nonsubjective" precipitants, concomitants, and
consequences of subjective events. As matters now stand, "gaps" are
narrowing in "time-space," but they are far from abolished in "figure"
(experienced content).

An appropriate continuing task for political scientists and physical scientists at a center would be to keep up with the operational
indexes employed by "self" and "other" observers in designating subjective and nonsubjective events.

We have said that the testimony of physical and biological scientists would be essential to the center if we were to anticipate the
shape of things to come and hence to give policy consideration to
contingencies before they have restricted our range of choice. A center
would undoubtedly draw on an unending succession of scientists and
engineers for brief reports such as do not necessitate resident membership.

But the principal goal to be served by the inclusion of scientists
in the work of the center is more fundamental to the growth of
knowledge than the anticipation of contingencies. We have directed
attention to the remarkable fact that a turning point has been reached
in the work of every scientific discipline. Even astronomy—and possibly nuclear physics—has come to involve the observer as part of the
phenomena. This involvement goes beyond the familiar point that the
observer, by affecting the immediate field of observation, influences
the records obtained by his instruments. The novelty in the case of
astronomy, for instance, is that human subjectivity is beginning to enter the data of astronomy, most obviously in the creation of "artificial" satellites.

If we postulate a universe of events, there can be no such phenomenon as an "artificial" event. Subjective events of goal formulation are in the universal manifold as surely as is the realized satellite.

The crucial point is that man is taking *all* evolution into his hands whether *his* evolution as a species, the planned introduction of novel forms of life, or the evolutionary future of the cosmos. The circuiting of events through the internal processes of man and other higher forms of life is the policy-making process through which evolution can be affected.

Given a potentiality of this kind, political science comes to play a crucial role in the clarification of goals and strategies within the decision process, not only for man, not only for such advanced forms of life as are created or discovered, but for the universe as a whole.

A Sample Theory:
The Cosmic Role of Decision

How shall we conceive of subjective events in the universal manifold? Undoubtedly, this question will continue to occupy a central position in the problems of man and his future. At present, the complex tasks that we recognize as rational problem-solving occur in organisms possessing a brain, namely, a central organ that appears to be the site of information input, initiation, and execution.

It cannot be said, however, that the presence of an intricate set of circuits is a sufficient explanation of the occurrence of complex subjectivity. An alternative hypothesis, for example, is that subjectivity is a specific energy localized only when certain catalytic preconditions occur, for example, when the concentration of circuits and of electrochemical energies reaches a necessary level.

A distinguishing mark of subjective events (in addition to "awareness") is referentiality, that is, referring in the present to events that may be at a distance in time-space and which may never have been brought to the focus of attention (of or by the referring ego) in previous sequences of subjective events. Subjective events of problem-solving clarify future operations and hence guide the processes of nature to the purposes conceived by one part of nature, namely, the part that achieves a focal center of circuiting. In principle, a continually redirected flow of events can be progressively subordinated to the goals conceived in central decision structures. Decision structures in which man participates may become exceedingly intricate, especially if forms of higher life are discovered or brought into existence.

In the light of these reflections on subjectivity, it seems that the principal role of subjective events is to redesign the future patterns of physicochemical energies and masses. Tampering with the future, then, is the distinguishing point or, to put it another way, tampering with time.

Imagine that the universe of events is an expression of one fundamental energy which we shall designate "duration," an operation that leaves the term "time" free to perform its everyday task of designating perceived sequences. Imagine, further, that the energy of duration is finite; that is, no matter how gigantic in terms of ordinary human experience the magnitudes involved, the universe will eventually become void.

The next step in the speculative construct is to allow for the possibility that the flow of duration toward voidness can be interfered with. Since all energy is postulated as duration, this requires us to imagine that duration becomes divided against itself and in so doing postpones the approach of voidness. Timing is paralyzed, as it were, into patterns that preclude the release of energy in the fundamental form of duration.

Hence we conceive of mechanical, chemical, electrical, in fact, all derived forms, of energy as patterns of captured and at least temporarily imprisoned duration. In accordance with the equivalence of mass and energy, the patterns of mass can be explained under various conditions that permit us to locate particles or waves in configurations of micro- or macromagnitude.

Although the evolution of the stars appears in universal perspective to be a grandiose means of organizing and retaining the energy of duration, nevertheless present knowledge suggests that astral bodies contain the seeds of their destruction and eventually fail to maintain themselves.[18]

The evolution of life seems to offer another strategy by which the approach to voidness can be deferred. Living forms are formidable fixers and users of energy. This has led to the description of life as an "open system," in contrast to the "closed systems" of physics and chemistry.[19] The open system is a site for the generation of energy on a huge scale; hence, we conceive of life as a highly successful means whereby the energy of duration is caught and held.

These considerations point to the distinctive role of higher forms of life in the universal manifold of events. The setting of goals and the adoption of strategies can defer the dissipation of the energy of duration into voidness. This may be accomplished by tapping the Niagara of duration energy to provide energy of subjectivity and to guide the future flow of other energies into patterns whose perpetuation forestalls dissipation into voidness.

A critical feature of the present speculative model is the generation of conflict in the stream of duration. What is the simplest postulate that would allow such contradictions to occur? We can generalize the image introduced by Planck, since jumps from various points in a random pattern of direction, length, and figure would contain conflicting possibilities.[20]

A Check-List of Value Projections

Among the immediate preoccupations at a center would be the task of estimating the impact of science and technology on fighting potential and hence on the balancing of power. I am among those who have long advocated spending billions to develop a less destructive system of weapons than we have traditionally employed in international politics and in police work. The "paralysis bomb" is presumably coming closer as our command of brain chemistry improves. The objective is to incapacitate the target temporarily and to permit him to revive with no organic damage from the experience.

As a denial device, the effect of the paralysis weapon resembles that of censorship on the mind. There are also in prospect chemical instruments whose role is more positive, hence akin to propaganda or indoctrination. It is generally agreed by qualified specialists at present that chemicals (drugs) do not enhance the capability of an individual, but that they may be of enormous importance in enabling a human being to live up to his highest potential.[21]

This modest proposition greatly understates the significance of the drugs now known or in prospect. Even a partial inventory calls attention to the alleviation of pain, the temporary or enduring cure of psychic and somatic ailments, the fostering of equable moods suitable to congenial human relations, the suspension of fatigue in periods of emergency, the encouragement of exhilarated moods of relaxed enjoyment, the stimulation of fantasy for purposes of creative thinking, the suspension or control of procreation, and the stimulation or control of sexual and other bodily appetites.

The use of combined chemical, communicative, and small-group controls for political purposes is a subject that has received a blaze of public attention in recent years, and properly so, since in the past the pertinent questions of public policy have been dealt with feebly or sporadically. It would be one of the main challenges of a multidisciplinary political science center to explore standards of authoritative prescription designed to safeguard at least a minimum sphere of responsibility. Which zones of privacy are to be protected against intrusion by official or unofficial persons?

A continuing preoccupation of political science centers would be to anticipate the significance of science and technology for production. In this context, a leading question is: How superfluous will most human beings become for other than a consumer's role? It is probable that technological innovations will provide in abundance the molecules required for human sustenance. Similarly, there are grounds for predicting that buildings and other structural forms can be put together, moved, or demolished with much the same nonchalance that some Pacific islanders show in manipulating a palm leaf.[22]

Political thinkers have traditionally approached the prospect of universal affluence with misgivings. In the United States, it is facile to suggest that the categorical imperative to work and save was intensified by the ideological and operational patterns of New England Puritans and that these social formations brought to the New World an outlook that was a peculiarly pure example of the capitalistic warp of Protestantism.[23] However this may be, a long-term cyclical movement in human culture may be upon us, and the elimination of work may be imminent. If we welcome the emancipation of man from work —in the sense of occupations imposed as a condition of livelihood— ingenuity will be required, since the transition to self-direction can precipitate the anxieties and uncertainties of which Erich Fromm memorably wrote. The task is a strategy of escape *to* freedom by overcoming the residues of past socialization.[24]

Archaeology, History, and Anthropology

That a political science center would draw on colleagues in history, archaeology, and the adjacent social sciences is to be taken for granted. The links between students of folk society—the distinctive subject matter of social anthropology—and political science have been closer in recent years as whirlwind modernization added to the turbulence of politics in Asia, Africa, South America, and many heretofore-isolated island communities.[25] In future years, the data of anthropology will be highly pertinent to the consideration of various problems that are likely to grow into large dimensions. We have already referred to the obsolescence of work. Some folk societies have long been accustomed to relative exemption from work. Is it true that they have devoted themselves assiduously to the cultivation of congenial human relationships and therefore achieved a sociable, affectionate, and lively style of life? Or, on the other hand, has exemption from serious responsibility favored the rise of sensual and tyrannical personalities who rule by intimidation? Perhaps we shall find that the dominance attained by the domineering element in society depends on the possibility of exploiting the fears that are kept alive by such occasional disasters as pestilence, flood, and earthquake. This source of tyranny will presumably recede as the scientific image of the world moves toward universality.

Anthropology, archaeology, and history are inexhaustible sources of data on every phase of man and culture, and political science will draw on various parts of this repository as problems gain in urgency. It is also true that the scientific advantage will not always be on one side. In the past, the questions raised by students of government and law have often provided a sense of priority for scholars who work in archaeology, history, and anthropology. Sometimes, it is true, political science has been slow to assimilate the answers given to its questions. This is partly because recent Western political theory has been caught between two dogmatic images of primitive man—the pastoral fantasy of Rousseau and the bellicose nightmare of Hobbes. As anthropological and archaeological data accumulate, the idea of a social contract seems inappropriate to preliterate people. It also seems to exaggerate the role of climactic events and of rational agreement in place of the incremental growth of culture.

It is possible to affirm today the the outline of a working synthesis between political science conceptions and the data of archaeology, history, and anthropology is in sight. Centers of political science would expedite the synthesis and draw further implications for policy and science.

Ideas that were dimly perceived or figuratively expressed in Western European theory have been greatly clarified by new knowledge. The bucolic image of primitive man does in fact approximate the style of life achieved by many folk societies. Listen to the late Robert Redfield's characterization of the folk community as a moral entity:

> The primitive and precivilized communities are held together essentially by common understandings as to the ultimate nature and purpose of life. . . . Humanity attained its characteristic, long-enduring nature as a multitude of different but equivalent systems of relationships and institutions each expressive of a view of the good. Each precivilized society was held together by largely undeclared but continually realized ethical conceptions.[26]

But this is not the whole story of early man. When we complete Redfield's picture, we find that the external arena in which folk societies interacted with one another resembles nothing so closely as Hobbes's image, if we edit it to show that it was the hand of the *group* that was raised against the foreign *group,* rather than the hand of each individual against every other. The syndrome of parochialism was precipitated by, and in turn consolidated in, the arena where the expectation of violence prevailed.

The conception of social contract becomes meaningful if we redefine it to refer, not to the beginning of orderly group life, but to the origin of urban culture or civilization, which carried with it literacy, legal codes, bureaucracy, taxation, and the concomitant weakening of kinship identifications. We have evidence that however drawn-out the preurban life of man, civilizations took shape with astonishing speed. The creativity of man flowered exuberantly in the opportunities that urban specialization could afford. The ideas of sudden development and of the important role played in urban life by rational methods of articulating and solving problems do not exaggerate the situation.

In company with many if not most Western thinkers, Rousseau and Hobbes were acutely conscious of their individuality and of their alienation from many of the traditional institutions of the society in which they lived. Under the stress of ego sensitivity, they gave currency to a dichotomy that readily lends itself to misinterpretation. They opposed an entity called the "individual" to an entity called "society," and they imagined that the origin of society was the mystery to be explained. It was this imagined need of explaining why gamboling lambs or bloodthirsty lions quit gamboling or pouncing that led to the conception of a social contract and varied its provisions accordingly.

Psychology

If archaeology, history, and anthropology have provided a corrected map of the past of organized politics, we must credit social psychology with helping to explain the mechanisms whereby interacting individuals achieve both culture and individuality. It is unthinkable that any center of political science would cut itself off from these disciplines.

The theoretical model that commends itself today recognizes that a social process of any kind, whether involving human actors or not, is a distinctive configuration within the universal manifold of events.

The distinctiveness of a social process resides in the traits of the actors and the traits of interaction. The participants are alive; we have already said that living systems are more than objects passively affected by their surroundings. On the contrary, they behave, and this means that they modify what they do by passing potential act-completions through an inner circuit. While passing through an inner circuit, the various influences originating in the environment are also integrated, as are all the predisposing features of the organism. The predispositions—such as demand for food—are residues of past interactions with the environment plus current demands arising in the system.

The social process of organisms of any kind is never adequately described as "individuals versus the whole." If the whole of any society is divided into two hostile parts, the situation is most clearly described as one group of "individuals" modified by collective factors versus another group of "individuals" modified by collective factors. If one biological organism seems to oppose all the others, the same point applies; it is an "individual" modified by collective factors who is opposing all other "individuals" modified by collective factors.

If we phrase the problem as "the individual versus society," we confuse by implying that society is *not* composed of individuals or that the individual is not shaped by interacting with others who compose society.

The traditional mode of opposing the individual to society is sometimes thought of as an opposition between "human nature" and "society," or "culture." The connotation is usually that the genetic constitution endows the individual with needs and capabilities that cannot be sufficiently gratified in social life. Hence, man is invariably at war with his own creation.

This theoretical model may serve to describe history without foreclosing the possibility that future cultures or genetic structures can be more smoothly adjusted to one another. Even in regard to the past, it is possible to call attention to many human beings living at many times and places who have given no indication of being dissatisfied with their societies. But it is also possible to call attention to millions of men and women who have given drastic evidence of dissatisfaction in the forms of rebellion, murder, or suicide. It is to be observed that much recorded dissatisfaction is not aimed at society, but at nature, for nature is often niggardly of fertile soil and propitious climate and is given to earthquake, flood, storm, poisonous plants and snakes, and to other dangerous animals and murderous micro-organisms.

As matters stand today, it is "original nature plus some patterns of culture plus some features of nature" that may culminate either in gratification or lack of it. Experimental psychology provides us with a picture of man's predispositions that confirms two points of relevance here—natural impulses at given stages of life may conflict, and mechanisms of conflict adjustment are themselves part of original nature.

One of the most dramatic confrontations of "man" and "society" in recent times was made by Freud when he portrayed the unconscious dimensions of man's original nature as constituted in such a way that it is almost unthinkable to imagine that man can ever achieve high levels of enduring gratification. It must be pointed out, however, that Freud's methods of research and therapy brought to light evidence of a different kind. His data were never demonstrably about original predispositions; they always referred to predispositions as modified by exposure to particular civilizations, classes, interests, and to systematic adjustment of personality. The data of psychoanalysis are "man plus particular patterns of culture plus particular exposures to nature." Any hypotheses about inborn predisposition, whether in reference to direction or to strength, are open to further investigation.[27]

A continuing question for any future center of political science is whether, as interdisciplinary data accumulate, the present balance of emphasis on "original nature" versus that on "culture" must be changed, especially in reference to such profoundly important and damaging institutions as the divided world arena. At present, the evidence weighs heavily on the side of cultural patterning. The present world arena appears to express the self-perpetuating strength of conflicting cultural syndromes of parochialism as they modify human beings.[28] The solution appears to lie in the rise of a civilization of universal identities, value demands, and pacific expectations.

At the same time, the microscopes of psychoanalysis and of other specialized forms of inquiry have traced in detail the destructive consequences of many social practices and institutions now prevailing on the globe. The implication is that changing constellations of destructive factors veto the tendencies working in favor of peaceful unification of world public order.

If a center of political science is to keep an informed eye on the changing map of institutional and cultural knowledge, it would be necessary to arrange for intermittent exposure to representative specialists in the various social institutions and regions of the world community.

Political scientists must themselves carry the primary burden of describing and explaining the flow of political institutions throughout the globe. This task is of such fundamental importance to the profession that we have given rather extended consideration in preceding chapters to the problems involved.

THE ROTATIONAL CYCLE

For the moment, it will suffice to call attention to major institutional specialties that must find a place in the rotational cycle of any such center. First, we mention specialists in the numbers and the physical and mental states of man and of any organisms in which man comes to have particular interest.

In the years immediately ahead, the significance of the population explosion and the feasibility of various policies in regard to it will continue to occupy the minds of people at any center. At the moment, chemical means and surgical devices for limiting conception are known. In estimating the wisdom of alternative programs, we must not lose sight of the fact, hinted in passing above, that progress in astronavigation and settlement may be used to alleviate the pressure of numbers on living standards.

Perhaps the most tantalizing long-run question for a center to think about is how to use scientific knowledge to design or redesign advanced forms of life. For instance, it has long been a favorite proposal of some that man's famous destructive potential should be tamed by genetic means. It is not out of the question to think of modifying the genetic message that is part of every germ cell in such a way that whole generations will be altered and tamed. Actually, the precise nature of the proposed modification is ambiguous. Furthermore, it is important to give weight to the point that, if a strain of men is bred which is inhibited from anger, rage, or strong self-assertion, though capable of love and gentleness, the result may be a flood of victims for unreconstructed members of the species and of other advanced forms of life.

Among the specialists at the center would be students of communication ranging from linguists to engineers. One long-range problem in this field relates to the design of life and society. Why not aim at forms of life able to exchange messages directly from brain to brain, dispensing with the clumsy installations now required to conduct mass and person-to-person communication? What consequences are likely to follow the acquisition of interbrain communicative capability? One immediate demand would presumably be to perfect the means of screening unwelcome messages. If "mind reading" goes along with the new technology, the demand for privacy will also become acute.

In this connection, the ability of individuals to achieve empathic relations with others would be of great importance for human understanding and solidarity. It is recognized by artists that empathy is not invariably associated with sympathy, since the divining of the inner experience of others is not always connected with willingness to enter into the moods and images of another person.[29] Brain-to-brain communication would probably identify those human beings who are limited in sympathy as well as in empathy, and this might result in a more refined process of social selection in which genuinely benevolent characters have an advantage.

A more immediate potentiality in the field of communication is the emancipation of the individual audience member from his present dependence on program directors. The ideal equipment for this purpose would enable each of us to send his "pick-up" equipment anywhere at any time. If one is *not* in the frame of mind to watch the debate on the floor, one may beam on the court or on the work of a commission.

Specialists in education would be of great importance at the center, since every important innovation in adult culture carries implications for the socializing practices of schools, families, neighborhoods, and in fact everyone who affects the preadult. Much time would be given to working out the most effective ways to employ "teaching machines" in society. What are the proper limits of "conditioning"? Questions similar to the problems of chemical or genetic taming of man and advanced forms of life occur here.

Political scientists have a tradition of great sensitivity to policies affecting love and sexuality, partly because factors of this kind have been notoriously difficult to subordinate to comprehensive visions of collective achievement. The loyalties generated in the small family and extended kin group are frequently in opposition to the state, which traditionally disrupts the private lives of men and women in the name of war, preparation for war, or devotion to projects that eliminate family life. Tension has been everlasting between large, community-wide organizations (church, army, civil service) and families or intermediate associations.

There is a possibility of emancipating sexuality from procreation and thereby eliminating some of the considerations traditionally invoked to justify the limitation of sexual interstimulation to married **partners and to oppose relations among unmarried partners of the** same or the opposite sex. Aside from measures designed to prevent violent quarrels, what can be said in terms of deference to man's freedom of choice about the norms appropriate to the emerging world?

REPRESENTATION ACCORDING TO INTELLECTUAL TASK

We may summarize the composition of centers of political science by calling attention to the variety of emphases that must obtain if all five intellectual tasks are to be performed with distinction. A rotating arrangement would presumably be necessary to achieve a sample of the intellectual division of labor and of the contemporary map of knowledge. If a nucleus of permanent members existed, the chief aim would be to supplement their approaches. In any case, the choice of personnel would be by much more exacting criteria than simply by subject matter. Intellectual alertness and scope are indispensable to the successful working of a collegial venture like the center. When these qualities are present, they hold in check the "occupational paranoia" not infrequently endemic among able scholars. After all, exaggerated estimates of the contributions of the self are only tenable when the mind is dull or the scope of a discipline is minuscule.

For the intellectual task of clarifying the goals of the center, we have indicated above that specialists in the *grounding* as well as in the *specification* of preferred outcomes would be consulted. In our society, we think at once of professional theologians, metaphysicians, ethical theorists, and mathematicians.

In connection with the examination of trend, condition, and projection every analytic-empirical specialty contains potential candidates. Some candidates would contribute mainly to problems of method that crop up in the task of forming theoretical models to guide research or in the gathering and processing of data at various observational standpoints in the manifold of events. In this context, we have in mind mathematicians, logicians, and statisticians, especially those accustomed to dealing with biological and social processes.

We would give prominence to the physical sciences at centers of political science largely because expert testimony by specialists in these various fields is indispensable to the projecting of contingencies. Some scientists deal with complex structures in the natural order. We have astronomers, and especially cosmologists, in mind. The earth sciences also come into this category, since geology, physiography, and meteorology deal with configurations of matter and energy in time. Strictly speaking an "earth science" is needed for every star, planet, and sat-

ellite, since each astral structure is a large, patterned sequence requiring individual study. The "life sciences" also belong among the
larger configurations and cross-refer to astronomy and paleontology
in connection with problems of evolution.

Physics and chemistry deal with the microstructures and functions of the processes of nature—molecules and atoms, mass and energy. Once an entity has been identified, the search begins to describe
its distribution throughout the cosmos, the earth, and all living forms.
Hence, our map of the universe is continually refined as more subtle
entities are identified and their configurations delineated.

Besides the members drawn from the physical and biological sciences, a vigorous center of political science would systematically include specialists in history, prehistory, and the other social sciences.

Psychology would require rotations within the field in order to
keep in touch with the changing views of the basic potentialities of
original nature and the distribution of predispositions among individual members of the species. Comparative psychology, physiology, neurology, and brain chemistry are among the disciplines that intersect
in the study of fundamental structures and functions.[30]

Prehistory, history, and social anthropology must be relied upon
to provide a map of the succession of human cultures.

Economic values and institutions are illuminated by all the social
sciences. However, it would be important to bring actively into a
center academic and business economists and economists with experience in stimulating economic growth in both socialist and capitalist
economies.

The study of communication today includes specialists in linguistics and on the engineering of communication networks specialized in
mass and particular media. Since the distinctive value outcome affected by communication is enlightenment, the study of current information grades over to organizations and persons who engage in
research.

Obviously, a center would draw continually on specialists in communication. It would also be important to associate with a center
population analysts and public health and social medicine specialists.
Social biology is an area necessitating close ties with biological sciences generally.

The study of occupational, professional, and artistic skill groups
is the province of sociologists, economists, political scientists, and particularly of educators. A center must include within its agenda specialists in all phases of socialization and professionalization.

The family and other institutions of intimacy seem likely to undergo profound changes. Hence, the center would draw on all who study these relationships.

That the respect structure of society should move toward mobility and the recognition of merit are axioms of all who accept human dignity as an overriding objective of policy. But caste forms are deeply entrenched, and the center would need to be in contact with scholars in touch with the social class systems of the world community.

The center would also draw on scholars who specialize in the history of religion and morality.

Political scientists would be recruited from the several fields within the profession, such as the history of doctrine; jurisprudence; law; and the structure of government, politics, and administration at international, national, provincial, and local levels.

THOUGHT AND ACTION

Although we have emphasized the place of political science in the intellectual community, it is not our intention to suggest that centers of political science restrict their membership to full-time scholars and scientists. On the contrary, we are favorably impressed by the mutual enrichment that follows when men of action and scholars are brought together in circumstances favorable to serious exchange of experiences and of views. In this interchange, it is not to be assumed that the division of labor between the men of action who report experience and the scholars who analyze and interpret will be clear-cut. Reflective and creative minds are not limited to full-time teachers, researchers, and advisors. Nor are significant experiences of active affairs a monopoly of the professional politician, businessman, and administrator. Personalities are too varied in motivation, skill, and exposure to life for the traditional images to apply. The modern intellectual is more likely to live at a communication center than in the isolation of a tower, whether ivory or glass, and the modern decision-maker usually has considerable professional background and remains in contact with specialists of many kinds. In future years, we expect the level of intellectual culture to continue to rise and at the same time to become more selective in arranging common maps of knowledge to be shared throughout life, irrespective of specialization.

At the principal centers of civilization, once-celebrated difficulties of communication are largely obsolete. At thousands of board and committee meetings and consultations, the technique of communication has been mastered on all sides, so that lawyers, engineers, scientists, investors, and managers get on with the problem at hand with little skill-consciousness or misinterpretation. It is true that, as one moves away from the top levels of New York, Washington, and Cambridge, for example, the traditional stumbling blocks appear, and this is as true of the lower echelons in the East as anywhere else. In coming years, however, fuller advantage should be taken of improved means of sharing experience.

The idea of centers of political science is to consolidate and improve the advances that have been made in integrating frames of reference among scholars and scientists and between them and the responsible decision-makers of government and other social institutions.

NOTES

[1] The literature of controversy over the role of universities in America includes, e.g., R. M. Hutchins, *The Higher Learning in America* (New Haven: Yale University Press, 1936); and H. D. Gideonse, *The Higher Learning in a Democracy,* "A Reply to President Hutchins' Critique of the American University" (New York: Farrar and Rinehart, 1937). An important interpretation of *Education in the Forming of American Society* is by B. Bailyn (New York: Vintage Books, 1960). Approaches attempting to portray the educational system "as it is" include T. Caplow and P. J. McGee, *The Academic Marketplace* (New York: Basic Books, 1958); and L. Wilson, *The Academic Man* (New York: Oxford University Press, 1942). Cf. also R. Thomas, *The Search for a Common Learning,* "General Education, 1800–1960" (New York: McGraw-Hill, 1962).

[2] For insight into the traditional outlook of various civilizations, cf. D. S. Nivison and A. F. Wright, eds., *Confucianism in Action* (Stanford: Stanford University Press, 1959); F. Rosenthal, trans., *Ibn Khaldûn, The Muquaddimah,* "An Introduction to History" (London: Routledge and Kegan Paul, 1958); W. Barclay, *Educational Ideals in the Ancient World* (London: Collins, 1959); W. Jaeger, *Paideia,* "The Ideals of Greek Culture," trans. G. Highet (2nd ed.; 3 vols.; New York: Oxford University Press, 1943); S. Radakrishnan and C. Moore, eds., *A Source Book in Indian Philosophy* (Princeton: Princeton University Press, 1957).

[3] A study of books and articles cited in advanced biological research showed that 50 per cent went no further back than five years; fewer than 10 per cent went back twenty years or more. Cf. P. Weiss, "Knowledge: A Growth Process," *Science,* 131 (1960), 1716–1719.

4 A. Flexner, *Universities, American, English, German* (New York: Oxford University Press, 1930).

5 Ralph Tyler has directed the center from the first. The driving initiative was taken by B. B. Berelson, then of the Ford Foundation. The spread of the term "behavioral sciences" owes much to the choice of label for the center. Many potential labels were rejected, partly because they had acquired unfortunate connotations in influential quarters, partly because they were identified with an existing—and somewhat circumscribed—set of organizations. Among the rejected expressions were "human relations" and "social sciences." In political science, the expression "behavioral" is sometimes facetiously, perhaps enviously, used to refer to the work of anyone who has a grant from Ford. More solemnly, the term is taken to refer to a strong emphasis on joining systematic theory with disciplined observation. Systematic theory does not ultimately close its eyes to historical data, nor are disciplined observational procedures restricted to field or laboratory studies of contemporary events.

6 At first, scientists of the modern era found it necessary to phrase what they did in terms of the Aristotelian categories as interpreted by contemporary theologians. Scientists thus concentrated on material, formal, and efficient causes and found increasing difficulty with "final causes." Final causes in Aristotelian usage were the purposes for which objects were designed. The designs, patterns, or forms— the formal causes—were regarded as open to direct observation. Final causes, however, could only be inferred from a comprehensive vision of the whole field of potential study. The construct of an ultimate designer and creator of materials, designs, and mechanisms —if treated as a hypothesis, not as an article of faith—is compatible with scientific inquiry. Traditionally, most theologians and ecclesiastical authorities have insisted on faith, not hypothesis, although they have often argued that the plausibility of various hypotheses—partially established empirically—justifies the leap to belief.

7 Cf. the discussion of possible contact with advanced forms of life in M. S. McDougal, H. D. Lasswell, and I. Vlasic, *The Public Order of Outer Space* (New Haven: Yale University Press, forthcoming).

8 Thomas Cooper (1759–1839) came to the United States from England with Joseph Priestley in 1794. His connection with South Carolina began in 1820.

9 Harlow Shapley, long director of the Harvard Observatory, actively promotes science clubs at the preparatory level and lectures untiringly on astronomy to audiences of every level of sophistication. For the general reader who would like direct access to an intelligible collection of historic landmarks, cf. Shapley, ed., *Source Book in Astronomy, 1900–1950* (Cambridge: Harvard University Press, 1960).

[10] C. P. Snow is an eminent exception. Cf. the controversy precipitated by *The Two Cultures and the Scientific Revolution* (Cambridge: University Press, 1959).

[11] New York: A Signet Book, 1956, p. 6.

[12] Author of *The Star Maker* and several other works.

[13] The early connections between the study of the heavens and the activities of the political elite were close. The standard histories of science —by G. Sarton, L. Thorndike, O. Neugebauer, and N. J. T. M. Needham, for instance—are informative on these connections. The timing of acts of state was deeply influenced by the testimony of experts on the heavens. Cf. D. J. de Solla Price, *Science since Babylon* (New Haven: Yale University Press, 1962).

[14] The connection between politics and alchemy was close in many civilizations. Sometimes the accent was on discovering means to immortality, sometimes on the making of metal—of interest to the treasury and the military.

[15] Stanley's contribution is put into context by I. Asimov, *The Intelligent Man's Guide to Science* (New York: Basic Books, 1960), Vol. II, Chap. 13.

[16] Cf. A. Einstein and L. Infeld, *The Evolution of Physics* (Cambridge: University Press, 1938).

[17] Cf. H. Hyden, "Biochemical Aspects of Brain Activity," in S. M. Farber and R. H. L. Wilson, eds., *Control of the Mind* (New York: McGraw-Hill, 1961).

[18] A concise review of current hypotheses can be found in J. Singh, *Great Ideas and Theories of Modern Cosmology* (New York: Dover Publications, 1961), describing the views of Schmidt, Hoyle, Weizsäcker, Kuiper, Alfén, Whipple, Urey, and many others. Also cf. M. K. Munitz, ed., *Theories of the Universe from Babylonian Myth to Modern Science* (Glencoe, Ill.: The Free Press-Falcon's Wing Press, 1957).

[19] Cf., e.g., L. Bertalanffy, *Modern Theories of Development,* "An Introduction to Theoretical Biology" (New York: Oxford University Press, 1933). Bertalanffy's general systems approach has influenced some biologists and social scientists.

[20] Cf. F. A. Lindemann, *The Physical Significance of The Quantum Theory* (Oxford: University Press, 1932). The map I have outlined suggests that the subjective event of reference, by bringing models of the past and future into the present, enlarges the context in regard to which behavior—hence social interaction—occurs. This carries with it the potentiality of orderly arrangement of subsequent contexts. The mass-energy preconditions of a specific set of subjective

events are trivial; however, the "trapping" of duration energies is accomplished by selective intervention in the unfolding future. Conflicting policy programs among living systems may nullify the potential for order by blocking integration within the inclusive context of interaction. Mass-energy units can be arranged in a hierarchy of magnitudes; subjective references can be described according to the time-space context alluded to and the complexity and integration of the arrangements referred to in the context; interaction sequences can be described according to the actualization of arrangements in context. Many currents in contemporary thought harmonize in varying degree with this speculative model; cf., e.g., Teilhard de Chardin, *The Phenomenon of Man* (New York: Harpers, 1959). Cf. also some trends that appear in philosophies of history. A convenient compendium is H. Meyerhoff, ed., *The Philosophy of History in Our Time,* "An Anthology" (New York: Harpers, 1959), with selections from Dilthey, Croce, Collingwood, Pirenne, Toynbee, Becker, Beard, Aron, Dewey, Lovejoy, White, Butterfield, Berlin, Popper, Jaspers, and others. The study of decision, as I conceive it, increases the probability of actualizing inclusive goals in the cosmic process, even if inclusive goals have not been achieved before.

[21] Cf. the section on "The Influence of Drugs on the Individual," especially the papers by S. S. Kety, J. G. Miller, and J. O. Cole, in S. M. Farber and R. H. L. Wilson, eds., *Control of the Mind* (New York: McGraw-Hill, 1961).

[22] Cf. the rather cautious essays authorized by Soviet scientists in M. Vassiliev and S. Gouschev, eds., *Life in the Twenty-First Century* (Baltimore: Penguin, 1961).

[23] Cf. P. Miller, *The New England Mind from Colony to Province* (Cambridge: Harvard University Press, 1953).

[24] An imaginative and informed reassessment is S. de Grazia, *Of Time, Work, and Leisure* (New York: Twentieth Century Fund, 1962).

[25] Cf. D. Lerner, *The Passing of Traditional Society* (Glencoe, Ill.: The Free Press, 1958).

[26] R. Redfield, *The Primitive World and Its Transformation* (Ithaca: Cornell University Press, 1953), pp. 12, 15.

[27] I note in passing that psychoanalytic formulations are being stated in ways that admit of more concentrated research. E.g., K. M. Colby, *Energy and Structure in Psychoanalysis* (New York: Ronald, 1955); D. Rapaport, "The Conceptual Model of Psychoanalysis," in *Theoretical Models and Personality Theory* (Durham, N.C.: Duke University Press, 1952). Applications of dynamic psychiatry and psychology to the study of politics are gradually gaining in volume and quality. Recent examples are L. Pye, *Politics, Personality, and Nation Building,* "Burma's Search for Identity" (New Haven: Yale

University Press, 1962), and, above all, the works of N. Leites, H. V. Dicks, and E. Erikson. Cf. L. W. Milbrath and W. W. Klein, "Personality Correlates of Politics," *Acta Sociologica,* 6 (1962), 53–66; L. W. Milbrath, "Predispositions toward Political Contention," *Western Political Quarterly,* 13 (1960), 5–18.

[28] But see the new genetic knowledge tersely summarized in C. H. Waddington, *The Nature of Life* (New York: Atheneum, 1962).

[29] The most refined examination of the relevant subjectivities is M. Scheler, *Zur Phänomenologie und Theorie der Sympathiegefühl und von Liebe und Hass* ("On the Phenomenology and Theory of Sympathy and of Love and Hatred"), with an Appendix on the reason for assuming the existence of other selves, *Gesammelte Schriften* (Berne: Franke, 1954), I.

[30] For new models of the brain, cf. G. S. Blum, *A Model of the Mind, Explored by Hypnotically Controlled Experiments and Examined for Its Psychodynamic Implications* (New York: Wiley, 1961); D. O. Hebb, *Organization of Behavior* (New York: Wiley, 1949); W. R. Ashby, *Design for a Brain* (New York: Wiley, 1952); and G. A. Miller, E. Galanter, and K. Pribram, *Plans and the Structure of Behavior* (New York: Holt, 1960).

11
Conclusion

The present inquiry comes at a time when great and accelerating changes multiply the problems that press on individuals and groups at every stage of national, international, and subnational life. There is obvious, pressing demand for the services of every person or profession believed competent to contribute to the solution of the vexing questions of public policy.

This discussion is addressed to all who concur in the fundamental importance of harmonizing our institutions with the requirements of human dignity and who recognize that the task calls for higher levels of performance by public and private agencies dealing with political intelligence and appraisal.

Explicitly, I am concerned with increasing the weight of factors that favor responsible freedom by giving more emphasis to the study of government. If the study of government is to make the impact of which it is capable, no government, no political party, and no private association can be allowed a monopoly on research, teaching, or consultation. In the huge urban civilizations of our day, an indispensable safeguard of freedom is enlightenment regarding the past and prospective role of government in the social process as a whole.

The prospects of democratic and responsible government are enhanced when the doings of governments and of every other influential participant in the political process are open to mutual inspection and appraisal. Inspection gains depth when immediate happenings are seen in the broader context of space and time. It is the distinctive task of professional students of government to supplement the news and views of the day in any locality by providing comprehensive and reliable maps of the larger currents of politics.

I have put the accent on the consideration of policies available to political scientists for improving the bases on which their inferences rest. Recognition has therefore been given to the perfecting of comprehensive, selective, and reliable surveys of contemporary and historical events and of supplementing surveys by strategies that exploit the potential returns from experimentation, prototyping, and intervention.

Acutely sensible to the sheer magnitude of pertinent detail, I have put forward a number of procedures intended to bring to the attention of any scholar, citizen, or official an intelligible image of the configuration of past, present, and future events in which he is enmeshed and with which he interacts. The decision seminar, the social planetarium, and related devices are tentative solutions to problems of preventing an overload on the network of political communication.

In anticipation of the persisting challenge to creativity that the future will undoubtedly contain, my discussion of professional training has centered on the cultivation of creativity. The relevant exercises of political imagination presuppose intimate familiarity with the most distinctive features of the era, and this points unmistakably to the roles of science and technology.

After the stage of induction into the professional study of government come the problems connected with careers devoted to research, teaching, consultation, administration, or public leadership. Since this book is directed mainly to questions posed by the rising level of intellectual excellence in our society, I have given extended treatment to the building of environments in which political science can be cultivated under optimal conditions. The idea of centers of political science is a specific example of an institutional means of adjusting our perspectives and operations to our emerging needs.

Many matters of no inconsiderable importance have been given scant attention or left to one side. This has sometimes been done in the hope of giving more extended consideration to the topic elsewhere. Such topics are strategies of general civic training, of collaboration in research and policy teams, and of giving and obtaining advice. Other topics could be usefully discussed in a factual setting that lies beyond the limits of the present sketch. I have in mind, for instance, the strategy of introducing the study of government to peoples of reviving ancient civilization whose traditional forms of political life are non-democratic, save possibly at the lowest levels, or the strategy of introducing political science to industrializing peoples whose cultural traditions are characteristic of folk societies. Another topic worthy of extended factual analysis and policy recommendation is the financing of political science and civic education at all age levels. What are the appropriate criteria for the allocation of manpower and facilities to research, training, consultation, and dissemination? This question, in particular, deserves exploratory study by a committee of the American Political Science Association.

I have, I trust, made it plain that the fundamental fact of politics is inextricable from human society, if by politics we mean the largest arena of interaction in which goals are clarified, degrees of achievement are described, conditioning factors are analyzed, future developments are projected, and policy alternatives are invented and evaluated.

In a specialized civilization, the case for the continuing study of government by an organized profession of scholars is persuasive. I am, however, among those who recognize that, under various circumstances, political scientists may make fewer significant contributions to the subject than other scientists or writers. This is the competitive thrust of life, and it is eminently reasonable that contemporary and future members of an identifiable profession measure up to competitive conditions. I have outlined some policies open to the profession, as presently constituted, that promise to contribute to the success of political science in years to come.

Whether a conventionally named body of scholars called "political scientists" will continue to play a prominent part in the study and appraisal of politics depends chiefly on its vigor and imagination. Can we improve the intelligence flow on which the profession must depend for the opportune performance of the teaching, consultative, research, and other tasks for which they are responsible? Can we achieve levels of personal competence that measure up to the formidable tasks of the twin ages of science and astropolitics?

The future in this, as in other dimensions, is partly open to direction through keener insight into the goals, assets, and liabilities of the self. The present inquiry is a phase of this continual self-appraisal. It is impossible to contemplate the present status of man without perceiving the cosmic roles that he and other advanced forms of life may eventually play. We are, perhaps, introducing self-awareness into cosmic process. With awareness of self come deliberate formation and pursuit of value goals. For tens of thousands of years, man was accustomed to living in relatively local environments and to cooperating on a parochial scale. Today we are on the verge of exploring a habitat far less circumscribed than earth. The need for a world-wide system of public order—a comprehensive plan of cooperation—is fearfully urgent. From the interplay of the study and practice of cooperation we may eventually move more wisely, if not more rapidly, toward fulfilling the as-yet-mysterious potentialities of the cosmic process.

INDEX